D1606190

Holy Joe

Missouri Biography Series
William E. Foley, Editor

Joseph W. Folk
State Historical Society of Missouri, Columbia

Holy Joe

Joseph W. Folk and the Missouri Idea

Steven L. Piott

University of Missouri Press
Columbia and London

Copyright © 1997 by
The Curators of the University of Missouri
University of Missouri Press, Columbia, Missouri 65201
Printed and bound in the United States of America
All rights reserved
5   4   3   2   1   01   00   99   98   97

Library of Congress Cataloging-in-Publication Data

Piott, Steven L.
    Holy Joe : Joseph W. Folk and the Missouri idea / Steven L. Piott.
      p.   cm. — (Missouri biography series)
    Includes bibliographical references and index.
    ISBN 0-8262-1130-5 (alk. paper)
    1. Folk, Joseph Wingate, 1869–1923.   2. Governors—Missouri—
Biography.   3. Politicians—Missouri—Saint Louis—Biography.
4. Missouri—Politics and government—1865–1950.   5. Saint Louis
(Mo.)—Politics and government.   I. Title.   II. Series.
F466.P58   1997
977.8'041'092—dc21
    [B]   97-18907
                                                                          CIP

♾ ™   This paper meets the requirements of the
American National Standard for Permanence of Paper
for Printed Library Materials, Z39.48, 1984.

Designer: Stephanie Foley
Typesetter: BOOKCOMP
Printer and binder: Thomson-Shore, Inc.
Typefaces: Adobe Garamond and Leawood

To Dave

Contents

Acknowledgments

G eneral thanks and credit should be given to the staffs of the editorial, reference, and newspaper departments of the State Historical Society of Missouri in Columbia; the Western Historical Manuscript Collection, Columbia, Missouri; the Missouri Historical Society in St. Louis; the Library of Congress Manuscript Division in Washington, D.C.; the Elma Ross Public Library in Brownsville, Tennessee; and the Memphis Shelby County Public Library in Memphis for their assistance on this project. I would also like to thank the State Historical Society of Missouri for granting permission to publish material that appeared in the July 1995 issue of the *Missouri Historical Review.*

I would also like to give special mention to Lana McClune, History Department Secretary, for her technical assistance and good humor; to John Bradbury, Manuscript Specialist at the Western Historical Manuscript Collection at the University of Missouri–Rolla, for facilitating access to the Folk Papers; and to Judy Bowser, Head of the Inter-Library Loan Office in the Clarion University Library, for patiently tracking down hard-to-find but invaluable sources.

Several other individuals played important parts in the preparation of this book. Lawrence O. Christensen and William E. Foley both read and commented on the final draft of the manuscript. I appreciate the time they took and the helpful suggestions they made. Christopher Gibbs took time to read the entire manuscript when I know he had better things to do. His comments once again proved invaluable. As a critic, wordsmith, and confidant, he provided more help than he realizes. Larry Gragg read each draft of the manuscript and tirelessly listened to endless interpretive and organizational questions. His calm counsel, irrepressible good humor, and sound judgment helped to keep the topic in focus. I could not ask for a better friend. Finally, I would like to thank David Thelen. He inspired an interest in the topic of American reform in graduate school that has not diminished over time.

Holy Joe

1

Brownsville

In his *Autobiography*, Lincoln Steffens, the noted journalist and crusader against urban corruption, recollects how he met Joseph W. Folk. Sent forth by his New York editor to find articles for *McClure's*, Steffens journeyed to the Midwest looking for material. His plan was to "take confused, local, serial news of the newspapers and report it all together in one long short story for the whole country." Hearing that someone by the name of Folk was "raising the deuce of a row about bribery in the board of aldermen" in St. Louis, Steffens traveled to that city in the summer of 1902 to check out the report. He met Folk, the circuit attorney pursuing the case, in a quiet corner of the lobby of the Planters Hotel. The two men were natural allies; Folk needed help and publicity in his campaign against corruption, while Steffens needed a compelling story. The reporter listened with rapt attention as the young attorney revealed to him the shocking evidence of municipal corruption he had uncovered. In the process, Steffens found himself drawn to the issue of exposure. "He startled my imagination," said Steffens. When the first installment of Steffens's landmark muckraking article, "Tweed Days in St. Louis," appeared in the October number of *McClure's*, it caused a national sensation. As the ongoing exposé gathered momentum in the press, particularly in the pages of *McClure's*, Folk became a national figure and, to many, Missouri's political savior.[1]

Steffens prided himself on being a student of men's characters as well as their politics, and, by his own admission, he found Folk fascinating. Intrigued by the young prosecutor's sense of duty, Steffens thought he had discovered the roots of that virtue in Folk's background: "A

---

1. Lincoln Steffens, *The Autobiography of Lincoln Steffens*, 368–73. See also Louis Filler, *Crusaders for American Liberalism: The Story of the Muckrakers*, 106–8.

1

southerner from Tennessee, he came of the race of southern Puritans who have the hard, righteous traits of their New England cousins. . . . He had the world all pictured for him in the schools of Tennessee and in his law studies. The Bible, the English common law, the Constitution of the United States . . . described things as they were—so he had believed when he came up from Tennessee to start his career. . . ."[2] Upbringing and environment created a frame of reference for Joseph Folk. Family life and the rural, small-town culture that surrounded him during his early years shaped his values and defined his world. These are essential elements in understanding the man who became Missouri's most celebrated reformer.

Haywood County, on the western slope of the West Tennessee plateau, dates its first permanent settlement to 1821 when Colonel R. Nixon arrived with his family. Other settlers followed apace, cleared the land, and cultivated corn and other cereals. In 1828 farmers in the county began to grow cotton, and Hiram Bradford built the first cotton gin at Brownsville. Cotton quickly became the leading commodity, and the construction of additional gins further encouraged its production. By 1830 the county's population had leaped to more than 5,000. In the mid- to late 1830s numerous migrants from Virginia and North Carolina entered the county. At first they attempted to cultivate tobacco, but failing to do so successfully they, too, turned to the production of cotton. Using either the Hatchie and Forked Deer Rivers or accessible wagon roads, local farmers easily shipped their crops to marketing points on the Mississippi River. High cotton prices sustained the industry in west Tennessee until the Civil War.

The hub of this growing and prospering county was Brownsville, sixty miles northeast of Memphis. A stop on the Memphis Division of the Louisville and Nashville Railroad and near the geographic center of Haywood County, Brownsville soon became both the county seat and a thriving commercial center of nearly 1,000 people by 1850. The Civil War disrupted Brownsville's commercial progress, and, at least temporarily, restricted individual opportunity. During the war nearly all the regular mercantile businesses in town suspended operations. Merchants sold out their stock and closed their shops rather than risk

---

2. Steffens, *Autobiography,* 368–69.

having them raided by marauding guerrilla bands. Immediately after the war, business again revived, stimulated by high cotton prices. Many boosters soon regarded the prospering town of Brownsville as a city in the making. Entrepreneurs and speculators became intoxicated with the possibilities of instant wealth and extended themselves accordingly.

The cotton-based southern economy, however, proved to be susceptible to economic downturns, and "bust" soon followed "boom" in Brownsville as cotton prices dropped in the early 1870s. Fortunes were lost, businesses failed, and, after 1872, Brownsville slid into a general commercial decline that persisted for almost a decade. The fate of the Brownsville Manufacturing Company indicates that the cotton industry remained troubled ten years later. When the company, a cotton mill with over 3,000 spindles, 125 looms, and 120 workers (of whom 80 were female), was destroyed by fire in 1882, it was not immediately rebuilt. But the census of 1880 reported that Haywood County still ranked third in the state in the production of cotton. By that date the economy had at least begun to recover, and, although cotton still remained the primary crop, some farmers had shifted to raising livestock or to cultivating cereals and grasses.

In addition to their faith in the American dream of opportunity, the earliest settlers of Haywood County and Brownsville also brought with them a fervent commitment to the principles of Christianity. Presbyterians, Methodists, and Baptists made up the primary denominations, and an evangelical Protestantism increasingly became the region's dominant religious characteristic. Adherents learned that personal redemption would come through faith, good works, and the Christian way of life and that an individual's most grievous sin would be a failure to conform to the moral law of God. As the county was settled, the number of churches multiplied as did the number of religious educational academies. Prominent among these was the Brownsville Female College, established in 1850 by the West Tennessee Baptist Convention. Brownsville was also home to the Wesleyan Female College, chartered in 1870, and the Union Female Seminary, established in 1884. Brownsville's boosters could also boast of an excellent high school and public school, ten churches, and one weekly newspaper, the *States-Democrat*. As one might expect of the culture in mid-nineteenth-century, traditional, small-town, Protestant western Tennessee, Brownsville also accommodated a Young Men's

Christian Association (Y.M.C.A.) and a Temperance Alliance, as well as a handful of fraternal orders and mutual aid societies.[3]

Joseph Wingate Folk was born into this community on October 28, 1869. One of ten children, "Joel," as he was known as a child, was the seventh son born to Henry Bate Folk and Martha Cornelia (Estes) Folk.[4] Henry Folk was a native of Windsor, Bertie County, North Carolina. His father owned a farm worked by half a dozen slaves. Orphaned at a young age, Henry and his older brother lived with relatives who migrated to Fayette County in western Tennessee. Henry later used money from his father's estate to attend Wake Forest College in North Carolina. Upon graduation in 1849, he returned to western Tennessee. Here, he taught school in Haywood and Lauderdale Counties, met Cornelia Estes, and, after her graduation from Brownsville Female College, married her in November 1855. Cornelia's family had roots in Virginia dating back to 1704. Her grandfather, Joel Estes, a captain in the War of 1812, led the family from Pittsylvania County, Virginia, to western Tennessee in 1824. A man of wealth and enterprise, Joel Estes established a plantation of approximately 5,000 acres in Haywood County. As a beneficiary of at least some of this wealth, Cornelia's father gave the young couple a farm near Brownsville as a wedding present. Henry, never a farmer, ran a private school on the property and studied law. Three years later he made a career move: he sold the farm, invested his money in commercial real estate in Brownsville, and moved to Memphis to practice law. But the Civil War disrupted his plans and forced him to return to teaching.

In 1865 Henry Folk purchased a home in Brownsville and resumed his law practice. He soon became one of the town's leading lawyers and served for years as attorney for the Louisville and Nashville Railroad. Known to most in town as "Judge," Henry Folk prospered, invested in business, and profited as owner of the town's illuminating gas plant. The Folks lived prosperously, but a yellow fever epidemic in 1878 further depressed property values in Brownsville and evidently caused the family

---

3. *History of Tennessee,* 818–29.

4. Joseph Folk was named after his uncle, Joel Henry Estes, who was a Confederate soldier, and Washington Manly Wingate, a close friend and college classmate of his father who later became president of Wake Forest College. Two of the Folks' ten children, a boy and a girl, died in infancy. See "Genealogy," n.d., in Joseph Wingate Folk Papers, Western Historical Manuscript Collection, Columbia, Mo.

some financial stress. Deeply religious, Henry Folk actively participated in the local Baptist church where he also taught Sunday school classes. In his later years he served as a member of the board of trustees of the Brownsville Female College. Just prior to his death in 1899, Henry Folk was ordained a Baptist minister.[5]

As staunch Baptists, Henry and Cornelia Folk strove to create a home environment in which their children would receive "proper" moral training. The Folk family lived comfortably among Brownsville's professional elite in an impressive two-story, four-columned mansion on five and one-half acres of land on West Main Street.[6] The Folks could afford to keep two or three domestic servants, and Cornelia Folk devoted most of her time to her children. She set firm rules of conduct and imposed rigorous family discipline, which was not unconventional training in Protestant, small-town America during the mid-nineteenth century. Attendance at church, Sunday school (where Cornelia Folk also taught classes), and prayer meeting was mandatory social behavior, and family prayer, daily Bible reading, and saying grace before meals were standard features of the family routine. Dancing and card playing were strictly forbidden in the Folk household. The one member of the family to stage a brief "rebellion" as a youth was Joel Folk. He reportedly resisted church attendance, refused to submit to baptism, and, according to historian Louis Geiger, once posed such searching questions to a traveling revivalist that he earned brief local notoriety as a suspected atheist. When Joel finally rejoined the Baptist church in his mid-twenties, it was more for social and professional reasons than for any sudden rebirth of religious conviction. Church attendance for the rest of his life was "regular" but always less than enthusiastic.[7]

---

5. Louis G. Geiger, *Joseph W. Folk of Missouri*, 7–9. Geiger's account—a revised version of his Ph.D. dissertation, "The Public Career of Joseph W. Folk," which he completed at the University of Missouri in 1948—is virtually the only expanded discussion of Folk's early years in Brownsville. Geiger conducted interviews with members and relatives of the Folk-Estes family during 1947 and 1948. These included conversations with Joseph W. Folk's sister, May Folk Webb, and his wife, Gertrude Folk. See also *Farmington (Mo.) Times and Herald*, February 5, 1904; *History of Tennessee*, 828; and "Genealogy," Folk Papers.

6. The Folk home still stands at 630 West Main Street in Brownsville.

7. Geiger, *Joseph W. Folk*, 9–10, 12. See also information on early childhood in Folk Papers.

Cornelia Folk was confident in her ability to engender proper conduct among her children, especially her sons. Later, her grown children encouraged her to publish a small volume entitled *Heart Thoughts,* a compilation of motherly wisdom that blended piety with practical advice. In the book she included a chapter on "How to Train Boys" and urged mothers to center the training of their sons on prayer and communion with God.

> Teach your boy to look upward; implant religious principles in his heart while young, if you would have him bear the fruits of righteousness and be held firmly on the ascent of life. Sublime heights are only reached by clinging trust in God. . . . Incite him to good deeds and noble actions. . . . From pleasant homes with manly principles instilled within their hearts, go forth heroes buoyed by hope, who will successfully battle with life. . . . Train him physically, mentally, morally, spiritually. Then will he keep on an upward career—be a hero in life's battles.

Cornelia Folk's efforts appear to have met with some success. All six of her sons eventually went on to establish successful careers, and three of them chose to pursue religious-oriented callings. Edgar Estes Folk graduated from Wake Forest College and the Southern Baptist Theological Seminary to become a Baptist minister and editor of *The Baptist and Reflector,* the official publication of Tennessee Baptists. Henry Bate Folk graduated from Wake Forest College, where he was valedictorian, to become a school principal in New Orleans and, later, a reporter for the *St. Louis Republic* before his death at the age of twenty-two. Reau Estes Folk attended Wake Forest College for two years before going on to newspaper work in Nashville and Memphis. He later became the state treasurer of Tennessee. Carey Albert Folk graduated from Richmond College and did graduate study at Johns Hopkins University before becoming president of Brownsville Female College. He was later president of Boscobel College for Young Ladies in Nashville. Humphrey Bate Folk graduated from the Southern Baptist Theological Seminary to become pastor of the Baptist church at Shelbyville, Tennessee.[8]

8. Mrs. H. B. [Cornelia] Folk, *Heart Thoughts: Papers and Addresses,* 23–27; Geiger, *Joseph W. Folk,* 175; *Farmington Times and Herald,* February 5, 1904.

Although young Joel may have resisted formal institutional attach-
ments to his church, he nevertheless developed a strong Christian sense
of proper moral behavior. Upon meeting Folk years later, the journalist
William Allen White found him to be ambitious ("though not very
frankly so"), but noted that his ambition did not "sap his moral sense."
White concluded that it was this strain of morality that was crucial to
understanding Joseph Folk and that set him apart from others. "Many
contemporary statesmen and moralists are pagans," said White. "They
have a philosophy of life deep and broad and cosmopolitan . . . and
they are Christians only because they have a sort of protective mimicry
of creed, that merges them into their environments. But Folk, without
much depth to his natural philosophy of life, is deeply pious, without
being in the least sanctimonious, and without any cant." White also
found Folk to be exceptionally honest and that his honesty seemed to
result from "a deliberate conviction, of faith or creed, that honesty is the
best policy."[9] This simple sense of right and wrong served as an ethical
compass throughout Folk's adult life, and one that would come under
attack only after he left the secure world of Brownsville.

Henry and Cornelia Folk also stressed the importance of education in
their household. Educational preparation at home was traditional and
perhaps somewhat sectarian and moralistic. The children memorized
famous quotations; the reading material in the Folk library included the
classics, general histories, and Biblical commentaries. Joel Folk attended
both public and private schools in his hometown and finished his early
education at the Brownsville Academy, graduating in 1885 at the age
of sixteen. Friends remember him as being smart, conscientious, and
proficient in mathematics.[10]

Deciding not to follow three of his older brothers to Wake Forest
College (perhaps due to the financial reverses of his father), Joel, instead,
went to work. Apparently convinced that adventure and opportunity
lay outside of Brownsville, Joel set out for Memphis. He found work
there as a clerk with the Southern Express Company, then as a salesman
of patent medicines, and finally as a bookkeeper in the retail department

9. William Allen White, "Folk: The Story of a Little Leaven in a Great Commonwealth," 121–22, 124.
10. Geiger, *Joseph W. Folk,* 10.

of Oliver, Fennin and Company, a grocery concern. A serious illness, however, forced his return to Brownsville in 1887. Upon recovery, Joel remained in Brownsville and read the law in the office of his cousin, J. W. E. Moore. As an indication that his life and professional direction were changing, Joel, without consulting his family, adopted the more formal "Joseph W. Folk" as the appellation he now preferred.[11]

Deciding that he might fancy a career as a lawyer, Joseph pooled savings, borrowed money, and entered the second year of a two-year course of study at the Vanderbilt University Law School in Nashville in the fall of 1889. Not much is known about his time at college. Former classmates remembered him as being intelligent and possessing a quick and accurate memory. His seriousness as a student and his naturally friendly disposition gained him many friends, recognition as a young man of promise, and membership in one of the leading fraternities on campus. Moot court trials at Vanderbilt offered young law students like Joseph some experience in trial procedure and in the argument of cases. Instruction valued argument over oratory. The resulting "style," which Folk later perfected as St. Louis circuit attorney, often took the form of an appeal in which the jury is persuaded by sincere yet forceful argument. Joseph graduated from law school in 1890 and was admitted to the bar that same year.[12]

After graduation Joseph returned to Brownsville, entered general practice as a lawyer in the office of his cousin with whom he had initially read the law, and eventually opened his own office. Years later, St. Louis newspaperman Claude Wetmore tried to imagine Folk's initial experience as a small town attorney:

> The practice in that town was mixed. . . . One day a civil suit, the next defending a criminal; stating a case plainly to a common-sense justice, addressing platitudinous remarks to a self-opinionated jury, delving deep in leather-covered volumes, in effort to discover something not known by an erudite judge—this was Mr. Folk's life for three years. It was a study of actual conditions. . . .

As a talented, affable, prominent young man, Joseph Folk began to broaden his horizons and do the things that upwardly mobile young

11. Ibid., 10–12; *Farmington Times and Herald*, February 5, 1904.
12. Geiger, *Joseph W. Folk*, 11–12; *Farmington Times and Herald*, February 12, 1904.

men are wont to do. He developed an interest in politics, became active in the Democratic Club of Brownsville, and, although he declined the offer, was even endorsed by Democrats in Haywood County for the office of state representative in the Tennessee legislature in 1892. As Folk continued his legal career and perhaps aspired to political office, he also gave speeches on special occasions and once assumed editorial duties on the local newspaper as a substitute for the regular editor. One notable editorial contribution involved the subject of "Good Citizenship," which was written in response to a minor outbreak of vandalism in which a number of small boys had thrown bricks through church windows. The theme—the importance of respecting the rights and property of others—was a natural one given his background, and one that he would return to later as prosecuting attorney in St. Louis. Socially active as well as politically involved, Folk also joined the Knights of Pythias Lodge and served as chancellor-commander of the local society.[13]

But for all his early success in Brownsville, Folk was still very much a man-on-the-make with an eye to more promising opportunities than could be had in Brownsville. When an uncle, Judge Frank M. Estes, offered him a law partnership in St. Louis, he eagerly accepted the offer. With experience in having read the law, with a course of college instruction, and with three years of general experience, Joseph Folk, at the age of twenty-four, moved to St. Louis in 1893. Leaving Brownsville, a town of 3,000 people at that time, for the big city of St. Louis was not unlike his earlier youthful sojourn to the not-so-big city of Memphis. This time, however, he was more prepared to make a success of it. But Folk took more than training, experience, and a respect for the law with him. Imbued with a strong sense of Protestant moral values, Folk left Brownsville with a set of moral precepts that would guide him throughout his professional life. And if the opportunity for a career in public office presented itself, the same moral imperatives could be applied. The principles of government and those of the Christian faith were one and the same.[14]

13. Claude Wetmore, *The Battle against Bribery: Being the Only Complete Narrative of Joseph W. Folk's Warfare on Boodlers,* 21; Geiger, *Joseph W. Folk,* 12–13; *Farmington Times and Herald,* February 12, 1904.
14. Geiger, *Joseph W. Folk,* 12.

Folk did not, however, sever all his ties to the town of his youth. He frequently returned to visit his family and to court blue-eyed, brown-haired Gertrude Glass. Historian Louis Geiger tells of early Saturday risers in Brownsville commonly observing Joseph Folk, just off the early morning train from St. Louis, "'struttin'" through town "'like he was the governor of St. Louis.'" Gertrude, whom he had known all his life at church, school, and social gatherings, was the daughter of Thomas E. Glass, a successful Brownsville druggist, and Sally Thomas, the daughter of a well-to-do planter. She was known locally for her interest in music, her skill on the piano, and her participation in musical activities. Reflecting on growing up in Brownsville years later, Gertrude Glass remembered her world as insulated and closed. "I was brought up by most conservative parents in a little Southern town, composed of a few families whose pedigrees were known by all, and a 'stranger within our gates' must have credentials or suffer the consequence." And while acknowledging that her future husband knew the political "game," she confessed to being "quite ignorant of the art of politics." In fact, she admitted to being brought up in a social environment that denigrated politicians. "We rather looked down on politicians because of the few we knew." After three years of commuter courtship, and Gertrude's graduation from the Brownsville Female College, the couple were married in a simple ceremony at the Glass home on November 10, 1896. At the time of his wedding, Joseph Folk had established himself as an attorney in St. Louis and had rekindled his interest in politics.[15]

15. Ibid., 13; Gertrude (Glass) Folk is quoted in Eleanora G. Park and Kate S. Morrow, *Women of the Mansion: Missouri, 1821–1936,* 292. See also article dated October 24, 1915, in Mrs. Joseph W. Folk vertical file, Missouri Historical Society, St. Louis.

2

St. Louis

When Joseph Folk moved to St. Louis in 1893 to make his mark as an attorney, he entered a city that was in the midst of a period of rapid and sustained economic development. As an axis for both rail and river traffic, St. Louis had become both a manufacturing center and commercial hub. By 1890 St. Louis ranked either fourth or fifth among major American cities in the gross value of its manufactured goods and in the amount of capital invested in manufacturing. Though other midwestern cities asserted themselves as meat-packing and milling centers, St. Louis held its own in brewing, clothing, boot, and shoe manufacturing, furniture making, and chewing and pipe tobacco production. Assisted by the Missouri Pacific Railroad system, St. Louis businesses had aggressively expanded their markets to the west and southwest. As a result, jobbers and retailers all along the rail and river network depended upon St. Louis wholesalers for their supplies.[1]

Folk's newly adopted city had also made tremendous gains in population as it matured into a thriving metropolis. From a population of 350,000 in 1880, the city had grown to 450,000 by 1890. In 1900 it ranked fourth behind New York, Chicago, and Philadelphia with a population nearing 600,000. The city also possessed a population and culture that was ethnically diverse. By 1900 almost 20 percent of its population were foreign-born, while almost 42 percent had foreign-born parents. Native whites amounted to 32 percent of the city's inhabitants, while native blacks were slightly more than 6 percent. Among the foreign-born, approximately 53 percent were German while roughly 18 percent were Irish. Most of the immigrant/ethnic population lived

1. James Neal Primm, *Lion of the Valley: St. Louis, Missouri*, 345–57.

in the poorer North and South Sides of the city. As the wealthier inhabitants responded to urban crowding, noise, crime, and commercial expansion by moving from the center of the city, single-family residences increasingly gave way to multifamily tenements. St. Louis ranked fourth nationally in residential density in 1900 with an average of seven persons per dwelling. By 1900 only 23 percent of St. Louis families would own their own homes.[2]

Like every other major American city groaning under the pressure of an expanding population during the late nineteenth century, St. Louis had a list of urban problems to confront. According to Orrick Johns, son of the noted *St. Louis Post-Dispatch* editor George Johns, "The city was a disgrace. Its sewerage system was inadequate, it was half-policed, its streets and even sidewalks were unpaved and sink-holes of mud. The town was practically in darkness at night. And the water! St. Louis water was notorious—an opaque, chocolate colored fluid as it came from the river, rich with infusoriae and sand." To his list Johns could have added another hazard of urban life in St. Louis—smoke—the result of the burning of Illinois soft coal by factories, railroads, and homeowners. Spurred on by women's organizations that regarded the pollution as a community health concern, the St. Louis Municipal Assembly responded by passing a smoke abatement ordinance in 1893. The new regulations resulted in some improvement to the city's air quality, but the state supreme court declared the ordinance unconstitutional in 1897. The court struck down the law on the grounds that the state had not officially granted cities the authority to extend their police powers in this manner. In 1901 the legislature gave the city of St. Louis the authority to declare its smoke a "nuisance." St. Louis's new smoke ordinance, enacted that same year, created the office of smoke inspector and gave that official the authority to prosecute violators.[3]

To promote further economic growth and cope with urban problems, St. Louisans placed their faith in their elected officials. In 1876 St. Louis gained the distinction of being the first American city to achieve

---

2. Ibid., 345, 357–58; U.S. Department of Interior, *Twelfth Census of the United States, 1900: Population,* lxix.

3. Orrick Johns, *Time of Our Lives: The Story of My Father and Myself,* 140; Primm, *Lion of the Valley,* 357–58; David Thelen, *Paths of Resistance: Tradition and Dignity in Industrializing Missouri,* 226–27.

municipal home rule. Its Municipal Assembly was bicameral. The upper house, or Council, had thirteen members elected at large, while the lower house, or House of Delegates, had one member elected from each of the city's twenty-eight wards. Executive functions were assigned to the mayor, who appointed most department heads. Proposals for public works to be contracted by the city had to originate in the six-member Board of Public Improvements. The Municipal Assembly, however, maintained the authority to decide which companies received public utility franchises. But even though the city's charter guaranteed home rule, the state retained control over the police department, municipal elections, and liquor licensing through metropolitan boards appointed by the governor. The arrangement allowed the state's dominant Democratic party to hinder local Republican influence in St. Louis.[4]

By the time Folk arrived in 1893, St. Louis had a competitive two-party political system even though the state was solidly Democratic. The Democratic party in the city drew its strength from a coalition of interest groups—blue-collar workers, Irish Catholics, middle-class professionals like Folk, and conservative upper-class businessmen. These groups often differed over local reform issues, and, during the mid-1890s, split into "silverites" and "goldbugs" in the national debate over monetary policy. St. Louis Republicans could also claim support that cut across class lines and were especially strong in the South Side German community. But the Republicans also suffered similar class, ethnic, and ideological divisions. Political success was possible for either party, but probably only through political compromise and successful coalition-building.[5]

One other characteristic of St. Louis's political culture during the 1890s was that it was controlled by a political machine. In St. Louis the machine was Democratic and directed by "Boss," or as he was deferentially known to many, "Colonel" Edward Butler. Born into a desperately poor family in Ireland in 1838, Butler decided to try and escape poverty by immigrating to the United States when he was eleven or twelve years old. His first job was shoeing horses at a trotting-horse

4. David Paul Nord, *Newspapers and New Politics: Midwestern Municipal Reform, 1890–1900,* 24; Jack David Muraskin, "Missouri Politics during the Progressive Era, 1896–1916," 20.

5. Nord, *Newspapers and New Politics,* 25.

dealer's in New York. Making his way to St. Louis just prior to the Civil War, Butler worked as a blacksmith's apprentice. He saved his money and soon opened his own horse-shoeing shop. He also secured the Western agency for the sale of a patented horseshoe. He ventured into politics when he realized that political preferment could gain him a lucrative shoeing contract as supplier to the horse-drawn street railway companies.[6] Even without any formal education, Butler quickly mastered the art of delivering votes. He soon had his own gang of "plug-uglies" and "rowdies" that became known as "Butler's Indians." They created election day chaos by "moving the polls," assaulting voters, intimidating election judges, and voting often ("repeating") for their candidate. Butler quickly discovered that electioneering could be the road to wealth. He multiplied his profits through shrewd investments, and enhanced his power and influence by providing loans, bail money, and other personal favors. By the 1890s Butler had established an elaborate organization and was known to most as the "Boss." Using his influence within the state Democratic organization, Butler established a working relationship with the Democratically controlled St. Louis police department and Democratically appointed election officials.

Even though Butler was nominally a Democrat, he could work with a Republican mayor if necessity dictated. Bipartisanship merely meant good business to Butler, even if it did occasionally make him a few enemies. Gaining control of the Municipal Assembly was relatively easy. It was said that over half the members of the House of Delegates and not a few of the members of the Council were saloon-keepers, and they knew which party controlled liquor licensing. As members of both houses earned only $25 a month in their official capacities, Butler found that by offering lucrative "fees," their allegiance could be purchased. Newspapers and those in the know referred to Butler's loyal supporters in the assembly as the "Combine." Butler personally negotiated with those seeking to obtain special privileges (such as coveted municipal fran-chises) or looking to kill an undesirable ordinance, bargained the specific "fee" per vote that would keep the Combine happy, and usually handled the finances himself. He also looked out for his own business interests, most notably the St. Louis Sanitary Company, which operated reduction

6. St. Louis did not convert to electric streetcars until the 1890s.

plants for the city's garbage, and the Excelsior Hauling Company, which collected the city's garbage and hauled it to the reduction plant.[7]

Several dozen bankers, investors, lawyers, merchants, and manufacturers who composed what would become known as the "Big Cinch" worked with Boss Butler as silent partners. A cross-section of St. Louis's business elite, this group looked to obtain the franchises or contracts that would allow them to make tremendous profits as the providers of necessary municipal services. Powerful and resourceful, they aspired to take full advantage of the city's economic growth. But to guarantee success, members of the Big Cinch realized they needed to accommodate individuals and groups outside their social and economic sphere. For that reason they placated Boss Butler and his Irish legions and were willing to bribe members of the Combine to obtain special privileges or to preserve the status quo. Most members of St. Louis's business elite never dealt directly with the Combine. But because the interests of banks, real estate companies, and utility corporations were so interconnected, it was virtually impossible for many in the business elite not to be indirectly involved with malfeasance in the Municipal Assembly.[8]

On occasion the party hierarchy could be challenged by an insurgent reformer who raised substantive economic questions and suggested fundamental reforms that threatened special interests. During the mid- to late 1890s that individual was Lee Meriwether. Meriwether was the state labor commissioner during 1895–1896. In January 1896 he released a preliminary report that compared the values of street railway franchises with the property taxes paid by those public service corporations. Meriwether's findings clearly showed that street railways were

7. Harold Zink, *City Bosses in the United States,* 302–11; Ernest Kirschten, *Catfish and Crystal,* 306–14; Johns, *Time of Our Lives,* 131–36; Thelen, *Paths of Resistance,* 21–22; Wetmore, *Battle against Bribery,* 13–19, 120; Geiger, "Public Career," 28–30. There is some dispute over Butler's age as well as the date when he arrived in the United States. The *Post-Dispatch* said he was sixty-six in 1902 and claimed he came to America when he was barely eighteen. See *St. Louis Post-Dispatch,* February 26, 1902.

8. Alexander Scott McConachie credits the journalist William Marion Reedy with being the first to identify the "Big Cinch" as early as 1900. For a discussion of the origins of the term "Big Cinch" and the manner in which it became lodged in the public mind in St. Louis, see Alexander Scott McConachie, "The 'Big Cinch': A Business Elite in the Life of a City, Saint Louis, 1895–1915," 139–89. See also Primm, *Lion of the Valley,* 367–69, 375–76.

grossly underassessed for purposes of taxation. While the city assessed general urban real property at approximately 40 percent, assessments for street railways ranged between 11 and 25 percent. The city, he argued, was not being fairly compensated for the monopolistic privileges it had bestowed. In November 1896 Meriwether released a final report that charged that street railways were guilty of tax dodging (having paid only $47,500 in local taxes when their tax bill should have been $1,478,582). His solution was simple: make those corporations pay their taxes and place them under stricter municipal regulation.[9]

Meriwether's attacks on public service corporations caught the attention of some within the St. Louis Civic Federation, generally an upper-class organization favoring efficiency and economy in government and election law reform. A faction within the federation, led by the secretary, Walter Vrooman, and the president, Reverend Willard W. Boyd, supported the idea of utility regulation. Vrooman was a Harvard-educated minister who had been actively involved in reform causes in several eastern cities before coming to St. Louis, while Reverend Boyd was pastor of the Second Baptist Church in St. Louis and had close ties to downtown business leaders. Sensing an opportunity for municipal reform, they urged Meriwether to run as a Democratic candidate for mayor of St. Louis in 1897. Boyd promised him the support of the St. Louis Civic Federation. When Meriwether publicly attacked the street railway corporations and suggested that compensation from those corporations should be used to fund public works projects to hire the unemployed, working-class St. Louisans rallied to his side as well.

Not everyone, however, liked what Meriwether had to say. His strident anticorporate rhetoric and tax radicalism alarmed both Boss Butler, who worried about threatened power and patronage, and the upper-class business elite who worried about fundamental changes to the status quo. As a result, Butler opted to support the return of former mayor Edward Noonan to office, while the business elite favored the candidacy of conservative businessman Edwin Harrison. Both Noonan

9. Nord, *Newspapers and New Politics,* 73, 79, 93–94; Primm, *Lion of the Valley,* 371; Thelen, *Paths of Resistance,* 223; Ronald L. F. Davis and Harry D. Holmes, "Insurgency and Municipal Reform in St. Louis, 1893–1904," 2; Jack David Muraskin, "St. Louis Municipal Reform in the 1890s: A Study in Failure," 45–46. See also Missouri *Eighteenth Annual Report of the Bureau of Labor Statistics,* 1–8.

and Harrison were allied with street railway interests, each having served in the Municipal Assembly as political agents for James Campbell, St. Louis's leading street railway magnate.

Meriwether had counted on the support of the Civic Federation and organized labor to carry him into office. But despite Boyd's assurances, the central council of the Federation, controlled by conservative, upper-class business and professional men, switched its support to Harrison, who ultimately emerged as the Democratic nominee. With the Democratic party divided, and with Meriwether deciding to stay in the race and run as an independent, the Republican candidate, veteran city politician Henry Ziegenhein, easily won the election. Ziegenhein, like Noonan and Harrison, was sympathetic to the interests of street railway corporations. Opponents charged that Ziegenhein, as city collector, had allowed street railways to cheat on their taxes.[10]

The election was over, but the debate over the issues that Meriwether had raised—regulation of public service corporations, tax reform, and corporate influence in municipal government—was not. In March 1898, less than one year after the election, the Municipal Assembly began consideration of a request made by the Central Traction Company for a fifty-year municipal streetcar franchise. The blanket franchise would allow the corporation the right to construct more than one hundred miles of track along lines paralleling those of the city's six major existing street railways. As compensation for the franchise, Central Traction agreed to pay the city $1,000,000 over the fifty-year franchise period.[11]

St. Louis's leading newspapers denounced the Central Traction proposal as a franchise "grab." Most regarded the giant franchise as unnecessary and considered the payment, stretched out over fifty years, as inadequate compensation for the city. The *Post-Dispatch* was especially vehement, denouncing the proposal as a swindle perpetrated by scoundrels. When the Municipal Assembly passed the franchise over the mayor's veto in April 1898, the *Post-Dispatch* charged bribery and demanded a grand jury investigation. The grand jury looked into the charges, but returned no indictments. Central Traction quickly sold its

10. Nord, *Newspapers and New Politics,* 94–95; Davis and Holmes, "Insurgency and Municipal Reform," 2–3; Muraskin, "St. Louis Municipal Reform," 46–48.

11. Nord, *Newspapers and New Politics,* 96, 108–9.

franchise to a group of local street railway men with financial backers
outside the state. During the spring and summer of 1899 the new United
Railways Company, in reality a national holding syndicate, formally
acquired the properties of all the city's independent railroad systems,
except for the St. Louis and Suburban Railway Company. Finally, on
September 30, 1899, the United Railways Company leased its newly
consolidated property to the St. Louis Transit Company. Under the
terms of the lease the St. Louis Transit Company was to operate the
lines, make the necessary repairs, improvements, and extensions, and
pay an annual rental.[12]

Surprisingly, there was no accompanying public indignation over the
episode. No mass meetings occurred. No rallies took place. Aside from
the Single Tax League and the Taxpayers' League, no middle-class reform
groups came to the front to join the *Post-Dispatch* in a counterattack.
One reason might have been the impending war with Spain. Perhaps
St. Louisans were still weary from the last election and more concerned
about Spanish atrocities in Cuba than streetcar franchises. For whatever
reason, a general city-wide interest in reform did not manifest itself in
1898. The time was not right. Four years later, however, when Joseph
Folk renewed charges of bribery and corruption, the popular mood had
changed.[13]

Joseph Folk, after only a few years in St. Louis, managed to build
up a successful civil law practice specializing in corporation law. He
also became increasingly active in Democratic politics, and joined a
group of young professional men with moderately reformist views in
organizing the Jefferson Club of St. Louis. Members of the Jefferson
Club generally disliked the influence of the machine element within
the Democratic party and tended to focus their collective attention on
how they might limit Boss Butler's influence on party nominations. Folk
made a name for himself in the organization when he led a successful
fight to keep the Jefferson Club in line behind William Jennings Bryan's
candidacy in 1896. Allowing his enthusiasm free rein, Folk became the
club's campaign manager during the election and began to establish a

12. Ibid., 109; Steven L. Piott, *The Anti-Monopoly Persuasion: Popular Resistance to
the Rise of Big Business in the Midwest*, 57–59.
13. Nord, *Newspapers and New Politics*, 110.

reputation as a forceful speaker. The opportunity to meet Bryan during the campaign only served to elevate his esteem in Folk's eyes, and Folk continued to be a loyal Bryan supporter even after his defeat. Folk's leadership in 1896 enhanced his stature in the Jefferson Club and was undoubtedly a contributing factor to his election as president of that body in 1898.[14]

After serving as president of the Jefferson Club for one year, Folk yielded the office to Harry Hawes, who had emerged as the dominant personality in the organization and a key figure in both state and local Democratic politics. Attempting to rebuild the Democratic party's political base in St. Louis and, thereby, reduce Boss Butler's influence, Governor Lon V. Stephens set out to unite all the anti-Butler factions under his control. To gain an organizational base in the city, Stephens decided to work in cooperation with the Jefferson Club. The governor hoped to use the club to achieve party unity, gain control over nominations, and win the confidence of the St. Louis business community. As a further step in that process, Stephens appointed Hawes president of the St. Louis Board of Police Commissioners in 1898. With his new position as police commissioner and a reputation as an organizer and political manipulator, Hawes was a natural replacement for Folk in Stephens's scheme. When Hawes became president of the Jefferson Club in 1899, he quickly transformed that body from a small association of devotees of Thomas Jefferson into a powerful organization of five thousand members. Successfully integrating ethnic and racial minorities, businessmen, and public utility speculators into the club, Hawes headed an efficient organization that could be manipulated for political purposes. As president of the police board, Hawes quickly converted the St. Louis police department into an arm of the Jefferson Club. The club soon had effective ties with every precinct and enough power and influence to have a strong say in the nominating process. But before the Jefferson Club could test its political strength in a municipal election, St. Louis was rocked by a major streetcar strike that altered not only the course of St. Louis politics but the public career of Joseph Folk as well.[15]

14. Geiger, *Joseph W. Folk*, 14–15.
15. Muraskin, "Missouri Politics," 50–53; Primm, *Lion of the Valley*, 373.

The transit strike was an outgrowth of the Central Traction/United Railways franchise consolidation scheme of 1898–1899. Confronted with wage cuts and a weakened bargaining position as a result of the consolidated transit system, unionized streetcar employees began a campaign to increase the number of members in their union, the Amalgamated Association of Street Railway Employees. During the first week in March 1900, the union, assisted by attorney Joseph W. Folk as its legal counsel during the negotiations, presented the St. Louis Transit Company with a list of demands that included recognition of the union, a ten-hour workday, reinstatement of men recently discharged for union activity, the elimination of split shifts, a standardized pay scale, and a grievance procedure. On March 10, company president Edwards Whitaker and his board agreed to reinstate fired workers and to accept a ten-hour workday. Company directors actually granted concessions only to buy time while they floated a bond issue. Nevertheless, a major strike had been averted. But within two months the agreement began to break down. Union leaders charged that the company had reneged on rehiring promises, had violated the ten-hour agreement, and had generally discriminated against the union. Convinced that company directors were not sincere, the union decided to act. On May 8, 1900, 3,325 union employees of the St. Louis Transit Company went on strike. All streetcar lines in the city were tied up, including the independent Suburban line where workers had actually struck over similar grievances one week before.[16]

Initially the strike took on the appearance of a simple labor versus capital confrontation with the crucial question being union recognition. President Whitaker thought he could break the union by continuing to run his cars with non-union workers, and police board president Harry Hawes thought he could minimize violence and protect company property and non-union employees by placing policemen on streetcars. But Whitaker and Hawes had misjudged both the union's determination and the public temper. From the very beginning of the strike, St. Louisans from all social backgrounds joined in support of a consumer boycott of the St. Louis Transit Company organized by the union. Commuters boarded furniture vans, carryalls, tallyhos, milk wagons, ice wagons,

16. Piott, *Anti-Monopoly Persuasion,* 59–60; Primm, *Lion of the Valley,* 380; Davis and Holmes, "Insurgency and Municipal Reform," 5; Geiger, *Joseph W. Folk,* 16.

sprinkling carts, hucksters' carts, and hacks rather than ride on the cars. Others, wearing badges on their coat lapels that read "I will walk until the streetcar companies settle," simply went on foot to take part in a common action of protest against the company. According to Emil Preetorius, editor of the German-language newspaper *Westliche Post,* the company got what it deserved for trying to turn local government into a servant "of monopoly, by monopoly, and for monopoly." The strike had awakened a consumer-taxpayer-citizen consciousness that reflected a renewed interest in the debate over public control of public service corporations that Lee Meriwether had started in 1897.[17]

After a few weeks the carnival atmosphere of the strike began to fade and matters became more serious. Strikers and their wives began to feel the insecurity of lost wages, small businessmen the pinch of declining sales, and commuters the inconveniences of supplemental transportation and inclement weather. To intensify matters the company began to bring strikebreakers or "scabs" into the city from as far away as Cleveland. As frustrations mounted, the violence increased. Both men and women threw bricks, stones, tin cans, and sticks at the passing cars, and shouted abuse at the motormen, conductors, and policemen who manned them. Protesters cut trolley wires, placed obstructions on the tracks, constructed barricades, and even set small dynamite charges in attempts to further disrupt service.

The actions of the protesters, however, soon forced the federal government to get involved and hasten an end to the strike. The federal government had contracts to send its mail over five of the St. Louis Transit Company lines, lines that were disrupted by the disturbances. On May 20, U.S. District Court Judge Elmer B. Adams issued an injunction to prevent further disruption of the mail. The injunction allowed for an increased force of deputy marshals or, if that proved insufficient, a posse could be sworn in to guarantee deliveries. When eleven people were injured in a disturbance between transit company employees and riotous crowds on May 29, police board president Hawes directed Sheriff John H. Pohlman to assemble a posse comitatus of 1,200 (later raised to 2,500) men to restore order.[18]

17. Emil Preetorius quoted in *St. Louis Post-Dispatch,* June 1, 1900; Piott, *Anti-Monopoly Persuasion,* 60–62; Thelen, *Paths of Resistance,* 222.
18. Piott, *Anti-Monopoly Persuasion,* 62–65.

In the end, the use of strikebreakers and the posse against the strikers was too much. On July 2, 1900, after two weeks of quiet negotiations conducted by attorney Joseph W. Folk and Reverend W. W. Boyd, a conference between the strikers' grievance committee and company representatives reached a "compromise" settlement.[19] The company agreed to make wage and hour concessions, to create a grievance committee, and to fill vacancies only from a union list of strikers. The company did not agree to grant formal recognition to the union. The arrangement, however, broke down after one week when the union discovered that the company had hired non-union men in violation of the agreement. The strike dragged on until September, but the union had been defeated.[20]

The St. Louis streetcar strike was significant on several levels. The strike highlighted inadequacies in another municipal service, underscored corporate arrogance and the power of monopoly, raised new questions concerning legislative corruption surrounding the original franchise award, revived the call for the fair taxation of public utility corporations, and reemphasized the need for adequate public control over quasi-public corporations. William Marion Reedy, editor of the *Mirror*, undoubtedly spoke for many angry consumer-taxpayer-citizens when he stated: "All the rottenness of our system is exposed in this strike—bribery in legislation, corruption in politics, bestowal of monopoly without compensation, concentration of power into irresponsible and incompetent hands. . . ."[21] As a defining event, the strike served to make municipal ownership of utilities a vital issue in the upcoming municipal elections in 1901.

The intense public animosity toward the street railway trust caused Lee Meriwether to renew his crusade to make the utility question the cornerstone of a new municipal reform campaign. Shifting from his earlier emphasis on street railway regulation and taxation, Meriwether

19. Boyd, despite having connections with the business community, was also interested in the Single Tax and was on friendly terms with local socialists and organized labor.

20. Piott, *Anti-Monopoly Persuasion*, 65–68; Primm, *Lion of the Valley*, 380–81. See also Dina M. Young, "The St. Louis Streetcar Strike of 1900: Pivotal Politics at the Century's Dawn."

21. William Marion Reedy, "Strikeography," 3.

now advocated municipal ownership as the best means of securing public control over quasi-public monopolies. In 1901 he helped organize the Public Ownership party and announced that he was entering the mayoral race as an independent. Democrats and Republicans blanched at the genuine possibility that he might be elected. In desperation both major parties attempted to co-opt his appeal by stealing his municipal ownership program and claiming it as their own idea. Preferring the more direct approach, Boss Butler allegedly offered Meriwether $25,000 if he would withdraw from the race. Such tactics, however, probably only served to generate support rather than diminish it.[22]

One other issue complicated the St. Louis municipal elections of 1901, and that was the upcoming St. Louis World's Fair that was scheduled to take place in 1904. David R. Francis is usually credited with having suggested the idea for the fair to local business leaders as early as 1896. Francis was a leading St. Louis grain merchant and stockbroker as well as a majority stockholder in the *St. Louis Republic,* the newspaper that most closely reflected the interests and concerns of the downtown business community. The World's Fair, boosted as a commemoration of the centennial of the Louisiana Purchase, was primarily a city-business promotion scheme. To facilitate their plan, St. Louis's business elite wanted an efficient city administration that would modernize the city for the fair. Because many of the leading fair boosters were also closely connected to the city's public utility corporations, they grew concerned when Lee Meriwether launched his Public Ownership party. St. Louis's business elite despised Meriwether for his abandonment of the Democratic party and feared him for his radical economic views. As a result, they were determined to defeat him. To that end, the Big Cinch made a deal with Jefferson Club president Harry Hawes and Democratic Boss Ed Butler. According to author Max Putzel, St. Louis utility magnate James Campbell originated the idea and agreed to act as the major financial underwriter for the campaign in return for the right to select the party's candidate for mayor. For their nominee, the Campbell-led business interests chose Rolla Wells, president of the American Steel and Foundry Company, an

22. Nord, *Newspapers and New Politics,* 116–17; Thelen, *Paths of Resistance,* 222–23.

investor in St. Louis utility companies, and a director of two downtown banks.[23]

The municipal election for mayor and assemblymen in April 1901 was a triumph for both partisanship and the Democratic party. Voters elected Democrat Rolla Wells, who received 39 percent of the vote; the Republican challenger George W. Parker received 31.5 percent and Public Ownership candidate Lee Meriwether received 27 percent. Of the forty-five contested seats in the Municipal Assembly, twenty-one went to the Democrats, sixteen to the Republicans, and six to the Public Ownership party. Hotly contested, the election seemed to exceed all others in allegations of widespread election fraud. Meriwether claimed that 13,000 more votes were cast for him than for Wells, but the Missouri Supreme Court refused to allow a recount or an inspection of the ballots. By fair means or foul, municipal ownership had been pushed aside for a commitment to the "New St. Louis"—a program of civic improvements aimed at showcasing the city during the World's Fair.[24]

The transit strike had another importance that went unnoticed at the time. It catapulted Joseph Folk to local prominence. Even though the strike settlement of July 2 was short-lived, it placed Folk's name in the newspapers, won him public praise for his efforts, and made him a friend of the unions. In fact, Folk had not been shy in his criticism of Whitaker's intransigence during the strike. When the head of the transit company rejected a compromise proposal on June 16 that had the support of both organized labor and the business community, Folk placed responsibility on the company directors and stated: "They seem to forget that the transit company is not a private corporation, but a quasi-public corporation in which the public has an interest. The public demands that some settlement be made." Such comments, and the fact that the agreement of July 2 allowed the union to claim at least a partial victory, did not go unnoticed among organized labor. At a meeting of the street railway union held at the West End Coliseum two days after the announced settlement, both Folk and Boyd appeared

---

23. Cosmo J. Pusateri, "A Businessman in Politics: David R. Francis, Missouri Democrat," 308–9; Nord, *Newspapers and New Politics,* 117–18; Davis and Holmes, "Insurgency and Municipal Reform," 7–8; Muraskin, "Missouri Politics," 75; Max Putzel, *The Man in the Mirror: William Marion Reedy and His Magazine,* 98–99.

24. Voting statistics are taken from Thelen, *Paths of Resistance,* 223–24.

in person to explain the terms of the agreement. At the close of their remarks, the meeting tendered both arbitrators a vote of thanks for their unselfish efforts in bringing about a fair settlement of the dispute. To Democratic power brokers like Harry Hawes, Folk had become a hot political prospect.[25]

The deal with the business elite still left the remainder of the Democratic ticket in the upcoming municipal elections to be filled, and Harry Hawes wanted Joseph Folk to be the party's candidate for circuit attorney. Folk's recent notoriety and his popularity with the unions were certainly factors in Hawes's decision, but the choice of Folk involved more complex considerations. On August 14, 1900, the *Post-Dispatch* reported that a faction within the Jefferson Club was demanding that Hawes resign as president. According to the *Post-Dispatch,* the faction, led by former club president and businessman John C. Roberts, was threatening to bolt and start a rival club if Hawes refused. The insurgents charged that under Hawes's direction the Jefferson Club had strayed from its founding principles, had become too dominated by Hawes as a result of his influence as president of the Board of Police Commissioners and had taken on the character of a political machine as a result, and had prostituted itself during the recent streetcar strike by accepting funds from the St. Louis Transit Company. For Hawes to survive as a Democratic power broker, it was imperative that he take some steps to placate his opposition. The nomination of Folk was a perfect way to quell the coup. Folk and Roberts were both from Tennessee, members of the Tennessee Society of St. Louis, and close friends. They would be political allies in the future. Folk, with a solid reputation as an attorney, also had the distinction of having served the Jefferson Club honorably as campaign manager and president. Coupled with his recent rise to prominence as a strike arbitrator and with his moral rectitude, the nomination of Folk as the city's chief criminal prosecutor made political sense on several levels.[26]

In spite of Hawes's eagerness to nominate his Jefferson Club colleague, Folk hesitated before accepting the offer. The position paid far less than

25. *St. Louis Post-Dispatch,* June 16, July 4, 1900.
26. Hawes survived the dissension and remained president of the Jefferson Club until 1905. Ibid., August 14, 1900.

he currently made as an attorney and required that he shift from civil to criminal law. Claude Wetmore recounts that it took a committee of businessmen to convince Folk that he should make a sacrifice for the party (part of the party's push to improve its image for the World's Fair). Municipal reformer Frederic C. Howe, who served as one of Mayor Tom Johnson's advisers in Cleveland, asserts that Folk yielded to their pressure only with the understanding that, if elected, he would be free to conduct his official duties without regard to party politics. In a slightly different account, the *Post-Dispatch* claimed that he demurred because he worried that an early political defeat might damage his career. According to the *Post-Dispatch*, he changed his mind only after gaining assurances that he would be nominated for a circuit judgeship at a future date. Harry Hawes recalled Folk's indecision in much the same way. He said that Folk wanted reassurance on three points—the cost of the campaign, the chances of winning, and the effect on his political career. Adding a bit of mystery to the decision is a comment made by close friend John C. Roberts in a letter to Joseph Folk's sister, Mrs. James A. Webb, shortly after Folk's death. Responding to her solicitation for information that might be helpful in writing a biography of her late brother, Roberts stated: "I doubt very much if there is anyone except myself, who knew what decided him in making up his mind to run for Circuit Attorney." But Roberts did not elaborate on this statement and if he did so in a later correspondence his response has either been lost or suppressed.[27]

With Folk willing to run as a candidate, the only remaining procedural step was to get the approval of the Democratic party's Boss Butler. The problem, however, was that Butler had already selected another man for the job! In an interview with journalist William Allen White, Butler told the often-repeated story of how this dilemma was resolved:

> I was going to nominate a man named Clark . . . when in comes Harry Hawes to my office one day an' says, "Colonel, how bad do you want that man Clark?" An' I says, "well—I dunno; I've promised it to him." "Well," Harry says, "I got a young feller

27. Wetmore, *Battle against Bribery*, 23; Frederic C. Howe, "Men of Honor and Stamina Who Make the Real Successes in Life: Joseph W. Folk," 554; Geiger, *Joseph W. Folk*, 23–24; letters from John C. Roberts to Mrs. James A. Webb dated September 6, October 6, 24, 1923, in Folk Papers.

name Folk I want to have it." . . . I says, "well, I'll see Clark and see what he says." And I seen him and he says he didn't need the office particularly, and I says, "well, if you don't, Harry Hawes's got a young feller name Folk that's been attorney for the Union Labor fellers and settled up their strike for 'em, and Harry kind o' wants to name him," and so the next time I seen Harry I says, "bring your little man around," and he done it and I looked him over, and there didn't seem to be anything the matter of him, so I says all right and he was nominated.

Looking back on events from the vantage point of 1925, Harry Hawes recalled the circumstances surrounding Folk's nomination in a slightly different manner:

> In the conferences that took place . . . Col. Butler urged the selection of Ben Clark as Circuit Attorney. Carl Otto was urged by the business men, and a deadlock in the conference resulted.
>
> I then presented to the conference the name of Joseph Folk. Strange as it may seem, there was not a single man in the conference that knew him excepting myself.
>
> After some two weeks conference, the deadlock still continuing between Col. Butler's men and Carl Otto, I was enabled to force the approval of Folk.

Ironically, eighteen months later Folk would be trying to send Butler to prison and he and Hawes would be bitter enemies.[28]

The Democratic party presented its platform and nominated its candidates at its convention on October 18, 1900. The platform (taking direct aim at the previous Republican Ziegenhein administration) piously proclaimed that the Democratic party's mission was to "redeem the municipality from corruption," and pledged its candidates to the "earnest, active and continuous effort to purify the entire administration of this city." The platform further promised that the party's judicial officers would be "governed by law and not by political dictation," and that administrative officers would "serve the public without reference to political affiliation." Folk took up the party's theme during his campaign

---

28. White, "Folk," 119; letter from Harry Hawes to K. G. Bellairs dated February 16, 1925, in Kenneth G. Bellairs Papers, Missouri Historical Society, St. Louis.

and promised a Jefferson Club gathering that he would "show up the straw men and dead men with which the city's payrolls are padded, and bring those guilty of this larceny of the people's money to justice."[29] There were probably few, however, who watched St. Louis politics closely that placed much faith in the vigorous pursuit of any of these promises.

As in the past, charges of voting fraud marred the municipal election held in November of 1900. "Butler's Indians" were reportedly out in force intimidating voters and election officials. False registrants and "repeaters" were said to be numerous, and Harry Hawes's police force was accused of assisting offenders. The Democrats carried every city office, including sheriff, circuit judges, coroner, public administrator, and circuit attorney: Folk defeated his opponent, Judge Eugene McQuillin, by a vote of 61,419 to 59,064.[30]

29. Quoted in Geiger, *Joseph W. Folk*, 24–25.
30. Ibid., 25; Kirschten, *Catfish and Crystal*, 318.

3

Boodle

During the political campaign, Folk had repeatedly reminded voters that, if elected, he would do his duty to enforce the law. What alarmed party managers, however, was that almost immediately after taking the oath of office on January 2, 1901, he began doing just that. Boss Butler felt that because he worked for the party's ticket, he deserved his usual patronage considerations. But when Butler entered Folk's office in early January and told him who to appoint as his assistants, the short, shy-mannered, young attorney with the cleft chin, round face, dark eyes, thin black hair, and studious spectacled look refused. On the surface one would think Folk had learned enough about St. Louis politics to have anticipated such a visit, but, according to journalist Lincoln Steffens, Folk later told him he was shocked that he was expected to turn himself, his office, and the law over to criminals. In defiance, Folk selected as his assistants Andrew C. Maroney and C. Orrick Bishop, two able criminal lawyers.

The young circuit attorney then instructed the grand jury to investigate the charges of fraud that surfaced during the recent municipal elections. To leaders of the Democratic machine, it looked as if Folk was disloyally turning on his party by setting out to arrest the very men who had worked for his own election. He was told to let Democratic "ballot-stuffers" go and to prosecute only those of the opposition. He was threatened with political ruin if he refused. But once again, stubbornly determined to uphold the law and give his office meaning, he persistently pressed forward with his cases. The grand jury eventually indicted sixteen individuals for crimes that included falsely and fraudulently impersonating registered and qualified voters, voting in more than one precinct, ballot tampering, and filing false election returns. If nothing else, Folk had established that he would not be the "innocent dupe" of the party machine. In defying Boss Butler and in pressing ahead with the election fraud cases, he had given the first indication that he possessed both principle and pertinacity.[1]

The public reaction to Folk's first attempts at honest politics was a conditioned one. According to Lincoln Steffens, "there was a sensation. But the stir was due to the novelty and incomprehensibility of such non-partisan conduct in public office." A few St. Louisans might have hoped for more from Folk, but he had only promised to enforce the law—not to reform St. Louis. And for the remainder of his first year in office, Folk did little else that drew attention to himself. Claude Wetmore, perhaps the most perceptive observer of St. Louis politics at that time, remembered that there were "mutterings against him [Folk] in the party ranks, occasionally a citizen would remark that the young lawyer was a man for the place, and occasionally a commendatory paragraph appeared in a newspaper. But ninety-nine out of a hundred St. Louisans had lost sight of the circuit attorney and he was unknown outside the city."[2]

In late January 1902 Folk took a bold step that changed not only his own public image but the course of St. Louis politics as well. On January 21, 1902, as he sat in his office reading the late editions of the local newspapers, he noticed a brief article on the back page of the *St. Louis Star.* The article suggested that an attempted bribery scheme involving directors of a certain street railway and members of the Municipal Assembly had apparently gone sour and that the parties involved were squabbling over unpaid bribe money. The article mentioned no names, identified no corporation, simply gave no details. The next day Folk called James M. "Red" Galvin, the reporter who wrote the article, to his office for a talk. Galvin had been a reporter for several St. Louis newspapers for years and had a reputation as a sort of "Jack-of-all-news" or "tipster." The novelist Theodore Dreiser, who worked with Galvin as a St. Louis reporter during the early to mid-1890s, remembered him as an "amateur detective, and political and

---

1. Wetmore, *Battle against Bribery,* 24–25; Steffens, *Autobiography,* 369; Filler, *Crusaders for American Liberalism,* 97; *St. Louis Post-Dispatch,* June 28, 1901; Johns, *Time of Our Lives,* 149.

2. Lincoln Steffens, "The Shamelessness of St. Louis," 554; Wetmore, *Battle against Bribery,* 26.

police hanger on" who "could glean news of things where other reporters could not. . . . By reason of his underworld connections many amazing details . . . of political and social jobbery came to light. . . ."[3] Such was apparently the case here.

Galvin was unable to supply much additional information, but he had heard that the negotiations with the Combine had not been conducted by the regular intermediary in such dealings, Boss Butler, but, instead, by Philip Stock, an experienced lobbyist and secretary for the St. Louis Brewers' Association. Because St. Louis only had two competing street railway lines—the St. Louis Transit Company and the St. Louis and Suburban Railway Company—Folk was able to discover that the Suburban was the only company to have recently requested a franchise extension from the Municipal Assembly. The circuit attorney also learned that the assembly had approved the ordinance (Council Bill No. 44, commonly known as the Suburban Railway bill) granting the extension, but that a court ruling had voided the new franchise at the last minute. Though the details were sketchy, Folk was convinced that a crime had been committed and that he knew both the bribing company and the company's agent.[4]

Folk immediately issued subpoenas to every member of the Municipal Assembly who had voted on the Suburban franchise bill and to officers of the street railway company to appear before the grand jury. He quickly found out that nobody was talking. In desperation, Folk decided to bluff. He called Charles H. Turner, president of the Suburban Railway Company, and Philip Stock to the grand jury room and boldly threatened them. Said Folk:

> Gentlemen, I have secured sufficient evidence to warrant the return of indictments against you for bribery, and I shall prosecute you to the full extent of the law and send you to the penitentiary unless you tell to this grand jury the complete history of the corruptionist methods employed by you to secure the passage of Ordinance No. 44. I shall give you three days to consider the matter. At the end of that time, if you have not returned here and

3. Theodore Dreiser, "Out of My Newspaper Days," 542.
4. Wetmore, *Battle against Bribery,* 27–29; Claude Wetmore and Lincoln Steffens, "Tweed Days in St. Louis," 580.

given us the information demanded, warrants will be issued for
your arrest.

Three days later, under advice of counsel, Turner and Stock turned
state's evidence and told both Folk and the grand jury the details of the
Suburban bribery scandal.[5]

The information that Turner and Stock subsequently gave to the
grand jury, and later in open court, revealed just how legislation was
"marketed" in St. Louis. In 1900 the Suburban Railway Company
desired to extend its lines west to Forest Park. The directors of the
Suburban, anticipating an eventual buyout by the larger St. Louis Transit
Company, believed that such an extension would double the property
value of the company and greatly enhance its selling price. To obtain
the franchise extension, however, Turner realized he would have to work
through the Combine in the Municipal Assembly. To initiate the process,
Turner approached Boss Butler who said he could guarantee that such
a bill could be passed for $145,000 (Butler referred to this as a "fee"
when interviewed by the press).

Turner, however, thought Butler's price was too high, and decided
instead to employ Philip Stock, who said he could get the bill through
the Municipal Assembly for $135,000: $60,000 for members of the
Council and $75,000 for members of the House of Delegates. Turner
borrowed the money on a note co-signed by Henry Nicolaus and Ellis
Wainwright, friends of Turner's and wealthy St. Louis businessmen.
Suspicious of each other's promises, the parties involved then agreed
that the money, in the appropriate amounts, should be placed in safety
deposit boxes in separate St. Louis banks. It was understood that bank
officials would require the presentation of two keys before allowing
the boxes to be opened. A key for each box was kept by Stock as
agent for the company. One duplicate key was given to Charles Kratz,
appointed by the Combine as their representative in the Council, the
other to John K. Murrell, the Combine's representative in the House of
Delegates. All parties agreed that payment would result when the new
franchise ordinance had been approved.

5. Folk quoted in Wetmore and Steffens, "Tweed Days," 580–81; Wetmore, *Battle
against Bribery,* 29–33.

Kratz and Murrell saw that the Suburban bill was then introduced in both houses of the assembly, and all parties anticipated quick passage. But there was one small hitch. Emil A. Meysenburg, a member of the Council's Committee on Railroads, had been financially burned as a shareholder in a failed concern in which Turner had been a director. Seeing an opportunity to recoup his loss, Meysenburg let it be known that he would allow the bill out of committee if Turner would agree to pay him $9,000 as compensation. Even though the $9,000 payment brought Turner's total to $144,000, only $1,000 below Butler's original offer, Turner consented. The bill then sailed through both houses of the Municipal Assembly. To protect his reputation as an honest politician who was not a member of the Combine and to deflect attention from his having accepted the $9,000, Meysenburg voted against Bill No. 44 when it came up for final vote in the Council. With the mayor's signature, it became an ordinance. But before the money could be distributed, a group of property owners adjacent to the proposed extension complained that the new ordinance violated the city's charter. They eventually won a court injunction that voided the ordinance. At that point the bribe-givers and bribe-takers began to bicker over the spoils. Kratz and Murrell claimed that the Combine had done its job and was entitled to its money. Turner, however, refused to allow Stock to release the money without having obtained the franchise extension. The rumor was that the Combine, impatient for its bribe money, had purposely leaked the initial story to the press in order to scare Turner and Stock.[6]

After hearing the testimony of Turner and Stock, Folk obtained bench warrants for the arrest of Charles Kratz, John Murrell, and Emil Meysenburg on charges of bribery. They were each released under bond while they awaited trial. Arrest warrants were also issued for Henry Nicolaus and Ellis Wainwright, Turner's cosigners, and for Julius Lehmann and Harry Faulkner, alleged members of the Combine, for having perjured themselves before the grand jury. Folk also, with rather melodramatic bravado and disregard for legal technicalities, compelled

6. Wetmore, *Battle against Bribery,* 34–40; Wetmore and Steffens, "Tweed Days," 581–82. See also *St. Louis Post-Dispatch,* January 26, 28, 1902; James L. Blair, "The St. Louis Disclosures," 91–94; and *St. Louis Post-Dispatch,* February 2, 1902.

the directors of the banks in which the bribe money had allegedly been deposited to open those safety deposit boxes (Folk threatened to have them indicted as accessories to the crime of bribery if they refused). He then, again without warrants, had the money seized as evidence. To complete his sensationalistic actions, Folk announced that he was expanding his investigation and that a new grand jury would begin a probe into previous charges of graft in municipal government.[7]

The initial investigation caused quite a stir in St. Louis. Folk became an instant celebrity. The *St. Louis Post-Dispatch* published an article entitled "Folk, The Man All Know Now Was Unknown To All In 1900." The account detailed how Folk, who just one year before had been comparatively unknown to the general public, had suddenly been thrust into the public spotlight. Just as surprising, however, was the abruptness with which Folk, described as possessing a "modest demeanor, a retiring disposition, and little taste for politics" when he entered public office, had become an aggressive, some might say grandstanding, prosecutor. What had motivated Folk to act as forcefully as he had, first in pressing election indictments that defied narrow partisanship and then in disrupting the political status quo in such a flamboyant manner? Was it, as his political enemies would soon charge, simply naked ambition? Or was it the exuberance of a youthful, extremely dutiful public servant whose strong moral imperatives had been aroused by evidence of shameful misconduct? Only two weeks into the investigation, it was too soon to tell. What was certain, however, was that Folk had truly seized the moment, and, emboldened by the notoriety, seemed determined to carry out an extensive probe of municipal corruption in St. Louis.[8]

The honest politician standing fast against the forces of corruption was exactly the story reform-minded newspapers wanted to celebrate. When asked by a *Post-Dispatch* reporter to describe the circuit attorney's character, Judge Frank M. Estes, Folk's uncle and former law partner, struck just the right chord and stated: "Joe's chief virtue lies in the fact that he cannot be handled. He is independent and believes in himself. He is the soul of honesty." Adopting the tone that the city

7. Wetmore, *Battle against Bribery,* 41–49; Wetmore and Steffens, "Tweed Days," 582; *St. Louis Post-Dispatch,* January 29–31, February 4, 1902.
8. *St. Louis Post-Dispatch,* January 29, 1902.

St. Louis Post-Dispatch, Jan. 31, 1902, State Historical Society of Missouri, Columbia

had finally received its savior, the *Post-Dispatch* reprinted a Thomas Nast cartoon from the 1880s in which a female figure representing liberty-freedom-justice-democracy is shown pushing aside two shady male characters identified simply as "briber" and "bribed." In addition to most newspapers, Folk received early support from civic-minded religious leaders like Reverend W. W. Boyd of the Second Baptist Church, the St. Louis Congregational ministers, and from many others with a serious long-standing interest in municipal reform.[9]

Folk soon realized, however, that his base of support, at least in St. Louis, was unstable. He became even more keenly aware of this as the bribery investigations continued. Reformer Frederic Howe, who visited Folk in the midst of his graft prosecutions, remembered asking the circuit attorney if he received any support from the press and the "well-to-do" classes in his fight. Said Folk:

> For a time I had the whole-hearted support of the press, the Chamber of Commerce, and the business men of the city. As long as I was after Boss Butler and the grafters in the city council, I was a hero. But when I started to prosecute bankers who were involved in a city franchise, the press turned against me. The prosecutions were bad for business, people began to say; they gave St. Louis a bad name; they should be dropped.

Lincoln Steffens also recalled that Folk met formidable resistance. According to Steffens: "Mr. Folk at once felt the pressure, and it was of a character to startle one. Statesmen, lawyers, merchants, clubmen, churchmen—in fact, men prominent in all walks of life—visited him at his office and at his home, and urged that he cease such activity against fellow townspeople. Political preferment was promised if he would yield; a political grave if he persisted." To the list of detractors could be added the obvious—machine politicians, who regarded him as an enemy, and party regulars, who scorned him as a traitor. Worse, Folk was threatened with bodily harm. Gertrude Folk remembered that her husband received so many anonymous death threats that they filled a trunk. He was forced to avoid walking alone in the city at night, and, for

---

9. Ibid.; Geiger, *Joseph W. Folk,* 31. The Nast cartoon can be found in *St. Louis Post-Dispatch,* January 31, 1902.

a brief period, even hired a bodyguard for protection. In January 1904 the *New York Times* carried a story to the effect that a group within the House of Delegates actually plotted to have Folk assassinated at an early point in the "boodle" investigations. The love-hate relationship that St. Louisans developed toward Folk would persist throughout his political career.[10]

The second investigation undertaken by Circuit Attorney Folk involved charges of bribery within the Municipal Assembly during consideration of the Central Traction franchise in 1898. The *Post-Dispatch* had leveled charges of bribery at the Combine in April 1898 and had called for a grand jury investigation. But the grand jury did not find anyone culpable and failed to return any indictments. The Folk-directed inquiry into the Central Traction case, however, was far more fruitful than the earlier one. Through testimony Folk learned that in March 1898 Robert M. Snyder, a Kansas City banker and speculator, began a campaign to obtain a franchise that would allow for the consolidation of all the street railway companies in St. Louis. Using the name Central Traction Company, Snyder requested a franchise that would allow his company to lay track for a competing streetcar line almost anywhere in the city. Snyder actually had no intention of doing this. He merely intended to sell the franchise to some other corporation willing to meet his asking price. The new corporation could then use the franchise as leverage to force the existing streetcar companies to sell out to them on reasonable terms or risk being run out of business as a result of the competitive advantage enjoyed by a unified system. On April 12, 1898, the Municipal Assembly passed the Central Traction bill over Mayor Henry Ziegenhein's veto. Snyder quickly sold his franchise privileges to the United Railways syndicate for $1,250,000.

Folk's investigation confirmed the earlier allegations of the *Post-Dispatch*—that Snyder obtained the Central Traction franchise by bribing members of the Municipal Assembly. Folk obtained testimony that Snyder paid approximately $250,000 to secure the franchise (twenty-

10. Frederic C. Howe, *Confessions of a Reformer*, 192; Wetmore and Steffens, "Tweed Days," 583; Wetmore, *Battle against Bribery*, 50–56; Geiger, *Joseph W. Folk*, 31–32; *St. Louis Post-Dispatch*, January 29, 31, 1902; *New York Times*, January 10, 1904. The *Times* ran a second story of a rumored plot to assassinate Folk during the Democratic State Convention at Jefferson City in July 1904. See also *New York Times*, July 19, 1904.

five members of the House of Delegates received bribes of $3,000 apiece and seven members of the Council accepted from $10,000 to $17,500 each for their votes). Although the circuit attorney had sufficient evidence to prosecute, he had a problem (one that would plague all his investigations) with the statute of limitations on such crimes. Missouri law prohibited the prosecution of individuals for bribery after three years. But the law also stipulated that permanent residency in Missouri was required for such immunity. In this particular case the bribe-takers had all remained in St. Louis, but the bribe-giver had moved to New York. When Folk learned that Snyder had maintained a residence at the Waldorf-Astoria Hotel in New York City for most of the time since 1898, he thought Snyder should still be liable under the law as a non-resident of Missouri. On that assumption he obtained a bench warrant for Snyder's arrest on February 15, 1902. Also arrested, and adding to the list of St. Louis businessmen accused of dealing with corrupt city government, was George J. Kobusch, president of the St. Louis Car Company, for perjury before the grand jury. Like Turner and Stock before him, Kobusch accepted immunity from prosecution in exchange for evidence that could be used in the case against Snyder.[11]

Folk's third major investigation, and the one many St. Louisans eagerly awaited, involved Boss Butler, the notorious symbol of the boodle and graft then plaguing city government. Rejected as the middleman in the Suburban franchise deal and saved by the statute of limitations in the Central Traction franchise scheme, Butler had managed to escape indictment during the first two bribery investigations. But on March 14, 1902, Butler was arrested and charged with attempting to bribe two members of the St. Louis Board of Health in connection with the awarding of the city's garbage disposal contract in September 1900. Butler was charged with having offered bribes of $2,500 each to Dr. Henry Chapman and Dr. Albert Merrell, both members of the Board of Health, to secure a three-year garbage contract for the St. Louis Sanitary Company of which he was a primary stockholder. The St. Louis Sanitary Company had held

11. Primm, *Lion of the Valley,* 387; Geiger, *Joseph W. Folk,* 33–34; Wetmore, *Battle against Bribery,* 57–65; Wetmore and Steffens, "Tweed Days," 583–85; "Municipal Corruption: An Interview with Joseph W. Folk," 2805; Howe, "Men of Honor and Stamina," 556; *St. Louis Post-Dispatch,* February 9, 15, 1902.

the city's garbage disposal contract since 1891. It was the only company in St. Louis to employ the Merz process of reduction as required by city ordinance, a process that reduced garbage by both chemical and mechanical means and yielded fertilizing material and grease as saleable by-products. Short of having another company convert to the Merz process, or having the city build and operate its own plant or have the garbage disposed of outside the city, the St. Louis Sanitary Company had a lock on the contract. The company's bid of $130,000 was double what the city had paid for the service under the old contract, but was, in fact, the only bid received. Ironically, Butler was nabbed bribing two public officials he did not have to bribe. The prosecution's case rested on the testimony of the two physicians, who interestingly enough had waited until the other boodle prosecutions had started before coming forth to tell their stories.[12]

In September 1902, during the trial of those implicated in the Suburban bribery case, Folk learned of another old scandal—the street lighting deal of 1899. The information triggered Folk's fourth major investigation. Like the Central Traction/United Railways scheme of 1898–1899, this scandal involved a New York syndicate that wanted to monopolize St. Louis's lighting business, which prior to 1899 had been divided among several companies. In October 1899, the Council approved a bill that allowed companies to submit bids for a ten-year contract to light the entire city of St. Louis. Members of the Combine in the House of Delegates looked upon this as another opportunity for remuneration when the bill came their way. The Combine let it be known that it would cost the bill's backers $75,000 to get the measure approved. When the bribe money did not appear, the Combine defeated the bill as a sort of object lesson. One week later, however, the Combine was persuaded to reconsider the bill and pass it. Delegates received $2,500 each for their votes. It was rumored that Boss Butler, with money provided by James Campbell, principle owner of the Welsbach Gas-Lighting Company, had distributed the bribe money to the members of the Combine.

12. John D. Lawson, ed., *American State Trials,* 492–500; Wetmore, *Battle against Bribery,* 110–12, 117; Geiger, *Joseph W. Folk,* 35; *St. Louis Post-Dispatch,* February 5, 16, 1902.

Sixteen members of the House of Delegates were indicted for bribery in both the Suburban street railway and lighting franchise deals, which became legally intertwined. Fifteen of the sixteen were charged with perjury as well. In addition, three other members of the Combine had already turned state's evidence in the Suburban scandal. What Folk needed was confirmation that it had been Boss Butler who had presented the $47,500 in bribe money to the nineteen members of the Combine in behalf of the bill's backers. To Folk's good fortune, three members of the House Combine already indicted in the Suburban investigation offered to make a deal. Unable to make bail and tired of prison martyrdom, they agreed to turn state's evidence in the lighting scandal and testify that it had been Boss Butler who delivered the bribe money. Butler was arrested for a second time on October 21, 1902, and again charged with bribery.[13]

Paralleling the investigations chronologically were the equally sensational trials. Folk realized that if he was to win popular support (and advance his own political career), he would have to convince skeptical St. Louisans that he could turn indictments into convictions. Eager to gain his first legal victory, Folk pressed to begin the trials of John Murrell and Charles Kratz, the Combine's agents in the Suburban deal. A victory in this case would provide momentum for related prosecutions and add force to his ongoing investigations as well. The trial of Murrell was to begin on February 17, 1902, and that of Kratz ten days later. But Folk's hopes for a quick victory were upset when lawyers for the defendants won delays. Murrell's trial was delayed twice—once for personal illness and then again when his lawyer fell victim to "nervous prostration." Kratz's lawyers won a continuance until early April. But delay soon turned to flight as first Murrell and then Kratz decided to forfeit bond and flee to Mexico.[14] Their escape was especially devastating to the circuit attorney as they were the only ones who could name the individual members in the Council and House of Delegates who had expected to receive a share of the bribe money. The Combine was safe as long as Murrell and Kratz

13. Wetmore, *Battle against Bribery,* 122–25; Geiger, *Joseph W. Folk,* 39–41; *St. Louis Post-Dispatch,* September 9, 1902.

14. Murrell's bond was $5,000. After his flight the court raised the bond for all the remaining defendants. When Kratz fled he forfeited $20,000. *St. Louis Post-Dispatch,* February 17, March 2, 11, 18, 20, April 7, 1902.

remained abroad. As a result, Folk had no choice but to prepare for the next trial on the court's docket, that of Emil Meysenburg, charged with accepting a bribe to facilitate passage of the Suburban franchise bill.[15]

The Meysenburg trial began on March 24, 1902. Lawyers for the defense admitted that their client had sold two hundred shares of stock in the defunct St. Louis Electrical Construction Company to Philip Stock for $9,000, but argued that it was a normal business transaction coincident to but independent of the Suburban bill. Defense attorneys added that Meysenburg's actions were consistently above board and that he made no attempt to hide his business dealings from his colleagues on the railroad committee. He had also accepted a check for the transaction instead of cash that might easily have been concealed. Character witnesses vouched for Meysenburg's integrity, while his lawyers sought to undermine the character of Turner and Stock as two confessed bribers who had turned informants to stay out of jail. Folk, on the other hand, argued that the $9,000 had been paid for stock that was known by all parties to be worthless, and could only have been granted to facilitate a corrupt arrangement. This was simply a case of money being paid to influence the conduct of a public official so that he would not oppose a bill. In an emotional appeal to the jury, Folk denounced bribery as a crime against democratic government. Said the circuit attorney:

> The legislator's vote and his influence is not private property, but that of his constituents. It is given him by the people as a sacred trust to be administered for the public good, and if there be in the category of crime one that is greater than all others, the unpardonable crime, it is the offense of him in whom such sacred trust has been reposed and who uses it for his private gain and enrichment.

Then, as he would do on many occasions during his closing remarks, Folk quoted from the Bible. In this instance his particular reference was to the familiar Biblical account from the gospel of Matthew describing how Jesus chased the money changers from the temple of God. "So there are in the temple in which our laws are made those who are trying

15. Geiger, *Joseph W. Folk*, 34–35; Wetmore, *Battle against Bribery*, 44–45.

to make an unholy profit out of the place, and it is for this jury to do like Christ did and run them out and keep them from making what should be the temple of law, a den of thieves, as it now is." The jury deliberated less than one hour before finding Meysenburg guilty and recommending a three-year prison sentence.[16]

The Meysenburg trial was the first opportunity many had to observe Folk's skills as a prosecutor. Though never described in terms of being a profound jurist, and prone to glossing over legal technicalities, Folk, nevertheless, impressed many with his abilities as a trial lawyer. Kenneth G. Bellairs, a reporter who covered the St. Louis boodle trials for the *St. Louis Star,* found him "superlatively active, resourceful and persuasive, always dangerous, with an uncanny and unerring faculty of finding and hammering the weak point in an adversary's case."[17] Other strengths, as consistently demonstrated throughout the boodle trials, were his poise (which he used to win the confidence of the jury), his propensity for biblical quotation (which he used to add import to his argument), and his mastery of the emotional appeal (which he used to bind the jury to him).

The conviction of Meysenburg enhanced Folk's reputation and added a sense of legitimacy to the investigations. So too did the report of the grand jury, issued on April 5 soon after the end of the Meysenburg trial. The report described the extent of graft in city government as "almost too appalling for belief," and depicted St. Louis as a city "completely at the mercy of faithless public servants." The report chronicled a ten-year period of franchise fraud and placed blame on the intelligent citizens of St. Louis who had, through their disinterest, allowed corruption to thrive in their city. The grand jury praised the efforts of Circuit Attorney Folk and called for the public and the press to support the investigations.[18]

The next trials to come up before the court's August recess were those of Julius Lehmann and Harry Faulkner for perjury in the Suburban case. In the Lehmann trial, which began on May 15, Folk used the testimony of two non-Combine members of the House of Delegates to prove guilt.

16. Folk quoted in Lawson, ed., *State Trials,* 406–7, 412; Geiger, *Joseph W. Folk,* 34–35; Wetmore, *Battle against Bribery,* 45–46; *St. Louis Post-Dispatch,* March 25–28, 1902. For complete trial record, see Lawson, ed., *State Trials,* 337–416.

17. K. G. Bellairs, "The Legal Side of Joseph W. Folk," 65.

18. Geiger, *Joseph W. Folk,* 36. See also *St. Louis Post-Dispatch,* April 5, 1902.

The witnesses confirmed the existence of a House Combine (composed of nineteen of the twenty-eight delegates) organized for the purpose of controlling legislation and acknowledged that Lehmann was a member. One of the witnesses swore that Lehmann had actually requested him to intervene in the dispute with Turner in an attempt to effect a settlement. Defense attorneys, on the other hand, held fast to the assertion that Lehmann was ignorant of the existence of a Combine and not a party to any alleged bribery scheme. Folk, in his summation to the jury, again called bribery "the greatest offense that can be committed against the people," implored the jury to "uphold the arms of the officers of the law and grand juries, or . . . render them powerless and helpless against the forces of evil," and asked the jury to convict Lehmann as an example. The jury quickly reached that same decision and recommended a two-year prison sentence.[19]

Faulkner's trial, which began on July 23, was merely a repeat of Lehmann's. Witnesses told the court that Faulkner had informed them of the Suburban bribery deal long before Faulkner denied any knowledge of this before the grand jury. The jury again returned a guilty verdict and recommended a minimum two-year prison term. Between January 21, 1902, when "Red" Galvin's story broke in the *Star*, and the end of July, when the court took its August recess, Folk initiated three major bribery investigations, examined approximately one thousand witnesses before several grand juries, and amassed over three thousand pages of typed testimony.[20]

While the public eagerly awaited the trials of Edward Butler and Robert Snyder, which had been postponed until late September and early October, Folk worked to procure the return of Murrell and Kratz from Mexico. This was a task made especially difficult because bribery was not included in the extradition treaty between the United States and Mexico. Folk, however, felt some sort of accommodation with the Mexican government might be reached, and he sent two officials to Mexico to see if they could negotiate the extradition of the fugitives. In the meantime, Folk, in cooperation with Senator Francis M. Cockrell of Missouri, petitioned Secretary of State John Hay to request extradition.

19. Lawson, ed., *State Trials,* 417–52; *St. Louis Post-Dispatch,* May 16–18, 1902.
20. *St. Louis Post-Dispatch,* July 23–24, 26, 31, 1902.

Hay was persuaded to make the request, only to be refused by the Mexican government. Undaunted, Folk then decided to lobby to get the extradition treaty with Mexico amended to include bribery. Meetings between Senator Cockrell, Secretary Hay, and Circuit Attorney Folk in Washington in May 1902 led to the almost immediate negotiation of an amendment to the treaty. The new agreement, signed by the U.S. Ambassador to Mexico and the Mexican Minister of Foreign Affairs on June 25, 1902, was ratified by the United States Senate in June of 1903. But because the treaty was not retroactive, it was of no immediate help to Folk in the Murrell-Kratz case.[21]

It appeared as if the only avenue open to Folk was to persuade the two fugitives to return on their own accord. It was reported that Kratz was financially secure and unwilling to consider such a proposal, but there were rumors that Murrell was ill, broke, and homesick and perhaps vulnerable to such a request. At that point, Folk received some unsolicited assistance from George Johns, editor of the *Post-Dispatch*. Johns proposed that the newspaper, at its own expense, would attempt to locate Murrell and make an effort to convince him to return for trial. Folk, glad to have Johns's assistance, gave the editor what information he had concerning the whereabouts of Murrell in Mexico. Johns then selected newspaperman Frank O'Neil for the job of finding and convincing Murrell. O'Neil was already famous for having persuaded Frank James, the brother of Jesse James, to surrender and stand trial. Working with a photograph of Murrell, O'Neil tracked his man to Mexico City. There, using arguments that had earlier proven successful with Frank James—that he could exchange a life of misery, sickness, and exile for a clear conscience, possible acquittal, and life at home among friends—he persuaded Murrell to give himself up.

Kept abreast of these events, Folk told no one of Murrell's return. He kept him hidden outside of St. Louis, stressed the likelihood of immunity from prosecution, and took down his full confession. At Murrell's trial, which began on September 8, 1902, Folk was able to prove the existence of a Combine in the House of Delegates and connect the Combine to Philip Stock and the $75,000 provided by Charles Turner. In addition,

21. Geiger, *Joseph W. Folk*, 38; *St. Louis Post-Dispatch*, May 2, 7, 9, 12–13, June 26, 1902.

Murrell provided information that linked the Combine to the lighting franchise deal of 1899. Sixteen members of the House of Delegates were indicted for bribery, while fifteen of the sixteen faced charges of perjury before the grand jury as well. Three delegates agreed to become witnesses for the state against Edward Butler in the lighting scandal. As valuable as Murrell's testimony was, he had only implicated members of the House of Delegates who had sold their votes in the Suburban deal. Council members who had committed the same crime were safe as long as Kratz remained in Mexico.[22]

The two remaining major trials awaiting Folk were those of Snyder and Butler. The trial of Robert Snyder, accused of bribing members of the Municipal Assembly in the Central Traction franchise scheme of 1898, began on September 29, 1902. The key witnesses in the trial were Councilman Frederick G. Uthoff and businessman George J. Kobusch. Uthoff testified that Snyder had paid him $50,000 for his vote in the Central Traction deal. Kobusch, who had turned state's evidence to escape a perjury conviction, corroborated Uthoff's testimony and swore that Snyder had told him he had paid $250,000 to members of the Municipal Assembly to secure the Central Traction franchise. Kobusch also recounted that he had personally delivered $10,000 from Snyder to one councilman. The defense made no attempt to refute the bribery charges.

As the statute of limitations in the case had expired, the legal contest hinged on whether or not Snyder had been a resident of Missouri since 1898. Folk was able to prove that Snyder had spent a great deal of time in New York, but Snyder's lawyers argued that their client had never relinquished residency in Kansas City, that he continued to maintain a home there, and that his children had always lived there. The circuit attorney had the weaker argument, but then Snyder's attorney, Henry S. Priest, made the mistake of uttering the most widely quoted comment to come out of the boodle investigations. Said Priest to the jury: "There are worse crimes than bribery; bribery is, after all, not such a serious crime. It is a conventional offense, . . . a trifling offense, a mere perversion of justice." To this, Folk responded with his equally famous line—"bribery

22. Geiger, *Joseph W. Folk,* 38–39; Wetmore, *Battle against Bribery,* 66–83; Johns, *Time of Our Lives,* 151–52; *St. Louis Post-Dispatch,* September 8, 14, October 5, 1902.

is treason, and the givers and takers of bribes are . . . traitors. . . ." In the final deliberations, the crucial legal question regarding Snyder's residency seemed to merit little importance in the minds of jurors. They found Snyder guilty of bribery and recommended a five-year sentence.[23]

The next trial to result from Folk's graft investigations involved Boss Edward Butler and charges that he had bribed two members of the Board of Health to win a garbage contract. All St. Louis was riveted to the proceedings. But because Butler had many enemies in St. Louis and had been subjected to such intense editorial abuse and cartoon ridicule in the newspapers, there was some question whether he could get a fair trial in the city. Using that basic argument, Butler's lawyers won a change of venue to Columbia, Missouri, the state's university town. When the trial opened in the Boone County Courthouse on October 13, 1902, the defense immediately requested a demurrer to the indictment. Using an argument that would later be significant, Butler's attorneys argued that the St. Louis Board of Health had not technically been given the authority to approve any contract providing for the reduction of the city's garbage. Accordingly, if Butler offered a bribe to this "unofficial" board, he was guilty of nothing. Judge John Hockaday, after a day's deliberation, overruled the motion and ordered the case to proceed. But before anyone was called to testify, the defense requested a continuance ostensibly to locate a missing witness. The request for a continuance was probably a ploy to gain Butler's release so that he could take an active part in the current election campaign in St. Louis in which his son, James Butler, was running for reelection to Congress. Wishing to be fair, Judge Hockaday granted a continuance in the trial until November 10. In doing so, he intensified high drama.[24]

When the Butler trial resumed four weeks later, both sides were prepared to present their cases to a jury composed almost entirely of farmers. The trial hinged on the testimony of the two prize witnesses, Drs. Chapman and Merrell. The defense, unable to shake the testimony of Chapman and Merrell, weakly claimed that Butler had actually been

23. Priest and Folk quoted in Lawson, ed., *State Trials*, 487, 490; Geiger, *Joseph W. Folk*, 43–44; Wetmore, *Battle against Bribery*, 64–65; *St. Louis Post-Dispatch*, October 3, 5, 1902. For complete trial record, see Lawson, ed., *State Trials*, 453–91.

24. Lawson, ed., *State Trials*, 498–507; Wetmore, *Battle against Bribery*, 112–16; Geiger, *Joseph W. Folk*, 44–45; *St. Louis Post-Dispatch*, June 5–9, October 13, 16, 1902.

bedridden at the time of the alleged bribe. They also argued that because the St. Louis Sanitary Company was the only concern legally empowered to reduce the city's garbage, no reason to offer a bribe existed.

Folk responded to the defense by arguing that Butler's financial involvement in both the Sanitary Company and the Hauling Company, which would have been ruined if the bid was not accepted, provided sufficient motive to bribe. Relying on the technique of emotional appeal that had served him so well before, he informed the jury that "the giver of bribes robs the entire community" and "poisons the very foundation of the law itself. . . ." Then, from what he may have remembered from his Sunday school days, Folk reminded the jury that: "The Children of Israel of old had the ark of the covenant of God, and whosoever would lay profane hands upon it must suffer death. The ark of the covenant of a free people is official virtue, and he who would corrupt it must suffer for his attempt. He must pay the penalty of the law." And, in a manner that echoed his mother's advice on raising boys, Folk rhetorically asked the jury, "What is the use of teaching that honesty is the best policy if a man like this defendant . . . is not made to suffer the penalty of his crime. What is the use of teaching your boys that it is better to be honest, if one guilty of such conduct is not made to pay the penalty of the law?" Then, in words that were often quoted after the trial, Folk implored the jury to return a guilty verdict: "I plead with you for the civic righteousness of many men. . . . I plead with you for the honor of the entire State. . . . Oh Missouri! Missouri! I am pleading for thee!" Folk then asked the jury to return a verdict that would "vindicate" the law and put an end to bribery in the state for years to come. He asked this, he said, "because it is just and because it is right."

> "Right is right, since God is God,
> And right the day must win;
> To doubt would be disloyalty;
> To falter would be sin."

It was a philosophy that came from the core of his being, one that had been molded in Brownsville and Nashville, tested by experience in St. Louis, and now confirmed by a jury of rural Missourians in Columbia who found Butler guilty and recommended a three-year prison sentence. After sentencing, Butler posted bond preparatory to filing an appeal to the Missouri Supreme Court.[25]

Almost immediately after the Butler conviction in the garbage removal case, Folk, who was acquiring an aura of invincibility in the courtroom, took up the case of Henry Nicolaus. The indictments of Ellis Wainwright and Henry Nicolaus, who had implicated themselves in the Suburban scandal as cosigners of the $135,000 note that Charles Turner intended to use to bribe the Combine in the Municipal Assembly, had generated a great deal of criticism among members of St. Louis's upper class. Wainwright and Nicolaus, both millionaire brewers, were highly respected, influential leaders in the business community. As a result, the friends of the two businessmen tried desperately to get the circuit attorney to dismiss the charges against them. Folk, however, claimed that it was up to the jury to decide their fate and that he was duty bound to bring them to trial.

When the trial began on December 2, only Nicolaus appeared in court. Wainwright was traveling in Europe and, apparently, unprepared to risk his day in court. The defense argued that Nicolaus, in signing the check, did not know for what use Turner intended the money, nor did he inquire. Nicolaus merely signed his name as a personal favor to Turner. Because he had no knowledge of Turner's plan, Nicolaus could not be charged with bribery. Folk argued that it was ridiculous to suppose that Nicolaus, a highly successful businessman, would put his signature to a $135,000 note without inquiring as to its purpose. Folk argued that it was impossible in this instance to prove with direct evidence that Nicolaus had "guilty knowledge." It was however, possible to connect "usual habits and actions with the circumstances that surrounded such actions." In other words, circumstantial evidence should be proof of intent. The judge refused to accept the circuit attorney's reasoning, finding that the state had failed to show knowledge or intent of bribery. As a result, the judge concluded that the case was

25. Folk quoted in Lawson, ed., *State Trials,* 559, 561–63; Geiger, *Joseph W. Folk,* 45–46; Wetmore, *Battle against Bribery,* 117–21; *St. Louis Post-Dispatch,* November 10, 14, 1902. For complete trial record, see Lawson, ed., *State Trials,* 507–66. An example that shows that Folk never forgot the value of the precepts first imparted to him by his mother and his church can be found in Joseph W. Folk, "Respect for Law."

not strong enough to be allowed to go to the jury and he instructed the jury to acquit.[26]

As disappointing as the Nicolaus trial must have been to Folk, he could still reflect upon a sensational year of accomplishment as a prosecuting attorney. The 1902 investigations had led to sixty-one indictments against twenty-four individuals (forty-three for bribery or attempted bribery and eighteen for perjury). His record at the end of 1902 stood at thirteen convictions and one acquittal, and he still had Butler under indictment for bribery in the lighting scandal. This exemplary record would not last forever. All the cases that resulted in convictions were taken on appeal to the Missouri Supreme Court. As an indication that the appeal process would be an agonizing one for Folk, the state's highest court, on December 16, 1902, reversed and remanded the case of Emil Meysenburg, which had come before it on appeal. Finding technical errors in the lower court's ruling, the higher court ordered the case to be retried. For the moment, however, Folk stood as a nearly invincible hero.[27]

Events in St. Louis were also attracting national attention and helping to generate a discussion concerning the health of the American polity in general. In October 1902, in the midst of the Butler trial, *McClure's* published the famous muckraking article by Claude Wetmore and Lincoln Steffens entitled "Tweed Days in St. Louis." Wetmore, city editor of the *Post-Dispatch* at the time, wrote the first draft of the article, but Steffens, who had interviewed Folk in the summer of 1902, revised it to suit his taste and *McClure's* style. Steffens was just beginning to gather information on municipal corruption that would eventually constitute his muckraking classic, *The Shame of the Cities,* and he found the events in St. Louis and the figure of Joseph Folk compelling.

According to Steffens, who recalled the incident in his *Autobiography,* the circuit attorney, six months into the graft investigations, confessed that he needed "help, publicity." Steffens remembered Folk telling him that up until that time the newspapers in St. Louis had been supportive,

26. Folk quoted in Wetmore, *Battle against Bribery,* 93–98; *St. Louis Post-Dispatch,* December 2–4, 1902. Wainwright finally returned to St. Louis in April 1911. His case was dropped in November of that year. Folk was out of office by then and his chief witness, Turner, was dead. *St. Louis Post-Dispatch,* November 6, 1911.

27. Geiger, *Joseph W. Folk,* 46; *St. Louis Post-Dispatch,* December 16–17, 20, 1902.

but that they did not yet know all that he knew. And Folk was worried: "The ramifications of this thing, the directions the trails of evidence are taking, the character of the opposition I encounter—I'm afraid I'll soon be losing all local support. . . . I warn you that what is coming is beyond belief. . . ." Folk then revealed to Steffens the most important and shocking discovery to come out of his investigations. Said Folk: "It is good business men that are corrupting our bad politicians; it is good business that causes bad government—in St. Louis." What Folk meant, and what Steffens and Wetmore tried to explain in their pathbreaking article, was that businessmen, so in need of special privileges and public franchises, misused politics for their own selfish ends. Soon bad politicians drove out good politicians and put the city up for sale. Bribery became the businessman's necessity, while bribe money came to be regarded as the legislator's legitimate perquisite. Steffens observed that Folk had managed to step back from his facts and had begun to discern larger truths—that bribery and corruption were systematic, that the city's best citizens were inextricably linked with its worst, and that the result threatened the existence of democratic government. To Folk, bribery was more than a violation of the law. It was a betrayal of public trust.[28]

In "Tweed Days in St. Louis," Steffens and Wetmore summarized the city's recent events for a national audience. And as Folk had hoped, their hard-hitting, uninhibited style allowed newspapers in St. Louis more freedom to support his antigraft campaign. The two journalists recounted St. Louis's descent into the netherworld of corruption and placed special emphasis on the years 1898–1900. That was the time, said the authors, in which foreign corporations invaded St. Louis to share in the city's "despoliation," while machine politicians gave away franchises, padded city payrolls with the names of people who did not exist, neglected public improvements, and allowed boodlers to siphon off public money. Steffens and Wetmore also retold the story of the Suburban Railway and Central Traction schemes, and recited the earliest convictions of both grafters and men of good standing.[29]

The authors of "Tweed Days in St. Louis," and Steffens alone five months later in "The Shamelessness of St. Louis," also attempted to

28. Steffens, *Autobiography,* 368–73; Wetmore and Steffens, "Tweed Days," 577.
29. Wetmore and Steffens, "Tweed Days," 579.

analyze the apparent breakdown in local democracy. They described the corruption that characterized St. Louis as *boodle*—the practice by which bankers, lawyers, corporation managers, and promoters bribed public officials to gain franchises, contracts, or low tax assessments. And they informed readers that its ramifications were complex. Boodle robbed the community, threatened free government, and jeopardized the sovereignty of the citizen. As Steffens later stated in *The Shame of the Cities:*

> The great truth I tried to make plain was that which Mr. Folk insists so constantly upon; that bribery is no ordinary felony, but treason, that the "corruption which breaks out here and there and now and then" is not an occasional offense, but a common practice, and that the effect of it is literally to change the form of our government from one that is representative of the people to an oligarchy, representative of special interests.

Completing their analysis, Wetmore and Steffens issued a warning— municipal corruption, as revealed by Folk in St. Louis, could be found anywhere.[30]

---

30. Lincoln Steffens, *The Shame of the Cities,* 17; Wetmore and Steffens, "Tweed Days," 577–86; Steffens, "Shamelessness," 545–60.

4

The System

By early 1903 Folk had become Missouri's most publicized political figure. While most Missourians knew of Folk's accomplishments, few knew much about the man himself. Journalist William Allen White described him as "pleasant and good-natured to a point of geniality, but . . . never humorous—never sarcastic, never flippant. He never lets himself loose. His countenance has a glow to it, but it is not of gaiety, but rather of kindness. He plays the game of life with a smiling face, but with his cards close to his vest buttons."[1] Folk's public persona during the highly publicized investigations and trials added to this impression. His professional demeanor throughout the proceedings underscored the seriousness of the moment, but not without adding an unemotional cast to his bearing. Some interpreted his cool, reserved, half-smiling manner as cold, calculating, and aloof. This was reinforced as compromising propositions and outright threats forced him to withdraw even further during the height of the boodle investigations. His penchant for somber, formal attire (Prince Albert coat, starched collar, black bow tie, and ever-present pince nez) added yet more weight to a dull, overly serious public image.

Folk provoked extreme responses from those who knew him or who worked closely with him. A few of his associates found him to be an egoist and somewhat of a publicity seeker. W. Scott Hancock, the elected assistant circuit attorney for St. Louis, complained that Folk monopolized the public spotlight and failed to share credit for some of the important secondary investigations in the circuit attorney's office. Orrick Johns, son of *St. Louis Post-Dispatch* editor George Johns, saw in the circuit attorney a similar pattern of "double-dealing" toward his

---

1. White, "Folk," 125.

associates. According to Johns, this was evident in Folk's failure to give the *Post-Dispatch* credit publicly for its efforts to secure the return of bail-jumpers Kratz and Murrell from Mexico. Such conflicts, generated by ego, ambition, or whatever, were undoubtedly exacerbated by journalists who preferred to herald the heroic actions of a lone crusader. But most of those who closely followed Folk's activities were impressed by his moral courage and acknowledged respect for him as a person. This was clearly the case with journalist Lincoln Steffens. In a letter written to his father in 1903, Steffens said of Folk: "There is a man!"[2]

Folk was also a remarkably self-contained individual. He had no "cronies" in the political sense, no confidants, no advisers, nor, for that matter, did he have many close friends. Claude Wetmore commented in 1904 that Folk was constantly hounded by individuals ("often from the most unexpected quarters") who wished him to show leniency to some wayward friend or who suggested that he neglect certain phases of his work. Placed in a position of being asked to compromise what he believed to be his duty, Folk gradually withdrew himself and shunned the society of others. Gertrude Folk recollected that she and her husband almost never entertained socially while he was circuit attorney. After a day at his office in the old Four Courts Building, the Folks usually dined at home. Occasionally, they attended a local theater within walking distance of their home. Folk liked to relax by listening to his wife play the piano. He also liked a good cigar. Once fond of history and historical literature, Folk read little besides the daily newspapers. He apparently kept up with all the major St. Louis dailies, and read them with a great deal of scrutiny. As historian Louis Geiger has accurately concluded, the basic Folk was a "tireless, persistent worker . . . whose consuming interest was his work and his career, for away from them he almost disappears from view."[3]

Folk was, in fact, busy day and night as circuit attorney. His workload continued to be heavy even after the hectic year of 1902. During 1903 and 1904 he continued to prosecute the boodle cases, and supervised the secondary investigations involving vice and gambling as well as

2. Geiger, *Joseph W. Folk*, 56; Johns, *Time of Our Lives*, 154–55; Ella Winter and Granville Hicks, eds., *The Letters of Lincoln Steffens*, 158.

3. Wetmore, *Battle against Bribery*, 56; Geiger, *Joseph W. Folk*, 57–58.

alleged corruption in the St. Louis Police Department. He also worked closely with Missouri Attorney General Edward C. Crow in a probe of bribery in the state legislature that became known as the alum scandal, and unofficially began his campaign for the Democratic gubernatorial nomination.

As Folk prepared for new boodle trials, he also had to deal with old ones. As previously mentioned, the Missouri Supreme Court had reversed and remanded the case of Emil Meysenburg (charged with bribery in the Suburban scandal) in December 1902. As they would in succeeding cases brought on appeal, the judges found defects in the indictment, in the evidence, and in the rulings and instructions of the trial judge. Judge James Gantt, who was one of Folk's most outspoken critics, reviewed the Meysenburg case and sharply criticized both the prosecutor and the trial judge: "[the case] occupies the bad pre-eminence of holding a larger number of errors than any other record in a criminal case I ever before examined; and if this record exhibits a sample of a fair trial, then let Justice be symbolized by something other than a blind goddess with sword and scales." The court's ruling shocked the prosecution and seemed to place all of Folk's prior convictions in jeopardy. The Meysenburg case, Folk's first conviction, was finally nol-prossed on November 23, 1903; further prosecution was abandoned.[4]

Equally frustrating were the findings of the Missouri Supreme Court in the appeals of Julius Lehmann, Harry Faulkner, and Robert Snyder. The cases against Lehmann and Faulkner, charged with perjury in the Suburban scandal, were reversed and remanded on technicalities in May 1903. This time, however, Folk was more fortunate. After a second mistrial, Faulkner was finally convicted and sentenced to three years imprisonment. While Lehmann awaited retrial for perjury, he was indicted and convicted of bribery and given a seven-year prison sentence. In the appeal case of Robert Snyder, who was accused of bribery in the Central Traction scandal, Folk was not so lucky. Once again the Missouri Supreme Court, on June 14, 1904, reversed and remanded the case, this time on grounds that the trial judge had improperly instructed the jury.

4. Quoted in *Missouri Reports*, vol. 171, 66–67; *St. Louis Post-Dispatch,* December 16–17, 1902, November 23, 1903. For complete trial record, see *Missouri Reports*, vol. 171, 1–67.

The case was nol-prossed in 1906, long after Folk had left office, when the state failed to produce its witnesses. Snyder was reindicted, but was killed in an automobile accident in October 1906 while awaiting trial.[5]

On December 9, 1903, the Missouri Supreme Court also set aside the conviction of Ed Butler, who was charged with attempting to bribe two members of the St. Louis Board of Health. The higher court accepted the argument made by Butler's lawyers—that the ordinance authorizing the Board of Health to award the garbage removal contract had not been officially signed by the mayor at the time of Butler's attempted bribery. In fact, even if the contract had been signed it would have been void because authority over garbage disposal really rested with the Board of Public Improvements and not the Board of Health, even though the latter agency had been awarding garbage contracts for years. As a result, the court held that money offered to members of the Board of Health in relation to that contract could not be construed as bribery.[6]

The Missouri Supreme Court's rather bizarre legal interpretation shocked many observers. Even President Theodore Roosevelt wrote to Folk that from his perspective the decision seemed "an outrage" and that judges had left the impression that they were "recreant to the cause of decent government." Folk was equally critical. Writing apparently in response to Roosevelt's letter, the circuit attorney revealed a little of his own legal philosophy as he vented his frustration. Said Folk:

> There are two kinds of Judges; one kind administers the law
> with a view of accomplishing the ends of justice desired; another
> kind, with a sort of distorted mental vision always hunting for
> loop holes and technical points to defeat the ends of justice. The
> State Appellate Courts, unfortunately, seem to have overlooked
> the purpose of the criminal law which is to protect society. They
> forget that the public has rights in a criminal prosecution, as well

5. *St. Louis Post-Dispatch,* May 19, July 16, 29, August 3, 6, 1903, June 14, 1904, October 28, 1906; *Missouri Reports,* vol. 175, 546–631, vol. 182, 462–528, vol. 185, 673–709; Lawson, ed., *State Trials,* 419, 576–92; Geiger, *Joseph W. Folk,* 48.

6. *Missouri Reports,* vol. 178, 272–347; *St. Louis Post-Dispatch,* December 9, 1903; Geiger, *Joseph W. Folk,* 47, 50; Kirschten, *Catfish and Crystal,* 325; Gerald T. Dunne, *The Missouri Supreme Court: From Dred Scott to Nancy Cruzan,* 89.

as the accused. The rights of the defendant are sacred and should be zealously safeguarded, but the rights of the public should not be lost sight of in doing so.

The theme that the public had rights that must be recognized and protected was one that Folk had first emphasized during the transit strike. It would be part of his legal philosophy throughout his public career.[7]

As for the new boodle trials, Folk won all five cases that went to the jury in 1903 and five of the six cases tried in 1904. The one exception, and a damaging one, was the second trial of Ed Butler for bribery. On February 6, 1904, the Calloway County Circuit Court (in Fulton) acquitted Butler on charges of having distributed a $47,500 boodle fund to members of the Combine in the House of Delegates in the street-lighting scandal. The *St. Louis Post-Dispatch* reported the jury foreman as saying, "jurors did not want to convict . . . on the testimony of boodlers and perjurers, whose statements were flatly contradicted by . . . men of good character." Claude Wetmore quoted another juror who had much the same opinion: "Had one man who was free from taint testified that Butler was on the floor of the house [of Delegates] that night [as a bribing agent], the result would have been different, but we would not convict a dog on the evidence of those fellows who betrayed their associates." In commenting on the decision to the *Post-Dispatch*, Folk stated that he thought the "evidence was as strong and clear as it is possible to furnish in a bribery case. There is no way to prove bribery except through polluted lips." Although Butler dodged a term in jail, he did not escape entirely unscathed. Public disclosures during the boodle investigations and trials diminished his influence. The ascendancy of both Rolla Wells and Harry Hawes as St. Louis power brokers hastened his decline. After 1904 he was never again a dominant player in St. Louis politics. As an added insult, the city refused to renew the garbage contract to his firms when it expired in 1904.[8]

7. Letters from Roosevelt to Folk dated December 12, 1903, and from Folk to Roosevelt dated December 23, 1903, Theodore Roosevelt Papers, Library of Congress, Manuscript Division, Washington, D.C.
8. *St. Louis Post-Dispatch*, February 6, 1904; Wetmore, *Battle against Bribery*, 133; Geiger, *Joseph W. Folk*, 47.

Folk attempted to rationalize the Butler verdict by stating that he had discharged his responsibility and that his conscience was clear. But the *Post-Dispatch*, in a ringing editorial three days after the trial, was not so sure. The editors, deeply disappointed by the verdict, censured Folk for "an apparent lack of thorough preparation and resolute aggression." What the editors meant by their charges was that Folk, well into his political campaign for the governorship, had divided his energies and in doing so compromised his "strength as a prosecutor of corrupt public officials and their influential allies." The editors saw the verdict as the most important of all the bribery cases, and worried that it might give "fresh encouragement to the corrupt combines in politics and in official circles." The overall trial record was even more disappointing. Of Folk's initial total of sixty-one indictments (forty-three for bribery and eighteen for perjury) against twenty-four individuals, only eight ever went to prison. In fact, all eight convictions involved only members of the House of Delegates, really the minor figures in St. Louis graft. Not a single member of the Council, nor any of the men who really ran the graft in St. Louis, ever served time in prison.[9]

Despite the editorial criticism, a number of factors combined to compromise the final results in the boodle cases. Folk allowed a large number of those accused to escape even short jail terms in return for evidence. Numerous prime offenders, for example, were let go to obtain evidence against Boss Butler. Ironically, the many deals Folk made actually hurt his later prosecutions as defense lawyers learned the value of questioning the character of the state's witnesses. Lengthy delays and the normally torturous pace of the legal process made it increasingly difficult for the state to produce witnesses, served to cool public indignation, and probably worked for the defendants. Folk's preoccupation with the gubernatorial campaign and his busy speaking schedule undoubtedly divided his attention and undercut time for legal preparation. Failure to pay attention to detail also played a part. As Folk noted in his letter to President Theodore Roosevelt after the first Butler trial, he valued the larger social significance of what he was doing at the expense of "loop holes and technical points." Sympathetic trial judges, undoubtedly as convinced as Folk of the guilt of those being tried, inadvertently

9. *St. Louis Post-Dispatch*, February 9, 1904; Geiger, *Joseph W. Folk*, 46–47.

assisted Folk to error by glossing over legal technicalities. The strict interpretation of the law taken by the justices of the Missouri Supreme Court was also a factor. The most evident example of their eagerness to observe every letter of the law was in their reversal of Butler's conviction in the garbage contract case.

One final factor that may have contributed to the surprising number of judicial reversals in the higher profile cases was partisanship. Missouri Supreme Court Justice James Gantt, who was openly critical of Folk's vigorous methods and the breadth of his investigations in St. Louis, was known to have political aspirations and was undoubtedly among those who perceived Folk as a traitor to his party. Gantt eventually became the machine-backed candidate for the Democratic nomination for governor against Folk in 1904. It is, of course, impossible to prove whether justices let partisanship blind their analysis. But Lincoln Steffens, for one, was certain that it had, and concluded that "the machinery of justice broke down under the strain of boodle pull." Orrick Johns agreed: "The machine whitewashed them [boodlers] in the highest court of the state." All this said, the supreme court's reversals probably helped Folk politically. People were not pleased to see boodlers escape punishment. As the *Gallatin Democrat* commented shortly after Butler's acquittal in the garbage contract case, "The common people . . . are getting mighty tired of technicalities. They don't understand the subtle legal complexities and circumlocutions that are pulling open the doors of our penitentiary to convicted boodlers. They want fewer decisions based upon hair-spun theories and brain-bewildering subtleties and more based upon justice." And if the solution seemed to be that reform would have to be carried to a higher level to be truly effective, many thought Folk was just the man to do it.[10]

One other boodle case, that of Charles Kratz, allegedly the Combine's agent in the upper chamber of the St. Louis Municipal Assembly in the Suburban scandal, is of some significance. It also provides an excellent example of one other aspect of Folk's character, his pertinacity. As mentioned in an earlier chapter, John Murrell's confession had

10. Steffens, *Autobiography,* 396; Johns, *Time of Our Lives,* 153; *Gallatin (Mo.) Democrat,* February 11, 1904. For a similar analysis of the boodle trial record, see Geiger, *Joseph W. Folk,* 49–50.

implicated members of the House of Delegates who had sold their votes in the Suburban franchise deal, but it failed to touch any members of the Council. Folk realized that he had reached an impasse in the case unless some way could be found to force Kratz's return. After ratification of the new extradition treaty with Mexico (which added bribery to the list of extraditable offenses but made no mention of whether the provision was retroactive) by the U.S. Senate in June 1903, Folk renewed his appeal to the U.S. State Department. As part of his effort to convince skeptics at the State Department that the "new" treaty with Mexico should be retroactive, Folk prepared a legal argument that rested on two tenets. First, under international law, extradition treaties were automatically retroactive unless they contained a clause that specifically stated otherwise. Second, the new wording covering bribery was merely a supplement to the original treaty and should have the force of the original.[11]

Determined to bring Kratz to justice, Folk continued to press his case in correspondence with Secretary of State John Hay throughout the summer and early fall of 1903. Finally, in early October, President Roosevelt (apparently at the urging of Lincoln Steffens who was eager to get Folk and Roosevelt together) invited Folk to the White House to discuss the matter. Perhaps the story is apocryphal, but reportedly, upon being told by Steffens of the details of Folk's campaign against boodlers in St. Louis and of his protracted efforts to secure the return of Kratz and others who had fled to escape prosecution, the president jumped up, slapped the desk with his hand, and exclaimed: "By Jove, we will get them!" After several conferences with President Roosevelt and further discussions with Secretary Hay, the participants sought the legal advice of Attorney General Philander Knox who determined that the treaty with Mexico was retroactive. Based on his opinion, Roosevelt ordered the State Department to request the extradition of Charles Kratz with the promise of reciprocity with Mexico under similar circumstances. Kratz was eventually arrested in Guadalajara, Mexico, on October 21, 1903. After final but futile legal attempts to escape extradition, Kratz finally returned to St. Louis on January 11, 1904, to stand trial. Charging prejudice against him in St. Louis, Kratz received a change of venue

11. Wetmore, *Battle against Bribery,* 99–102.

to Butler, Missouri. There, after numerous delays (Kratz had to have an operation for appendicitis) and charges of jury tampering, his trial finally began on February 20, 1905.[12]

Once under way, the Kratz trial challenged the skills of attorneys on both sides. Arthur N. Sager, who had succeeded Folk as circuit attorney after Folk had been elected governor, presented the prosecution's case. Sager argued that Kratz had accepted a bribe from Philip Stock, agent for the Suburban Railway Company, to persuade other members of the Combine in the upper chamber of the St. Louis Municipal Assembly to vote for the bill granting a franchise extension to that company. Sager produced testimony from Stock and two other witnesses who had previously turned state's evidence to support his case. Defense lawyers, on the other hand, produced a number of reputable businessmen who testified in Kratz's behalf, and argued that the defendant had never met with Stock to arrange a bribe and knew nothing of the $60,000 bribe fund. In explaining his prolonged flight from the law, Kratz, who looked "pale, thin and noticeably meek" during the trial, testified that he had fled to Mexico only to wait for an opportunity for an unprejudiced hearing.

In the end, the jury found Kratz innocent. In defending the verdict, members of the jury concluded that there was insufficient evidence to support a conviction and felt that Kratz was merely a victim of a conspiracy. Said one juror: "I came to think that there was a put-up job of bigger fellows to blame everything on Kratz. The evidence showed that there was boodling, but it did not show that Kratz did it." Others found the evidence presented by the state to be "of the wrong class." In language and reasoning similar to that expressed by the jury in the second Butler trial, jurors reported that they "found for the defendant principally because we didn't place much credence in the testimony of state's witnesses. . . ." "[We] didn't take much stock in the evidence of a lot of men [either indicted or convicted of bribery and/or perjury] like the state brought here." To many who had followed the Kratz case for over three years, the verdict came as a severe disappointment. The

---

12. *St. Louis Post-Dispatch,* August 24, October 8–10, 1903, January 11, February 26, September 26–27, 1904, May 28, 1923; Wetmore, *Battle against Bribery,* 102–9. The Roosevelt story can be found in the *St. Louis Post-Dispatch,* October 11, 1903.

Post-Dispatch, which had criticized Folk for the failure to convict Butler, angrily blamed the jury for Kratz's acquittal: "twelve small men . . . with strabismic mental vision and atrophied reasoning faculties, nullified all the efforts of the state and nation to vindicate justice and gave King Boodle a vigorous boost."[13]

Although the boodle investigations established Folk's reputation as a crusading prosecuting attorney and triggered the groundswell of public support that would elevate him to the governor's office, they were only the most spectacular of many investigations that issued forth from the circuit attorney's office during Folk's tenure. His office put out of business a group of fraudulent investment companies that had come to St. Louis because directors had heard that it was a "safe town"; spearheaded raids on policy shops, vice dens, and gambling establishments; and investigated corruption in the St. Louis Police Department. These actions added to the list of St. Louisans who disliked Folk, and further estranged Folk's relations with members of his own party at both the local and state levels. This was particularly true of his office's investigation of police connections to vice and gambling. The police department was the personal domain of party kingpin Harry Hawes and a part of the bureaucracy still controlled by the Democratic state administration. Folk, in what his opponents charged to be a politically motivated maneuver, further embarrassed his party by forcing the indictment of the excise commissioner of St. Louis, a Democratic appointee, for hindering enforcement of the liquor laws.[14]

What Folk and Steffens had learned from the St. Louis boodle investigations, and what Steffens articulated so well for a national audience through the pages of *McClure's,* was: that big business corrupted politics by bribing politicians; that municipal government was conducted for the interests of private business and not for the common good; and that corruption in municipal government was a problem of national proportions that threatened the very existence of democratic government. In raking the political muck of St. Louis, the circuit attorney and the journalist had come to some startling conclusions concerning the

13. *St. Louis Post-Dispatch,* February 24–25, 1905. For details of the Kratz trial, see *St. Louis Post-Dispatch,* February 20–25, 1905.
14. Geiger, *Joseph W. Folk,* 54.

pattern of corruption in municipal politics. But was the scope of this corruption confined to city politics, or did it extend to the state level as well? Most informed Missourians had heard charges that numerous recent actions of the state legislature had been tainted by scandal. And if the terms "Combine" and "Big Cinch" were common expressions used by those in-the-know in St. Louis to describe special interest politics, the term "Lobby" struck a similar resonance in the state capital.[15] As Folk probed St. Louis and gossiped with boodlers and newspapermen, he heard rumors that corruption ran as deep in the state legislature as it did in the St. Louis Municipal Assembly. But the state capitol was outside the circuit attorney's immediate jurisdiction, and he would have to find some other way to confirm his suspicions. According to Steffens, "helpless, but informed, Folk watched and waited, till at last his chance came."[16]

Shortly after the election of 1902, the *Post-Dispatch* renewed allegations of corruption in the state legislature. This time the charges centered on the popular William J. Stone, the former governor who was currently between jobs in public office, and reflected the newspaper's determination to block the nomination of Stone to the United States Senate. Crusaders for honest government and supporters of the Democratic party in Missouri, of which the *Post-Dispatch* certainly qualified, found Stone's activities as a lobbyist for various corporations doing business in Missouri unacceptable. The editors hoped that one final exposé of Stone's actions as legislative agent for corporations seeking special privileges from state lawmakers would bring about his defeat and the selection of a more acceptable candidate. To that end, the *Post-Dispatch* assigned reporter Joseph J. McAuliffe to investigate. His findings triggered Folk's involvement in what came to be known as the alum scandal, and all but assured Folk's nomination and election as Missouri's next governor.[17]

15. For information on the Lobby, see "The Great American Lobby: The Typical Example of Missouri"; and Lincoln Steffens, "Enemies of the Republic." The Steffens article was later reissued as a chapter in Lincoln Steffens, *The Struggle for Self-Government*, 3–39.

16. Steffens, "Enemies of the Republic," 589.

17. For details of Stone's involvement in this case, see Ruth Warner Towne, *Senator William J. Stone and the Politics of Compromise*, 50–63. The *St. Louis Post-Dispatch* began

The legislative origins of the alum scandal date to the 1899 session of the Missouri legislature when that body passed a so-called pure food law that prohibited the use of arsenic, calomel, bismuth, ammonia, or alum in the manufacture of any food product. The intent of the law, to eliminate poisonous substances in foodstuffs, was evident. Not so clear, however, was whether the substance alum (used in small amounts in baking powder) was a poison or whether, as many argued, it lost its impurity during the cooking process. Complicating the debate was the revelation that the secret sponsor of the original bill was none other than the Royal Baking Powder Company, the only concern using cream of tartar rather than alum as a leavening agent. To alum manufacturers, the passage of the law was a blatant attempt on the part of one company (Royal) to ensure a monopoly by raising a bogus health issue. Caught off guard by the abruptness of this maneuver, alum manufacturers could do little except form their own lobby, mount their own publicity campaign, and begin plans to seek repeal of the law at the next session of the legislature in 1901.[18]

While the alum interests prepared their repeal campaign, the Royal Baking Powder Company and its president William Ziegler took steps to defend the existing law. They employed a promoter by the name of Daniel J. Kelley, editor of the *American Queen,* a mail-order publication that served as the organ of the so-called Baking Powder Trust. Seeking to set up a front organization to conceal his machinations, Kelley organized the National Health Society in New York City. The society became the central agency behind a propaganda campaign against the harmful effects of alum. Kelley then hired William J. Stone to serve as attorney for the newly created Missouri Health Society, a branch of the national body, which was to carry on the fight against repeal of the pure food law in Missouri. Despite Stone's later claims to contrary, membership in the Missouri society, a dummy agency organized to hide Royal Baking Powder's participation in the anti-repeal campaign, never included more than Stone, his son Kimbrough, and a clerk in Stone's law office. Stone

---

publishing details of Stone's involvement on January 21, 1903, the day the Democratic majority cast its vote for Stone to succeed George Vest as Missouri's U.S. Senator.

18. Wetmore, *Battle against Bribery,* 145–46; Steffens, "Enemies of the Republic," 594, 596–97; Towne, *William J. Stone,* 52–53.

wrote letters reminding prosecuting attorneys that violators of the pure food law should be prosecuted, and employed chemists to test alum-based baking powders and then release their findings to state authorities for use as evidence in those prosecutions.[19]

As the 1901 legislative session neared, Kelley made an arrangement with newly elected Lieutenant Governor John A. Lee to assist the Baking Powder Trust in its efforts to block repeal of the pure food law. Lee was known to many St. Louis businessmen as the president of the Travelers' Protective Association and as owner-editor of the *Interstate Grocer,* a weekly trade journal that relied heavily on Royal Baking Powder advertisements and loudly denounced the evils of alum. But it was Lee's political influence that Kelley was after. As lieutenant governor, Lee also served as president of the senate. This position carried with it the power to make committee assignments and to determine to which committees bills would be referred.[20]

One of the first tasks of the 1901 Missouri legislature was to consider repeal of what was now being called the anti-alum law. Without wasting any time, members of the house unanimously voted to overturn the law and sent the measure on to the senate. In the senate, however, the outcome was different. Lee had the bill referred to the Committee on Criminal Jurisprudence, whose membership he had personally selected. The committee then allowed former Governor Stone to speak before it as counsel for the Missouri Health Society. Stone used the opportunity to argue that repeal would be a threat to public health. He also distributed a printed version of his arguments to each member of the senate. The *Post-Dispatch* later accused the Baking Powder Trust of using Stone's arguments to deflect suspicion of wrongdoing when the committee voted against repeal. "To be plainer," said the editors, "a corrupt legislator was to be placed in the position of yielding his vote to a forcible argument from a Democrat who had been twice a congressman, a governor of Missouri, the sitting member of the Democratic National Committee, and the leading candidate for United States senator." In the language of the streets, the newspaper accused Stone of acting as a "stall."

19. Wetmore, *Battle against Bribery,* 147–49; Steffens, "Enemies of the Republic," 596–97; Towne, *William J. Stone,* 52.
20. Wetmore, *Battle against Bribery,* 147, 150.

Following Stone's appearance, the committee, for reasons unknown, decided not to proceed immediately to a vote and, instead, sat on the measure until the legislature was about to adjourn. Finally, lacking any time for reconsideration, the committee reported the bill adversely. The surprising action of the committee, and Stone's prominent role before it, suggested that conspiracy had taken place and that Stone had used his influence to cover the operations of the Baking Powder Trust.[21]

Advocates for repeal of the anti-alum law tried again during the 1903 legislative session. This time the house passed a bill that would have removed alum from the list of impure food substances. In the senate, however, the Committee on Criminal Jurisprudence reported a substitute measure that required baking powder manufacturers to label their products with a list of chemical ingredients. Opponents charged that the revised measure was simply a trick on the part of the Baking Powder Trust to defeat the real purpose of the repeal bill by continuing the deception that alum was unsafe. When the bill finally came to a vote in the full senate, there was a tie. Lieutenant Governor Lee broke the deadlock by casting his ballot for the labeling bill.[22]

On December 31, 1902, just days before the forty-second general assembly convened, J. J. McAuliffe, who had worked as a *Post-Dispatch* staff correspondent for two sessions of the Missouri legislature, met with Circuit Attorney Folk and informed him he had evidence of bribery. McAuliffe told Folk that he knew that Lieutenant Governor John Lee controlled a boodle fund, supplied by the Baking Powder Trust, and that he had distributed money among members of the legislature to influence legislation in 1901. Of special interest to Folk, who was just completing a sensational year of boodle trials, was news that the "payoffs" had actually taken place at the Laclede Hotel in St. Louis. If such information could be substantiated, the circuit attorney could claim jurisdiction and order a grand jury investigation. During the winter months, while the legislature was in session, Folk made several trips to Jefferson City and conducted his own inquiry. The more he investigated the more certain

21. *St. Louis Post-Dispatch,* May 3, 1903; Wetmore, *Battle against Bribery,* 150–51; " 'Boodle' Investigation in Missouri"; Steffens, "Enemies of the Republic," 597; Towne, *William J. Stone,* 52–53.
22. Towne, *William J. Stone,* 58.

he became that the alum story was one of legislative malfeasance. As he pursued further evidence, Folk consulted frequently with Attorney General Crow. Crow, no novice in the area of criminal prosecution of corporations, had previously won antitrust suits against the Firemen's Fund and seventy-two other insurance companies for conspiring to fix rates and against the major meatpacking firms for forming a trust that controlled 90 percent of the trade in Missouri and for selling meat at fixed prices to the general public.[23]

In March 1903, in the midst of increased allegations and rumors, Circuit Judge James Hazell called a special session of the Cole County grand jury (in Jefferson City) to begin an investigation into what had become known as the alum scandal. At the urging of Folk, reporter McAuliffe shared his evidence with Attorney General Crow who took charge of the inquiry at the state capital. Since the distribution of bribe money had taken place in St. Louis, the circuit attorney began a second grand jury probe in that city. As Folk disclosed in an interview published in the *Independent,* testimony revealed that "thousand dollar bills and lesser 'drift-wood,' as it was called, have been the purchase price of laws in the State for years." The report of the Cole County grand jury confirmed these findings:

> The extent of the venality existing among the makers of our State laws is alarming to those who believe in free government. Our investigations have gone back for twelve years, and during that time the evidence before us shows that corruption has been the usual and accepted thing in State legislation. . . .
>
> Laws have been sold to the highest bidder in numerous instances. . . . Senators have been on the pay-roll of lobbyists and served special interests instead of the public good.

The grand jury's indictment of state governance was every bit as damning as Folk's earlier findings in St. Louis.[24]

---

23. Wetmore, *Battle against Bribery,* 154–57. Information on Crow's triumphs as attorney general can be found in the *St. Louis Post-Dispatch,* November 15, 1903; and Piott, *Anti-Monopoly Persuasion,* 33–54, 72–88.

24. "Municipal Corruption," 2805; Cole County grand jury quoted in Howe, "Men of Honor and Stamina," 555.

St. Louis Post-Dispatch, June 28, 1903, State Historical Society of Missouri, Columbia

After denials, delay, and a brief flight from the state, Lieutenant Governor Lee confessed the details of the crime. According to Lee, Daniel Kelley had given him $8,500 to be divided among members of the criminal jurisprudence committee to insure their votes against repeal of the anti-alum/pure food law in 1901. Indictments were eventually returned against Daniel Kelley, John Lee, William Ziegler, and four state senators for bribery, but none were convicted. When Kelley, evidently to get even with Lee for "peaching," made public a number of letters Lee had written him that proved that Lee had solicited bribes and engaged in blackmail, Lee resigned his office in disgrace. United States Senator-elect Stone, who had unwittingly triggered the investigation in the first place, was found to have violated no laws but suffered further humiliation as an influence peddler masquerading as a lawyer.[25]

25. Wetmore, *Battle against Bribery,* 158–79; "More Corruption Exposed in Missouri"; Steffens, "Enemies of the Republic," 597–98; Towne, *William J. Stone,* 58–59,

Folk's role in the alum investigation was secondary, but not without consequence. Aided by McAuliffe (who had the confidence in Folk to bring him the initial allegations), Folk followed his leads, quietly carried on his own inquiry, provided the information that launched the major investigation, worked closely with Attorney General Crow, and found a legal opening to convene his own grand jury probe. Although Crow deserves the credit for pressing the investigation throughout 1903, Folk shared in the notoriety. And in 1903 Folk, the illustrious St. Louis prosecutor, was unofficially running for governor while Crow, the dutiful attorney general, was not. Even Finley Peter Dunne heaped praise on Folk through his national column. In the words of Dunne's talkative yet perceptive Irishman, Mr. Dooley:

> Folk is th' noblest chaser iv thim all. Set him on a boodler's trail an' he's a whole pack iv trained bloodhounds. With tireless energy an' exalted enthusiasm he chases a boodler up hill an' down dale, into th' woods, across th' pasture, around th' barn, back iv th' pig pen an' into th' hin house, where he pins him to th' wall with a pitchforruk. "Villain," says Folk to th' boodler, "villain, confess now an' I'll be lenient with ye. Confess to all yer infamies an' all yer thousand-dollar bills an' all yer associates in fraud and corruption, an', so help me, I will ask the coort to give ye not more than 40 or 50 years," says Folk, as he deftly wiggles th' pitchforruk in th' boodler's vitals. "I do confess," says th' boodler. . . . "And now that I have confessed will ye have th' kindness to pull th' harpoon out iv me vitals an' let me take me chances with the Missouri Supreme Court."[26]

The alum scandal was important for several reasons: it gave Folk added publicity and increased his popularity with voters around the state; it further condemned him in the eyes of many within the party as all the major offenders in the affair were Democrats; it provided Folk, as a reform candidate for governor, with the evidence to make a convincing

61–62. To trace the ongoing coverage of the scandal in the *Post-Dispatch*, see accounts on April 6, 8–14, 16–22, 24, 26, 28, May 3–5, 9–10, 17, 30, July 9, 22–23, November 4, 1903.

26. Quoted in Duane Meyer, *The Heritage of Missouri: A History,* 544; and in Geiger, *Joseph W. Folk,* 55–56.

argument that municipal reform without state reform was meaningless; and it gave Folk and his confidant Lincoln Steffens the opportunity to expand their theory on political corruption. As Steffens stated in another famous article that appeared in *McClure's* in April 1904 entitled "Enemies of the Republic": "Our political corruption is a system . . . by which our political leaders are hired, by bribery, by the license to loot, and by quiet moral support, to conduct the government . . . not for the common good, but for the special interests of private business." "Just as in the city, the system in the state is corruption settled into a 'custom of the country'; betrayal of trust established as the form of government." As Steffens later recalled in his *Autobiography:*

> The business corruption of politics and government in Missouri was the same as in the city of St. Louis—the same methods, the same motives, purposes, and men, all to the same end: to make the State officials . . . part of a system representing the special interest of bribers, corruptionists, and criminals; that acts of bribery and corruption . . . form a continuous process which transforms the theoretically democratic government of the State and its cities into a plutocratic system which disserves the people and serves the seekers of privileges.[27]

As Lincoln Steffens continued to grapple with the causes of political corruption for the readers of *McClure's,* Joseph Folk set his sights on the governor's office and began to articulate a political doctrine that his friend Steffens called the "new patriotism"—that government rests upon the law and the law rests upon its officers; that public office must be held for the public good and not for private gain; that bribery was the most dangerous of crimes because it struck at the foundation of all law and was, in reality, treason; that both the bribe-taking public official and the bribe-giving businessman were traitors; and that the role of the patriot is to stamp out corruption. The challenge that confronted Folk, as he positioned himself as a candidate for governor, was to turn this doctrine into a winning political platform.[28]

27. Steffens, "Enemies of the Republic," 587, 590; Steffens, *Autobiography,* 445–46.
28. See Steffens, "Enemies of the Republic," 599.

5

The Missouri Idea

Near the turn of the century, gubernatorial campaigns in Missouri began early, often more than a year before the state nominating conventions and nearly eighteen months before the election itself. The 1904 campaign was no different. Newspaper editors seriously began to weigh the merits of a possible Folk candidacy for governor on the Democratic ticket during the spring of 1903. For his part Folk remained noncommittal but said nothing to dampen enthusiasm. Perhaps hoping to pressure Folk into making a decision, a delegation of businessmen from St. Louis's wholesale district came to his office in the Four Courts Building on March 28, 1903, and presented him with a resolution commending his work as circuit attorney. Conspicuously, the group included a number of friends and former Tennesseans whom Folk had come to know in the St. Louis Tennessee Society, which he had served as president in 1902. The document represented the sentiments of only one section of the St. Louis business community (most St. Louis businessmen were not as commendatory), but the thirteen hundred signatures affixed to the resolution suggested that support among the shoe manufacturers and merchants of Washington Avenue ran deep.[1]

The gesture, coming from friends, political supporters, and successful businessmen with the potential to contribute heavily to a political campaign was significant. Throughout his political career, Folk never entered any political campaign without first being certain that he had a solid base of support and a cadre of loyal, influential individuals behind him. Although there is evidence that Folk had actually begun to entertain the idea of running for governor much earlier (journalist Lincoln Steffens recounts that he and Folk had discussed the possibility

1. *St. Louis Post-Dispatch,* March 29, 1903.

as early as the summer or early fall of 1902), it is not known when he finally made up his mind to try for higher office. The visit from a segment of the St. Louis business community must certainly have influenced his decision. Not long after that meeting, and certainly with Folk's acquiescence, this same group of businessmen established a "Folk for Governor" bureau. The campaign organization was spearheaded by fellow Tennessean John C. Roberts, a close friend and supporter from earlier Jefferson Club days and the president of the Roberts, Johnson and Rand Shoe Company; Nelson W. McLeod, also from Tennessee and a partner in the Grayson-McLeod Lumber Company; and Murray Carleton, a dry-goods manufacturer. McLeod was secretary in charge. The Folk Bureau immediately began to collect a campaign fund, generate Folk literature, and promote "Folk clubs" throughout Missouri (there would be 125 by the end of July).

By midsummer Folk was being "groomed" for governor in a number of Missouri newspapers (the *Kansas City Times* listed seventy-nine state newspapers that supported him). Apparently as part of a deliberate strategy designed to make his campaign appear to be a grassroots effort, Folk remained silent during these early maneuverings. He cautiously waited until his campaign could be cast in terms of responding to a call from the people of Missouri. He did not have to wait long. The editor of the pro-Folk *Pineville Democrat,* for example, proclaimed that "Folk is not running for the nomination for Governor. The people are running him." Even if he had not formally declared his candidacy, Folk was certainly positioning himself for the race. As further evidence that an orchestrated effort was being made in the circuit attorney's behalf, his office released a schedule of "Good Government" speeches that he would make over the next three months. The speaking tour would allow Folk to test his popularity in all parts of the state.[2]

Folk presented his first speech on good government at the twenty-second reunion of the Old Settlers Association of Montgomery County in New Florence on August 1, 1903. The occasion, an annual picnic in

---

2. *Pineville (Mo.) Democrat* quoted in Frances Patton Landen, "The Joseph W. Folk Campaign for Governor in 1904 as Reflected in the Rural Press of Missouri," 71; Steffens, *Autobiography,* 390–91; *St. Louis Post-Dispatch,* July 12, 15, 30, 1903; Geiger, *Joseph W. Folk,* 61; J. J. McAuliffe, "Fighting the Good Fight in Missouri," 204; *The Nation* 77 (July 30, 1903): 85; Primm, *Lion of the Valley,* 392.

which farm families brought their own dinner baskets to the festivities, featured a baby show, a public wedding, a spinning wheel contest, and, as always, a keynote speaker. But the arrival of Joe Folk was something extraordinary. Special trains brought spectators from distant points, and some farmers drove thirty miles to hear the famous enemy of the boodlers. It provided the first opportunity for many to see the celebrated prosecutor about whom they had read so much, and not a few were surprised at Folk's calm manner, boyish appearance, and pleasant demeanor. Said one observer, "I thought he was a terror to boodlers. I don't see anything very terrible about him. He looks kind." Gatekeepers estimated that between ten and fifteen thousand people gathered to hear Folk. Thousands of buttons with his picture and the slogan "Folk for Good Government" could be found amongst the crowd as well as many white badges proclaiming "Joseph W. Folk for Governor, 1904."[3]

In his New Florence address, entitled "Civic Righteousness," Folk evaded the question of his candidacy, shunned partisan attacks, and avoided any mention of party politics. He did, however, use the opportunity to hit the themes he and Steffens had been emphasizing—the need to eradicate bribery and to fight commercialism in politics. Folk told the crowd that although many problems confronted the American people, none was more serious than bribery. He reminded his listeners, as he had jurors on numerous occasions during the boodle trials, that while other questions concerned the functions of government, bribery undermined the foundation of government itself. "Bribery, if allowed to go on, would be fatal to the civic life of any people," said Folk. "No government can long exist where it is tolerated." Borrowing Steffens's famous phrase, Folk referred to bribe-givers and bribe-takers as "the enemies of the Republic, . . . for when legislation becomes a commodity the liberties of the people will be lost." The corrupt state of affairs that had allowed civic honor to be pushed aside was, said Folk (again echoing Steffens), the "outgrowth of the commercialism of our times." "The . . . mania for speculation has caused a departure from the divine injunction 'in the sweat of thy face shalt thou eat bread.' Too many men seek wealth without the corresponding inclination to labor for its

---

3. *St. Louis Post-Dispatch,* August 1–2, 1903.

achievement. Political commercialism has taken the place in many men's minds of patriotism."

But these problems could be remedied, suggested Folk, through the establishment of a new patriotism and the vigorous enforcement of the law. "We need more of the patriotism of peace in private and public life. There must be a revival of civic righteousness in state and municipal affairs." It was humiliating, he said, to know that so much corruption had been allowed to go on for so long without restraint, but it was "more patriotic to apply the knife of the law to the cancerous growth than by tolerance to allow it to . . . destroy civic life." In concluding his hour-long address, Folk provided a reaffirmation of his own deep-rooted evangelical morality. He reminded Missourians that they had been given a noble opportunity to fight against public evils. "It is a battle of right against wrong; of the true against the false. Evil has been arrogant, but the day of reckoning has come."[4]

At the dedication of the Confederate monument at Palmyra two weeks later, Folk gave his second major political address. Using the occasion to reiterate his earlier political themes, Folk again suggested that the thrust of his campaign would be emotional—a moral crusade against the evil forces of corruption and special privilege. Again, he offered his listeners his prescription for good government: fight bribery and commercialism in politics, awaken a new civic consciousness (patriotism) in the people, and enforce the law. He referred to this program as the "Missouri Idea" and suggested that it could serve as an example for other states to follow.

As defined by Folk, the Missouri Idea necessitated the unrelenting exposure and punishment of official grafters and the transformation of public office into a public trust where elected officials would work for civic good and not for private gain. "Unless laws are strictly enforced," said Folk, "one toleration leads to another, and general wrong is the result. . . . The object of the law against bribery is to preserve official acts from the taint of corruption in order that officials may be influenced alone by the public good." Corruptionists, said Folk, were shrewd, but they feared an aroused public conscience more than anything. "They tremble now as they hear with ever-increasing distinctness the distant

4. Ibid., August 2, 1903.

rumbling of public indignation, but their hope is that the people will soon forget." Then, once again exchanging the pat phrases of a politician for the language of a revivalist preacher, Folk exhorted his political congregation to act. "May those who place civic honor above sordid greed, who despise wrong and hate corruption, march in solid phalanx against the forces of error, and, keeping step to the music of righteousness, make this their battle cry: 'Lord God of hosts, be with us yet, / Lest we forget—lest we forget!' "[5]

In each of his early speeches—at New Florence and Palmyra in August and again at Moberly and Shelbyville in September—voters responded enthusiastically to the man and to what he had to say. The circuit attorney, frequently referred to as the "Honest Man of Missouri," and his speeches, largely emotional expositions on good citizenship, represented the moral ideal in politics. In fact, his presentations were sermons on public morality. To the reporter J. J. McAuliffe, the message was simply, "Thou shalt not steal." Lincoln Steffens, who helped Folk write many of his campaign speeches, explained the intent: "Our purpose was . . . to arrange the overwhelming mass of evidence, confessions, and underworld gossip so as to paint a picture of the government as it actually was on the canvas of the old picture of Missouri as the Missourians thought it was." And to Steffens, Folk was an expert painter: "His speeches . . . were masterly statements; they were good pictures. He was a cool, appealing, rather gentle orator, very moving, but his imagination was the force that carried his audiences, his ability to . . . draw his outline of the corrupted government." Others agreed. "Each sentence [of a Folk speech]," said one observer, "was a nugget of axiomatic political truth, and was deliberately spoken clearly and emphatically. There was no answer except to agree with him or say nothing."[6]

Never a great orator in the sense of possessing grandiloquence or charismatic presence, Folk's primary speaking assets were his sincerity and intensity. He held audiences and juries with his devotion to principle, his earnestness, and his moral passion. The editor of the *Sturgeon Leader* described Folk as being "reserved . . . hard to get acquainted

5. Ibid., August 16, 1903.

6. McAuliffe, "Fighting the Good Fight," 207; Steffens, *Autobiography,* 444–45; A. L. Thurman, Jr., "Joseph Wingate Folk: The Politician as Speaker and Public Servant," 189.

with, and yet there is something in his make-up—that inexplainable something—which leads you to believe that he is the sincere and honest man he professes to be." Farmers especially trusted him. J. J. McAuliffe recalled that Folk once told him that he believed every rural Missouri Democrat with a beard longer than two inches was "with him." And Folk enhanced his appeal by casting himself as a politician who had confidence in the common man. As he liked to remind his listeners: "The power is with the people to preserve our institutions. All true reforms come from the masses." He was witnessing the religion of democracy, and it seemed to be taking hold.[7]

Another theme Folk struck in his early speeches, and one with which other Democratic gubernatorial candidates uniformly took issue, was that honesty was more important than party. The St. Louis prosecutor's repeated warnings that there could be no "truckling to boodle influences," and "no compromise with public plunderers" might have been acceptable to organization Democrats if he had left it at that. But when he suggested that "if a party cannot get along without rascals, the people should get along without that party," he sounded like a traitor to many party regulars. And to those schooled on partisanship as the basis of turn-of-the-century American politics, such a statement was tantamount to blasphemy. Folk intended his comment to mean that excessive partisanship or blind allegiance to party had facilitated the current state of American politics by sustaining the corrupt elements in it. In essence, Folk criticized a political culture that exalted loyalty over integrity. His questioning of party loyalties only confirmed what many machine Democrats had always suspected—Folk was not a party man. It was a problem with no solution, and one that would plague Folk throughout his political career. The harder he campaigned against corruption, the more he alienated party regulars who charged that such actions derived from personal ambition and served only to hurt the organization.[8]

By the time Folk formally announced his candidacy with a speech in St. Joseph on October 24, 1903, it seemed as if he had decided to seek

7. *Sturgeon (Mo.) Leader* quoted in Thurman, "Joseph Wingate Folk," 174; McAuliffe, "Fighting the Good Fight," 207; Folk quoted in *St. Louis Post-Dispatch*, August 16, 1903.

8. *St. Louis Post-Dispatch*, September 13, 1903.

the nomination without the aid of the party "organization." Corruption would be the issue of his campaign: "Bribery is more fatal to civic life than any other crime. It aims at the assassination of the commonwealth itself. It makes the passage of laws mere matters of bargain and sale, thwarts justice, enthrones iniquity and makes lawful government impossible." He would tell voters that he would continue to prosecute corruptionists: "The laws are made to be enforced, not to be disregarded. . . . When some laws are not enforced, lack of respect for all law is engendered. . . . I would like to see the law administered in Missouri so . . . that no man will be above or below the law." And he would redefine partisanship in reformist terms and run on principle:

> Partisanship does not mean the condoning of offenses by those calling themselves Democrats, for they are Democrats in name only. Some partisans insist that the test of loyalty is to stand by the party right or wrong; to defend the corrupt members regardless of decency . . . . The man who sees no more in democracy than this does not know what democracy means. He mistakes policy for principle.

In his own mind he was true to his party, and he would accuse his critics within the party as being the ones who were overly ambitious. "Organizations," said Folk, "deteriorate into machines when they are controlled by men who desire to use the party for personal ends, regardless of the party's welfare. . . ." In defiance, he would run for the Democratic nomination as a "democrat." "The best machine any individual can have," said Folk, "is the heart and conscience of the people."9

The outlines of what promised to be a hard-fought political campaign became apparent as the other challengers entered the race. The first to do so was Judge James B. Gantt in July 1903. Gantt, a Confederate Civil War veteran who had never held a political office, had spent the last thirteen years as a justice of the Missouri Supreme Court and had been openly critical of Folk's handling of the boodle trials. The judge's prominent role in overturning several of the boodle convictions on technical points and his outspoken defense of the court's rulings in

9. Ibid., October 25, 1903.

those cases had earned him a reputation for strongly catering to the Democratic machine in St.Louis. He was also said to be on confidential terms with the current Democratic state administration and very much in sympathy with their administrative policies. Not surprisingly, Gantt was a defender of the status quo and very anti-Folk. In one of his earliest speeches, the judge exclaimed: "My God, haven't we had honest government for the past thirty years? If there is anything I abhor it is the man who comes to Missouri to get rich out of the state and who slanders our fair name by talking about robbery and boodling." Gantt added little of substance to the political debate and never mounted an aggressive campaign, but he stood ready as a possible compromise candidate should the party's nominating convention end in a deadlock.[10]

James A. Reed, former prosecuting attorney of Jackson County and then mayor of Kansas City, announced his candidacy in September 1903 and quickly proved equally disappointing as a contender for the nomination. Despite a reputation as a capable prosecutor, an aggressive politician, an outstanding speaker, and a power in western Missouri, Reed stumbled badly from the start. Deprecating Folk's achievements as circuit attorney and ridiculing his effort to make "boodleism" the central issue in the campaign, Reed seemed to be either under inept political guidance or hopelessly out of touch with public opinion.[11]

Folk's third rival for the Democratic nomination was Harry B. Hawes, the shrewd political leader of the St. Louis Democrats. Hawes had first gained prominence as leader of the Jefferson Club and then as president of the Board of Police Commissioners in St. Louis. Although Hawes had engineered Folk's nomination as circuit attorney in 1900, they had quarreled over Folk's vigorous prosecution of Democrats accused of election frauds in 1901 and then openly split when the boodle investigations heaped further embarrassment upon the party. Hawes saw Folk as a political opportunist and self-promoter who cared little for the party. Writing years later, Hawes traced the origins of their feud

10. Ibid., July 12, 1903; Floyd C. Shoemaker, ed., *Missouri and Missourians: Land of Contrasts and People of Achievements,* 225; Gantt quoted in Geiger, *Joseph W. Folk,* 66; William R. Jackson, *Missouri Democracy: A History of the Party and Its Representative Members,* 1:288.

11. McAuliffe, "Fighting the Good Fight," 204; Geiger, *Joseph W. Folk,* 66; Jackson, *Missouri Democracy,* 2:907–8.

to Folk's refusal to share credit for his victory over corruption with the Democratic party that had sponsored him. In recounting the incident to newspaperman Kenneth Bellairs, Hawes gave the party and, indirectly, himself more credit than either deserved:

> The platform which nominated Folk pointed this [that a corrupt "ring" had long existed in St. Louis] out in detail and pledged that, if he was elected, the corruption would be exposed and punished. . . .
>
> He had been in office but a short while before the evidence commenced to come in, but unfortunately he had some friends who insisted that the credit of the exposure should be personal instead of given to the party which had placed Mr. Folk in office, pledging him to perform exactly this work.

But was challenging Folk a politically astute move for Hawes to make? William Marion Reedy, the editor of the St. Louis *Mirror* and a close friend of Hawes, advised against it. Reedy worried that if Hawes ran against Folk, he risked becoming associated with the very men that Folk attacked—convicted boodlers and their implicated associates, members of the state machine whose political supremacy was threatened, and representatives of liquor and gambling interests who feared that Folk would put the lid on their operations if elected. "To put Mr. Hawes to the front in such an attitude now," said Reedy, "is simply to ruin his career." Hawes delayed the formal announcement of his candidacy until January 1904, but in the end he decided to make it a contest. For party esteem and possible long-term reward, perhaps slugging it out with Folk was the right move to make.[12]

Once the Folk forces saw who their intraparty opposition would be and heard the first collective blast of anti-Folk rhetoric, they accused Gantt, Reed, and Hawes of collusion in an effort to defeat their candidate at any cost. When Folk's three opponents refrained from attacking each other or from even campaigning in each other's territory, Folk's supporters suspected a conspiracy. They charged that the old political guard, having given up any hope of defeating Folk in the statewide contest for delegates, had decided to use the cumulative strengths of

12. Letter from Harry Hawes to K. G. Bellairs dated February 16, 1925, in Bellairs Papers; Reedy quoted in Wetmore, *Battle against Bribery,* 182–83.

his opponents to deny him the nomination in a deadlocked state convention. Mayor Reed would carry Kansas City, St. Joseph, and several other western counties, Hawes would control the large St. Louis delegation, while Judge Gantt, with a few rural delegates, or someone else, could be brought forward as a compromise candidate. It began to look as if Folk's march to the nomination would be treacherous.[13]

The closing weeks of 1903 witnessed the real opening of the campaign. On November 18 Hawes made his first major address in Hannibal and quickly put Folk on the defensive. Hawes charged that Folk was not a good party man, and that he deliberately bartered away party loyalty to gain Republican support. In later speeches Hawes sharply assailed Folk as a "party traitor," a "renegade," a "masked Republican," a "bogus Democrat," and an "ambitious demagogue" and "self-appointed Moses" who promised deliverance for others but sought only advancement for himself. He brought his assault on Folk to a head in a speech formally launching his candidacy in St. Louis on January 16, 1904. Said Hawes: "If the price of Missouri's Governorship depends upon making the people believe that Democracy means dishonesty, then I, for one, find the price too high. Between the man who corrupts a legislature to secure a franchise and a man who corrupts public opinion to secure an office, I find but little difference." The bitterness of Hawes's attack on Folk, as well as Folk's angry responses, gave credence to the forebodings of those in the party who had warned that a Folk candidacy would split the party and give the advantage to the Republicans.[14]

Folk received criticisms from other fronts as well. The *St. Louis Post-Dispatch,* normally very supportive, suggested that Folk, in his effort to make the eradication of corruption the sole issue in the campaign, was missing an opportunity to promote a broader agenda of needed reforms. Three days after his St. Joseph address, the *Post-Dispatch* editorially charged that "Folk plays a harp with a single string; he sings a song with but one refrain—boodle." Pressing the point further, the editors listed five basic issues and suggested that Folk should add them to his

13. See Wetmore, *Battle against Bribery,* 181, 183; Geiger, *Joseph W. Folk,* 67; and McAuliffe, "Fighting the Good Fight," 208.

14. *St. Louis Republic,* November 19, 1903; *St. Louis Post-Dispatch,* January 17, 1904; Landen, "Folk Campaign," 85–87; Geiger, *Joseph W. Folk,* 66–68.

platform. These included commitments to: reorganize the Democratic party to exclude trust influences; separate the St. Louis police from politics; revise existing election laws; drive the Lobby from the state capitol; and compel corporations to pay their fair share of taxation. Folk responded in writing that he would support each of the points raised; however, the incident was more than a minor embarrassment. To run as a reform candidate and yet appear to need prodding to develop a full-fledged reform program suggested that Folk had not yet matured as a true progressive. The Missouri Idea was still in its infancy.[15]

Folk quickly responded to his opponent and most vociferous critic. During a series of speeches at Carrollton, Plattsburg, Macon, Warrensburg, and Independence in November and December of 1903, Folk responded to Hawes's charges that he was not a good Democrat by admitting that he was not Hawes's kind of Democrat—one who had previously joined hands with Boss Ed Butler when it suited his political purposes and who would allow corruptionists to remain in the party for the same reason. At various times he referred to Hawes as "Ed Butler's man," as "the would-be Dick Croker of St. Louis," as "the gangster's chief," and as "the machine-made product of ward-heeler politics," and charged him with being the self-constituted "dictator" and self-proclaimed "censor" for the Democratic party in Missouri. Folk labeled Hawes's brand of Democracy as the "product of machinery," and accused Hawes of regarding no man as a good Democrat who did not wear his brand of collar. "I do not believe," said Folk, "that party loyalty demands the support of corrupt men, nor the condoning of offenses committed by members of the party. If that be party treason then I say make the most of it."[16]

Folk's supporters also began to boom his campaign. At a meeting in St. Louis in late November, they formally inaugurated a state organization and advanced plans for the creation of Folk clubs in each of Missouri's counties. At the invitation of former congressman W. D. Vandiver, chairman of the Folk executive committee, delegations

15. *St. Louis Post-Dispatch*, October 27, November 5, 1903; Geiger, *Joseph W. Folk*, 65.

16. *St. Louis Post-Dispatch*, November 22, December 6, 13, 20, 1903, January 17, 1904.

representing each congressional district met again in the city on January 2 to complete a statewide organization for the campaign. A keynote address by Folk climaxed the second meeting. During his speech, which was interrupted twice by a heckler who shouted "Hawes" and then "Are you a Democrat?" Folk again lashed out at his adversaries in the party by questioning their motives. "Dishonest men," said the circuit attorney, "always try to hide behind the shield of the party and try to make it appear that attacks on them are slanders on the party."[17]

Folk again used his speech to stress that the paramount issue of the campaign was the elimination of governmental corruption. He also embraced a variation of the five-point reform program suggested by the *Post-Dispatch* in October. Realizing that he had been too cautious in his political judgment and too narrow in his political vision, Folk expanded his agenda and promised to destroy the Lobby at Jefferson City; grant municipal home rule to St. Louis, Kansas City, and St. Joseph (that is, take control of police and election boards from the governor and give it to the cities); take the police out of municipal politics; adopt laws that would guarantee fair elections; and revise tax laws to equalize tax assessments and require that all corporations, including public service ones, pay their fair tax share. In more sharply defining these reform issues, Folk, under the pressure of a campaign, took a major step forward in the creation of a broad program and announced his desire to lead a genuine reform movement.[18]

The campaign for the Democratic nomination entered its final phase during the spring of 1904 when party members in county conventions elected delegates to the state nominating convention to be held in Jefferson City in mid-July. At the St. Louis County convention in Clayton on March 1, Folk supporters received their first lesson in rough-and-tumble ward politics. On the night of the convention, a band of Hawes men, referred to by the press as either "Butler Indians" or "ruffians wearing Hawes badges," stormed the hall and caused a riot. After evicting all Folk sympathizers, they took control of the meeting and elected delegates favorable to Hawes. While contesting the actions

17. Ibid., January 3, 1904.
18. Ibid., November 29, 1903, January 1–3, 10, 1904; Geiger, *Joseph W. Folk,* 65; "A Slogan for Civic Righteousness."

of the Hawes bullies at Clayton, Folk's supporters reconvened four days later at Kirkwood and selected their own slate of delegates. It was left to the state convention to decide which delegation would be seated.[19]

The Folk forces fared no better in the Democratic primary held in St. Louis on March 12. Those in Folk's inner circle had conceded that Hawes—who controlled the party machinery in the city—would win easily, but they were shocked by the margin. Hawes won by a vote of 13,205 to 2,801 and carried every contested ward. He collected 111 of the 121 St. Louis delegates, almost one-third of the number needed for nomination. Folk's meager tally of ten delegates came solely from South St. Louis, where he had the support of ward leader A. C. "Tony" Steuver and ran uncontested.[20]

More than dismayed by the results, the Folk supporters cried fraud. They charged that "Butler Indians" or "saloon gangs" voted repeatedly and under false names and that "thugs" roughed up suspected Folk voters waiting in line to vote. Numerous voters reported that the police stood idly by and watched the manhandling. The charges took on added validity when several prominent St. Louisans claimed to have been assaulted in the fashionable West End section of the city. Outraged, Folk supporters charged that republican institutions had been trampled by criminal contempt of the law. Angry citizens held a highly publicized indignation meeting; over one hundred ministers signed a public petition denouncing the "outrages"; and Reverend Frank G. Tyrrell, pastor of the Mount Cabanne Christian Church, published a 228-page diatribe entitled *Political Thuggery; or, Missouri's Battle with the Boodlers* to draw broader attention to the incident and to rally Missourians behind Folk's campaign.[21]

Folk used the incidents in St. Louis to accuse Democratic Governor Alexander Dockery of complicity with the Democratic political machine

19. *St. Louis Post-Dispatch,* March 1, 6, 1904; Geiger, *Joseph W. Folk,* 69; Wetmore, *Battle against Bribery,* 184–87; McAuliffe, "Fighting the Good Fight," 207.

20. *St. Louis Post-Dispatch,* July 16, 1903, March 13, 1904; Geiger, *Joseph W. Folk,* 69.

21. *St. Louis Post-Dispatch,* March 12–13, 1904; Geiger, *Joseph W. Folk,* 69–70; Wetmore, *Battle against Bribery,* 188–94; McAuliffe, "Fighting the Good Fight," 208; Frank G. Tyrrell, *Political Thuggery; or, Missouri's Battle with the Boodlers.*

in that city. Despite statements from Dockery proclaiming his neutrality in the campaign, Folk charged that the governor had allowed his political appointees to work behind the scenes against his candidacy. He also claimed that Dockery was either too incompetent to control the St. Louis police or had secretly cooperated with the Democratic machine to prevent a fair vote in the city. Provoked by the charges, Dockery revealed his true position:

> For the first time in 30 years we are confronted . . . with the spectacle of an ambitious politician endeavoring to elevate himself to the position of chief executive by unfairly and unjustly assailing the administration of his party. . . .
>
> Mr. Folk has been badly beaten in his own home city because of his effort to gain personal advantage at the expense of the party which honored him with preferment.[22]

Several days later, although he denied issuing any direct orders, Dockery admitted that his political appointees in St. Louis and Kansas City had been working for Hawes and Reed. Dockery was caught in one final embarrassment when the grand jury investigating charges of election frauds indicted seventeen policemen and one Democratic central committeeman and criticized the governor for "allowing the St. Louis police department to be used as a political machine." In the end, the Folk forces had managed to turn the defeat into a triumph. They had linked Hawes with bossism, tied the standpat state administration to the machine in St. Louis, further enhanced Folk's political image as an outsider, and emphasized important elements of Folk's reform platform: get the police out of politics; remove the governor's control of police and election boards; adopt laws that would guarantee fair elections; and enforce the law.[23]

The Clayton riot and the St. Louis primary marked the turning point in the campaign. Folk used the positive publicity he received to put pressure on his opponents. While his headquarters continued to generate large quantities of campaign literature, he continued to stump the state. By mid-April he had traveled some 4,000 miles by train and

22. *St. Louis Post-Dispatch*, March 17, 1904.
23. Ibid., March 15, 17–18, 31, 1904; Geiger, *Joseph W. Folk*, 70.

over 300 miles by stage or other conveyance and delivered approximately 125 speeches (200 by the end of May), which reached approximately 250,000 people. Folk's popularity in the agricultural districts proved to be unmatched as county after county expressed their preference for him. Rural voters liked his repeated references to the common man, his attacks on corruption and special privilege, and his evangelical fervor. Hawes, too closely identified with machine politics, failed to collect a single delegate after the St. Louis primary, while Reed, unable to strike a popular chord with the voters, suffered setbacks in counties where he supposedly had strength.[24]

As it became increasingly apparent that Folk's "whirlwind" campaign could not be stopped, many tried to account for his apparent triumph. William Marion Reedy, a Hawes supporter, had predicted in mid-February that the odds were five to one against Folk's nomination. Dismayed by the turn in events, Reedy suggested in early April that the candidate had misrepresented himself. He angrily compared the Folk campaign to the Bryan campaign of 1896 in its "irresponsible, hysterical, malevolent mendacity, and in its demagogic assumption of monopoly of all the virtues." To Reedy, the voters had been duped. But by the third week in April, Reedy had resigned himself to the inevitable—predicting that Folk would win the election by one hundred thousand votes—and advised the circuit attorney's rivals to admit defeat. Judge Gantt exited the race first, followed by Hawes on April 28 and Reed on May 11. Reed immediately released his delegates to Folk, but Hawes refused. In bowing out Hawes lamented, "I thought I understood the people." Embittered by a vituperative campaign, Hawes warned Missourians that they were following an "ideal and imaginary" Folk. Hawes never understood, and journalist William Allen White thought he knew why.

> It was plain to everyone but the machine leaders that there was something in the air of Missouri other than politics. A great moral issue was moving among the people. That issue concerned the enforcement or the annulment of law, and Folk dramatized it. His

24. *St. Louis Post-Dispatch*, April 18, May 22, 1904; *New York Times*, April 18, 1904; Geiger, *Joseph W. Folk*, 70.

career, and the fight made upon him for that issue, cast him as the hero, and Americans never fail to applaud the hero and hiss the villain.[25]

On July 19 the Democratic state convention opened in Jefferson City. Folk and his followers seemed confident and in control, yet aware that they governed in an uneasy truce with party regulars and the old guard state committee. Now that the moral crusader headed the party ticket, regular Democrats seemed resigned to stand by any convention pledges for "moral advancement" that the candidate wanted to make. As a result, the preamble to the party platform reiterated the oft-repeated Folk dictum that the "paramount issue before the people of Missouri is the eradication of bribery from public life in this State." The party platform was also very much a Folk document and, in large part, a discourse on the Missouri Idea. The Democrats promised the passage of laws that would make it a felony for an official to solicit a bribe; compel witnesses to bribery to testify and grant them immunity from prosecution based on their testimony; void all franchises obtained by bribery; extend the statute of limitations in bribery cases to five years; require the prompt investigation of all allegations of bribery and the prosecution of all offenders; authorize the governor, through the attorney general, to take charge of any grand jury for the purpose of investigating corruption; make professional lobbying in the state legislature a felony; and protect all interests from "sandbag" measures or special interest legislation.

The Democrats went beyond this detailed commitment to fight corruption in suggesting additional reforms that included the initiative and referendum, a state primary, the abolition of corporate tax privileges, support for municipal home rule and the removal of the police from politics, good roads, and the strict enforcement of statutes prohibiting state officials from accepting free railroad passes. Many of the party's reform recommendations seemed more a reflection of the broader national progressive reform debate than Folk-inspired additions. In

25. William Marion Reedy, "Folk Boom's Progressive Demoralization"; William Marion Reedy, "Mr. Folk's Apparent Cinch," 1; William Marion Reedy, "The Fake Cry of Home Rule"; Hawes quoted in Wetmore, *Battle against Bribery,* 184; White, "Folk," 126; Geiger, *Joseph W. Folk,* 70–71.

fact, the candidate had failed to address many of the points during the nominating campaign. It appeared that Folk had still not caught up with the march of the reform movement.[26]

The euphoria felt by the reform forces over the nomination of their candidate and the adoption of a party platform that essentially enunciated their concerns quickly vanished as delegates got down to the business of deciding the remainder of the party's ticket. Many Folk supporters wanted a reform ticket nominated from top to bottom, but the party's old guard had different ideas. Reaching a workable "compromise" on this question pointed out the weaknesses of a campaign centered on personal popularity and moral fervor. Folk's amazing personal appeal had obscured his lack of backing by any tightly knit state organization with the power to impose a complete slate of candidates. Though perhaps foreseen by some, the consequences came as a surprise to many. While the Folk forces celebrated, party regulars continued to work, lining up delegate support for candidates who were closely identified with the state machine and had worked against Folk's nomination during the campaign.[27] Folk was essentially powerless to prevent the process. The party ticket, as finally approved by the convention at-large, featured a curious mix of reform Democrats and machine Democrats— an embarrassment both to Folk and reformers in general. According to historian Louis Geiger: "Folk carefully avoided any specific endorsement of the ticket, to convey, no doubt, that it had been forced upon him."[28]

Meeting in St. Joseph shortly after the Democratic conclave in Jefferson City, the Republicans nominated Cyrus P. Walbridge, president of the Bell Telephone Company of St. Louis, to be their standard-bearer. Walbridge had been a member of both the St. Louis House of Delegates (1881–1883) and the St. Louis Council (1889–1893), and had served as mayor of St. Louis from 1893 to 1897. Evidently, collective party wisdom thought that he could win the support of conservative voters and, perhaps, staunch anti-Folk Democrats, while the party's national hero, Theodore Roosevelt, would attract progressive voters. Walbridge,

26. Missouri Secretary of State, *Official Manual of the State of Missouri, 1905–1906*, 254–56; Geiger, *Joseph W. Folk*, 75–77.

27. The two individuals most prominently identified with the state machine were Sam B. Cook, the candidate for secretary of state, and Albert O. Allen, the candidate for state auditor. See "Mr. Folk for Governor," 173.

28. Geiger, *Joseph W. Folk*, 72–73, 79.

however, had held public office at a time when corruption ran unchecked in the Municipal Assembly. Although never personally implicated in any wrongdoing, he had done nothing to expose it. With his background in St. Louis machine politics, the choice of Walbridge appeared to be a shortsighted one.[29]

By pitting Walbridge against Folk, the Republicans really painted themselves into a corner. The Republican platform, in attempting to address some reform issues—favoring home rule for major cities in the areas of police governance and control over elections, condemning the continued use of free railroad passes by politicians, and taking a strong stance against corruption—probably served to embarrass Walbridge more than to help him. The same held true for the party's campaign strategy, which attempted to label the Democrats as the party of corruption and sought to discredit Folk by accusing him of caving in to the machine element within his party. The charges were patently untrue. The Republicans had been as guilty of political corruption as the Democrats, while Folk had obviously won the nomination against the will of the party machine and had withheld any endorsement of the full ticket. Besides, the impetus for reform had started within the Democratic party not the Republican. Endorsements of Folk by some prominent Republicans further damaged the party's cause. In St. Louis Chauncey Filley, head of the Good Government Republican Club, openly campaigned against Walbridge; in Kansas City the influential *Kansas City Star* supported both Roosevelt and Folk and encouraged Missouri voters to split their tickets. Outside the state, reform governor Robert M. La Follette of Wisconsin placed the question above party and endorsed Folk, while William Allen White, editor of the *Emporia (Kansas) Gazette* commented that it was "better to be a bolter than a traitor to a state." The rumor circulated, and on good authority, that even President Roosevelt wanted to see Folk elected.[30]

Folk and the Democrats opened their campaign against the Republicans at Springfield's Baldwin Opera House on September 1. There, sharing the platform with national party hero William Jennings Bryan, and with most other leading state Democrats in attendance, Folk outlined

29. Ibid., 79.
30. Ibid., 79, 81–83. Samuel Hopkins Adams apparently started the rumor in *Collier's Weekly.*

St. Louis Post-Dispatch, Sept. 22, 1904, State Historical Society of Missouri, Columbia

the issues upon which the final campaign would be fought. The key element in that fight, said Folk, whose inflexible sense of moral purpose had held him to a single-minded goal throughout the canvass, was the Missouri Idea. And he reminded his audience that the Missouri Idea had come to be known everywhere as the unrelenting exposure and punishment of bribe-givers and bribe-takers. He also vowed for the first time to support his party's ticket but qualified his endorsement by stating that he did so with the understanding that every candidate on the ticket had pledged to support a platform that declared unceasing warfare against corruptionists. As one historian aptly said: "Outwardly there was party harmony, but inwardly there were misgivings and suspicions."[31]

31. Quoted in Homer Clevenger, "Missouri Becomes a Doubtful State," 554; *St. Louis Post-Dispatch,* September 1, 1904.

Over the next two months Folk tirelessly stumped the state, hitting at Walbridge and the Republicans in their most vulnerable points. Folk's comments before a crowd of twelve thousand at the St. Louis Exposition Coliseum on October 29 were typical. There, at the close of the campaign, he rhetorically asked his audience how it could be expected that his opponent would be any more efficient as governor than he had been as mayor of St. Louis "when corruption was at its height and Walbridge failed to see it, or seeing it, failed to expose it." Supportive newspapers like the *Post-Dispatch* reinforced this theme through editorial comments and political cartoons that contrasted the two candidates. Walbridge, inattentive as mayor, slept while franchise grabbers looted the city treasury; Folk, vigilant as circuit attorney, used his big reform stick to rout grafters, boodlers and bribe-givers. To Reedy, there was no contest: "They [the Republicans] can't beat Folk. . . . Why? Simply because they can't beat the Ten Commandments. Mr Folk is identified with, almost incarnates . . . the moral law." Although voters continued to come out in great numbers to hear the defender of the moral law, they appeared less enthusiastic about the rest of the state ticket. It was also evident that Judge Alton B. Parker, at the head of the national Democratic ticket, was no match for Teddy Roosevelt in the minds of most Missouri voters.[32]

On November 9—election day—Folk won an emphatic victory. Running 23,000 votes ahead of the state ticket, Folk bested Walbridge by 30,000 votes. But the rest of the state and national tickets suffered a resounding defeat. The Republicans carried every other state office, nine of fifteen contested congressional seats, and the lower house of the state legislature. They also controlled a majority of the legislature in joint session. Roosevelt beat Parker by 25,000 votes. Surprisingly, a great deal of Folk's voting strength came from the major urban centers of St. Louis, Kansas City, and St. Joseph. In fact, Folk ran only 7,000 votes ahead of Walbridge in rural Missouri and carried only two more counties. A closer look at the election returns suggests that Democratic declines rather than Republican advances shaped the outcome. The overall Democratic vote in 1904 was 55,000 less than in 1900. In

32. *St. Louis Post-Dispatch,* September 22, 30, 1904; William Marion Reedy, "Why Walbridge Won't Win," 2.

the Democratic stronghold of Little Dixie (north-central Missouri), Democratic majorities dropped precipitously in several counties. This occurred without any corresponding Republican gains. Folk polled 23,000 fewer votes than Democrat Alexander Dockery had in 1900, while Walbridge tallied 21,000 fewer votes than the previous Republican gubernatorial candidate.

The *St. Louis Republic* attributed Democratic losses in rural counties to a large "stay at home" vote and to lingering bitterness from the vitriolic Democratic primary. Several historians have offered similar explanations, placing the blame on Parker (unappealing to many Bryan Democrats) and on bitter party factionalism (organization Democrats could not convince themselves to vote for Folk). In the final accounting, rural Democrats tended not to vote, while Republicans seemed willing to scratch their ballots and vote for Folk. As the editor of the *Kirksville Graphic* observed: "The Democrats won Missouri for Roosevelt, and the Republicans elected Folk." Though a disaster for the Democratic party, the election was a tremendous personal triumph for Folk and a victory for reform.[33]

33. *Kirksville (Mo.) Graphic* quoted in Landen, "Folk Campaign," 148–53; Missouri *Official Manual, 1901–1902* 12–13; Missouri *Official Manual, 1905–1906,* 442–43; Geiger, *Joseph W. Folk,* 83; Muraskin, "Missouri Politics," 174–75; Shoemaker, *Missouri and Missourians,* 226. This was the election in which John McCutcheon's famous cartoon in the *Chicago Tribune* announced that Missouri ("The Mysterious Stranger") had joined the Republican ranks.

6

The Lid

The inauguration of Joseph Folk as governor of Missouri on January 9, 1905, was more than merely a celebratory moment. To emphasize the importance of his triumph, the state party invited William Jennings Bryan, the idol of popular democracy, to make a special address to the General Assembly. Bryan told reporters that he accepted the invitation because he was interested in the "purification of politics" and in the issues involved in the election of Folk. "His triumph," said Bryan, "is one of good government, and whenever that triumphs I would do everything in my power to emphasize the fact. . . . Lovers of good government should make hard paths easier by rendering every moral assistance they can to the leaders of reform." Projecting national significance onto Folk's triumph, Bryan assured his listeners that the election of Folk would have beneficial effects in many states beyond Missouri.[1]

William Marion Reedy, the perceptive editor of the St. Louis *Mirror,* suggested that perhaps there was more selfishness than selflessness behind the Great Commoner's pronouncements. "Mr. Bryan is very much interested in Missouri. Why? Because he sees in Folk a possible rallying point for the party as reorganized by Bryan in 1908. Mr. Bryan finds Folk in sympathy with him on most matters and Mr. Bryan is not above taking advantage of Folk's popularity to get the party together in the future to advocate the Bryan ideas."[2] In hindsight, Reedy's theory was prescient. But it raised other questions as well. Could Folk maintain his

1. Nicholas Clare Burckel, "Progressive Governors in the Border States: Reform Governors of Missouri, Kentucky, West Virginia, and Maryland, 1900–1918," 68; *Cole County (Mo.) Democrat,* January 10, 1905.
2. William Marion Reedy, "Mr. Bryan and Mr. Folk."

popularity? Now that he had attracted the reform spotlight, could he keep it?

In his inaugural address, Governor Folk reiterated the ideas he had advocated in his campaign, stated the principles upon which he planned to run his office, and prescribed the rules of conduct he hoped would guide every legislator in the performance of his official duty. The dominant themes from the recent political campaign remained unchanged: patriotism (defined by Folk to mean civic righteousness) should triumph over partisanship; the war on bribery and corruption would continue; and the laws must be enforced. Then, before revealing his legislative agenda, the governor encouraged lawmakers to act boldly as he echoed Bryan's belief that national attention was on Missouri:

> Missouri has set an example in good government for other states, and the example must be kept up. The eyes of the whole world are on Missouri to see what is going to be done here. Those who believe in the righteousness of the people are looking to see their theory vindicated; those who hold that corruption is a necessary incident of government, and that the "Missouri Idea" is only a passing virtuous spasm, are awaiting the result to sustain their position. Missouri is now on trial.[3]

Folk's specific recommendations to the legislature closely followed the party's platform and his own campaign themes. On the topic of bribery, Folk asked for laws to compel witnesses to testify in bribery cases but to exempt them from prosecution for their testimony. He also requested that the statute of limitations in bribery cases be extended from three years to five years, and called for the voiding of all franchises obtained by bribery. Emphasizing the importance of law enforcement, Folk pledged to enforce all laws currently on the statute books, proclaimed that the state should not license gambling in any form, and urged that the law prohibiting the issuance of free railroad passes to politicians be strictly enforced. Determined to restore honesty to the electoral process, Folk asked that more authority be granted to election commissioners to guarantee fair election procedures. Convinced that the existing machine-dominated, caucus/convention method of nominating candidates could

3. Sarah Guitar and Floyd C. Shoemaker, eds., *The Messages and Proclamations of the Governors of the State of Missouri*, 282–86, 293–94.

be improved by giving voters more direct participation, he favored the enactment of a statewide primary law as well as a constitutional amendment authorizing the direct election of senators.

Several of Folk's recommendations were rather radical departures from the norm. Believing that the exercise of the franchise was "the highest duty of citizenship" and that there existed a pressing need "to remedy the evil of civic indifference that is the weakness of a republican form of government," Folk boldly proposed that voting be made compulsory. Certain that the presence of a professional lobby at Jefferson City facilitated corruption and should not be permitted, Folk declared that such unrestricted activity should be made a crime. Conceding that "railroads and all interests, quasi-public and private," should have the right to appear before legislative committees and argue for or against pending legislation, he believed there was a proper code of conduct that lobbyists should be made to follow. Though not detailed in his address, the program envisioned by Folk involved requiring "legitimate" lobbyists to register with his office and restrict their presence at the capitol to thirty hours.

The governor also addressed the politically charged question of increased home-rule for the cities of St. Louis, Kansas City, and St. Joseph. Under existing law, the police departments of those cities were under state control and supervised by boards appointed by the governor. The vote-getting potential of home-rule for Missouri's major cities had caused Democrats to include it as a plank in their state platform and Folk had favored the idea in his campaign. But now, as governor, he qualified his previous support for any change that would allow the "criminal classes" to gain undue political influence and diminish his control. Implying that some sort of political compromise could be eventually worked out, the governor advised further consideration and study of the question. Until that time, Folk recommended that police departments in all cities be placed under civil service and that promotion be awarded solely on merit. For his part, the governor pledged to keep the police out of politics.

Other topics received the governor's attention as well. In the area of labor reform, Folk promised that his office would become more actively involved in the arbitration of disputes between capital and labor that affected the public welfare. He also asked that a remedy be sought in cases involving the negligent (job-related) death of unmarried adults whereby dependent parents might obtain the right to sue. He proposed the passage of a bill placing the state road system on the same basis as the public school system—financed via a state tax and placed under the control of a state superintendent. He also requested that the state build a reformatory for first-time criminal offenders so that they might be separated from the more hardened criminals in the state penitentiary, and recommended that a commission be established to revise the state's statutes. The only items in the platform that failed to receive the governor's attention were the volatile issues of direct legislation (the initiative and referendum) and the abolition of corporate tax privileges. In the case of direct legislation, Folk probably considered it wise not to press the issue in 1905. A constitutional amendment to establish the initiative and referendum had been submitted to the voters in 1904, but had been decisively defeated. Of the 643,969 who voted for governor in 1904, only 285,022 (44 percent) voted on the amendment, which lost by 53,540 votes. It was the first time that voters in any state had failed to approve a direct legislation amendment after the question had been put before them.[4]

Despite this exhaustive list of legislative recommendations, some of Folk's staunchest supporters remained dissatisfied. The editors of the *St. Louis Post-Dispatch* were especially critical. They called much of Folk's program "indefinite," chided him for offering only general reflections on the topics of labor and capital, home rule, and election law reform, and took special issue with his failure to strike a direct blow at the so-called Breeders' Law of 1897, which the *Post-Dispatch* had been attacking editorially. Though Folk had spoken out against licensed gambling in any form, his failure to condemn this statute, by which the state legalized racetrack gambling under the guise of racehorse breeding, left him open to censure.[5]

Those who questioned Folk's commitment to law enforcement, however, especially in the area of "morality" statutes, underestimated the new governor's moral fervor. Shortly after his inauguration, Folk appointed Alphonso Stewart president of the St. Louis Board of Police

4. Ibid., 281–97; *St. Louis Post-Dispatch,* January 18, 1905; Steven L. Piott, "Giving Voters A Voice: The Struggle for Initiative and Referendum in Missouri," 27–28.
5. *St. Louis Post-Dispatch,* January 10, 1905.

Commissioners. Stewart, an attorney by profession, was, like Folk, insistent upon the proper interpretation of the laws and their rigid enforcement. Stewart's activistic public statements suggested that he intended to suppress crimes of any sort, but he seemed especially intent on monitoring the operations of disorderly saloons, illicit winerooms, and gambling dens. Another of the serious-minded reformers with whom Folk surrounded himself was Thomas E. Mulvihill, who Folk appointed to the office of St. Louis Excise Commissioner. The position was an important one, as the commissioner was authorized to control licensing in the city. Mulvihill warred against the liquor traffic in St. Louis with a special zeal that earned both him and Folk more enemies than friends.

With his own men in control of police and licensing, Folk proceeded to command Chief of Police Matthew Kiely to begin to enforce the law against illegal winerooms and gambling houses in St. Louis. This order was broadened in mid-April to include enforcement of the long-dormant "Sunday Closing Law" (passed in 1855), which prevented saloons, dramshops, and beer gardens from selling liquor on Sunday. Although rural districts generally complied with restrictions on alcohol-related amusements ("blue law" statutes) on Sundays, the major urban areas, especially St. Louis with its large German population, largely ignored it. Before Folk's first month in office had been completed, Chief Kiely's "morality squad" had begun conducting regular raids on suspected establishments. As a final step in the process, and as an indication of his resolve to see what newspapers were now commonly calling "the lid" properly maintained, Folk directed Chief Kiely to take steps to divorce the police department from politics. Folk requested that the police force be purged of men holding positions obtained as a result of political "pull" and that policemen and detectives who failed to execute their duty by refusing to enforce the laws against gambling and other statute violations be held strictly accountable. When a St. Louis grand jury issued a report critical of the police later in the year, Folk took immediate action and removed two members of the police board.[6]

6. Ibid., January 13, 15, 21, 29–30, 1905; Geiger, *Joseph W. Folk,* 102; *St. Louis Republic,* January 22–24, 29–30, 1905; Thelen, *Paths of Resistance,* 239–40; Burckel, "Progressive Governors," 77–78. After a long series of investigations that brought further embarrassment to the police department, Folk ousted the popular Chief Kiely in

While Folk redefined the scope of blue law enforcement in St. Louis (he had ordered similar action to be taken in Kansas City and St. Joseph as well), the *Post-Dispatch* conducted its own campaign for repeal of the nefarious Breeders' Law in early December 1904. In assailing the gambling syndicate that ran the Delmar racetrack in St. Louis, the newspaper accused the racetrack interests of having a corrupting influence on St. Louis politics and called attention to the moral evils permitted by the law. The *Post-Dispatch* alleged that the syndicate maintained a number of local Democratic bosses on their payroll as well as a powerful lobby at Jefferson City. As a result, it had enough pull in the city to block any legislation that might have destroyed its racing monopoly or trimmed its schedule, and influence sufficient at the state capitol to defeat any bills that might have increased tax assessments on its properties. More damning than the syndicate's alleged political influence, however, was the question of the moral evil engendered by racetrack gambling. When the newspaper linked gambling to crime, family deprivation, and the corruption of youth, it found that letters poured into its offices from outraged citizens who encouraged the editors to continue their crusade. To crystallize public discontent, the newspaper encouraged citizens to join together in a popular demand for repeal of the Breeders' Law.[7]

Civic and religious groups quickly responded to the appeal. The St. Louis Businessmen's League, the Evangelical Alliance, and the Christian Endeavor all held organizational meetings and passed resolutions favoring repeal of the law. On January 28, these various groups merged into an umbrella organization that called itself the Citizens' Organization for the Suppression of Racetrack Gambling. Conspicuous on the executive committee of the group were Nelson McLeod, who had served as secretary of the initial "Folk for Governor" bureau, and George Johns, who had worked closely with Folk in the Murrell-Kratz boodle case as editor of the *Post-Dispatch*. The committee mailed a thousand letters

---

September 1906. See Geiger, *Joseph W. Folk,* 101–2. Confronted with evidence of police corruption in Kansas City in 1907, Folk dismissed one of the police commissioners and the chief of police and promised that there would be further reforms in the department. See *St. Louis Post-Dispatch,* May 5, 16–18, July 30, August 4, 1907.

7. *St. Louis Post-Dispatch,* March 12, 1905.

to leading citizens in all parts of the state seeking their cooperation and sent telegrams to every state senator and representative requesting a public statement of their position on the Breeders' Law. Influential citizens urged Governor Folk to lend his support for repeal as well.[8]

This well-orchestrated campaign quickly generated a response from the legislature. After submission of a repeal bill, the House Committee on Criminal Jurisprudence held a series of public hearings at which the measure was considered at some length. The final boost for passage of the repeal bill came on February 7 when Governor Folk, evidently yielding to political pressure and his own deeply felt evangelical sympathies, announced that he supported the measure. In sending a special message to the legislature, the governor unequivocally stated that it was wrong to license gambling at all and called for repeal of the Breeders' Law. The state was actually caught in an embarrassing position as a portion of the licensing fees gained from racetrack gambling went to underwrite the cost of funding the Missouri State Fair. Then, as if to anticipate the charges of his critics that the special request for the elimination of racetrack gambling might signal the beginning of a broader vice crusade, Folk assured them that this was "not the demand of a frenzied morality, but of a sound and healthy public sentiment that will not tolerate the state sharing in the profits of vicious practices."[9]

Folk's enthusiastic enforcement of laws aimed at controlling gambling, vice, and liquor placed him at the center of controversy and generated questions concerning both his character and his potential as a broad-minded, progressive reformer. Was he—the enemy of boodlers, the antagonist of special interest politics, and the defender of ethical governance—simply a modern-day Puritan bent on imposing his moral values on others? Was the law nothing more than another form of Christian rectitude to him?

None of those questions had been answered, but many in the press who tended to find Folk "self-centered" and "unimaginative" to begin with were wondering out loud if perhaps he was not displaying more zeal than good sense. The *St. Louis Republic* editorially supported the

8. Ibid., January 29, March 12, 1905; *St. Louis Republic,* January 31, 1905.
9. *St. Louis Post-Dispatch,* January 29, February 7, March 12, 1905; *St. Louis Republic,* January 27, 31, February 1, 8, 1905.

initial police raids and felt the public would support such actions as long as they perceived that the law was being fairly and impartially enforced. But the editors also warned Folk that he might encounter resistance: "It is usually the case in matters concerning public morals that stern action is looked upon as an infringement on standing or virtually recognized privileges. Raiding, from the offender's point of view, is a revolution." Conceding that Missouri was in the midst of a great moral awakening, the St. Louis *Censor,* an independent weekly edited by George C. Dyer and devoted to "current comment" and "political gossip," raised the specter of intolerance. Dyer warned Folk not to be "pushed into the old rut of a fanatic zeal to moralize people by invading their personal liberties." He also suggested that the people had voted for Folk because they thought he was a real reformer "ready to go after big crooks and real criminals instead of raising a fog of dust by trying to suppress various kinds of conduct . . . which is nearly always the sole method of all fake reformers."[10]

One other vocal critic of Folk's new policy was William Marion Reedy, the colorful editor of the St. Louis *Mirror.* Reedy, who married a famous St. Louis madam and had a reputation as an ardent drinker and raconteur, advised Folk that the people of St. Louis would not tolerate Sunday closing of saloons and places of amusement. Described by his biographer, Max Putzel, as a man who "espoused reform while deriding its righteous excesses," Reedy was quick to offer Folk some advice. "The enforcement of the law," said Reedy, "must not be made a punishment upon decent people. Pleasure must not be treated as a crime. 'Reform' must not become persecution and repression." And Reedy had a warning for the new governor: "All Blue Law legislation . . . will be used to hurt Mr. Folk. He should not be entrapped into standing for bigotry and ultra-puritanical repression. The saying, 'enforce all the laws' can be carried too far. . . . This is not a Blue Law State. Governor Folk will offend nine out of ten natives and residents by trying to make it so."[11]

Others regarded Folk's efforts to impose the lid as an exercise in folly and futility. The National-German Alliance circulated a petition

10. Kirschten, *Catfish and Crystal,* 330; *St. Louis Republic,* January 24, 1905; *St. Louis Censor,* February 16, 23, 1905.

11. William Marion Reedy, "Reform Raids"; William Marion Reedy, "Not a Blue Law State"; Putzel, *Man in the Mirror,* 292.

of protest against Sunday closing, calling it a futile attempt "to resurrect a long-forgotten, antiquated and odious law" that narrowly reflected the will of certain religious denominations. Cornered by a *Post-Dispatch* reporter as he changed trains in St. Louis, William T. Jerome, District Attorney of New York City, was asked whether he thought Folk's attempts to enforce Sunday closing in St. Louis would be successful. With experience derived from similar unsuccessful attempts at enforcing blue law statutes in his city, Jerome offered little encouragement: "A Sunday closing law is impractical in a big city because it interferes with the political equilibrium of a city. Our experience . . . has taught us that it is political destruction to force upon a cosmopolitan community moral laws contrary to the wishes and desires of the people. . . . The morals of a cosmopolitan community cannot be governed by penal statutes." Taken together the comments suggested that Folk risked diverting attention from the Missouri Idea and compromising his political future by his actions.[12]

While Folk became mired in the debate over the enforcement of sumptuary laws, the Missouri legislature continued to tackle the broader policy issues suggested in the governor's inaugural address. As a result of the recent election, the Republicans controlled the lower house of the legislature while the Democrats maintained a majority in the senate. But the fact that legislative control was divided seemed to matter little. The eager, young, reform-minded Republicans and Democrats who entered the legislature in 1905 appeared both receptive to Folk's appeal to suppress partisanship and willing to approve measures that reflected Folk's popular mandate and the spirit of the 1904 campaign that brought about their own victories. Obstructionists, and there were a few, resided in the senate and represented Folk's old nemesis—the "old guard" holdovers within the Democratic party. Accommodating his personality to his need to work with the legislature, Folk adopted an individualistic style of lobbying for important bills. Meeting privately with one or two key legislators at a time, he counted on his persuasive powers to win them over.[13]

When the forty-third General Assembly finally adjourned on March 18, 1905, it had approved many important bills and most of

12. *St. Louis Post-Dispatch*, May 28, July 9, 1905.
13. Geiger, *Joseph W. Folk*, 91, 97; Burckel, "Progressive Governors," 71.

Folk's immediate political program. The governor's top priority, an antibribery bill, sailed through the house by a vote of 120 to 1, but met with opposition from the old guard in the senate who argued that the part of the bill forcing witnesses to testify against themselves (even with a guarantee of immunity) was unconstitutional. In the end, despite assurances from the state's attorney general that the measure was constitutional and a second special message of his own to the legislature, Folk was forced to settle for a much weaker measure. The final bill extended the statute of limitations to five years but deferred questions regarding testimony and forfeiture of charters obtained by bribery. In a related move, the legislature repealed the anti-alum law that had triggered the investigation into charges of bribery and corruption during the 1903 session of the state legislature and resulted in the resignation of Lieutenant Governor John A. Lee.

The legislature took a tougher stance on law enforcement by repealing the Breeders' Law and enacting a statute that made bookmaking and poolselling a felony, and by adding additional assistants and deputies to the offices of the circuit attorney and attorney general respectively. The legislature also passed a maximum freight-rate bill, the first in thirty years, and ten other minor statutes regulating the operation of common carriers in the state. A boon to shippers, the freight-rate measure reduced rates by 15 to 40 percent on all commodities transported by rail except coal. Attorneys for the railroad argued that the law was unreasonable if not confiscatory in nature and won an injunction while they challenged the law in court. And even though the legislature failed to pass an antilobby law or a tougher antipass law, corporate lobbyists chose not to challenge Folk's thirty-hour rule and railroads did not tempt legislators with free passes.

The legislature actually got out in front of the governor on legislation granting "home rule" and on measures relating to the welfare of workers and children. Though the legislature passed a bill granting local control of police to the city of St. Louis, Folk vetoed it on grounds that it placed too much appointive power in the hands of the mayor, who would be empowered to appoint all four members to the police board, and who would sit as ex-officio chairman of that body as well. The bill, as structured, effectively eliminated the governor's power to remove corrupt officials or prevent local politicians from using the police force for political ends. It was simply a transferral of power to which Folk could not acquiesce. In completing its work the legislature also passed a maximum hours law for railroad workers (no more than sixteen straight hours on the job without at least eight hours of rest), a bill granting the father or mother of an unmarried worker the right to sue for damages in the negligent death of a son, a child labor law prohibiting the employment of children under the age of fourteen in factories, an eight-hour law for workers in mines and smelters, a compulsory school attendance law for children between the ages of 8 and 14, and the establishment of places of detention (known as parental schools) for delinquent and dependent children.[14]

Missing from the list of legislative accomplishments in 1905 were measures relating to election law reform (the state primary), good roads, and corporate tax reform. Overall, however, the list of legislative accomplishments was an impressive one. Folk commended the legislature and declared it "free from the evil of the railroad pass, and [one] in which corruption had no part. . . . A dozen or more reform bills were passed, every one of which would be worth a campaign to secure." Others gave credit to Folk. The associate editor of the *St. Louis Globe-Democrat* found the governor to be "by far the most attractive personality which the Democratic party has at this moment. As a reformer he has done more than Tilden or Cleveland." And there were grounds for optimism as well. Legislative disappointments, especially the failure to pass a stronger antibribery law, would become campaign issues in 1906, while the opportunity to expand Folk's reform program would come with the legislative session of 1907.[15]

Two weeks after the close of the legislative session, the Missouri Society of New York invited Governor Folk to speak at its annual banquet in New York City. Folk's address, entitled "Patriotism of Peace,"

14. *Laws of Missouri Passed at the Forty-third General Assembly,* 51–52, 54–62, 102–4, 112, 130–31, 236–37; *St. Louis Republic,* March 11, 14, 18, 20, 26, 1905; *St. Louis Post-Dispatch,* March 15, 18, 1905; Burckel, "Progressive Governors," 71–76; Geiger, *Joseph W. Folk,* 93–94, 99–100; Charles M. Harvey, "Reform in Missouri: What Governor Folk Has Accomplished During the First Year of His Administration"; W. D. Vandiver, "What Governor Folk Has Done."

15. *St. Louis Republic,* March 29, 1905; *St. Louis Globe-Democrat* quoted in Harvey, "Reform in Missouri," 600.

provided him with the opportunity to bring his reform ideology up-to-date and to place his recent law enforcement actions in a broader political context. Folk's point of departure was again the Missouri Idea, which he now defined in terms of a new citizenship and a respect for the law. "Citizenship," said Folk, "implies a civic obligation to enforce the performance of every public trust by holding every public official to strict accountability . . . for all official acts." And it was the government that provided the measure of the people. "No government," said Folk, "was ever better than the people made it, or worse than they suffered it to become." One lesson that he had learned as circuit attorney was that civic indifference bred corruption. "When the people grow lax in the discharge of their civic obligations the government grows corrupt, and the very foundations of national life are poisoned, justice is thwarted and iniquity is enthroned." The remedy, said Folk, was the "patriotism of peace"—the patriotism of citizen activism, the patriotism of the ballot. But for the system to work, the law had to be enforced. "If the law be bad the remedy is to repeal, not to ignore it. . . . Disregard for one law breeds disrespect for all law. In allowing some laws [sumptuary laws?] to go unenforced we reap a harvest in having all laws broken."[16]

During the summer and fall of 1905 Folk extended his public speaking sphere. Still regarded as a "hero" by the national press (one New York reporter likened his accomplishments to Samuel Tilden's eradication of "Tweedism" from Gotham), Folk looked to maintain his political image. In an effort designed to cultivate national attention and supplement his meager salary as governor ($5,000 a year plus a maintenance for upkeep on the governor's mansion and for servant hire), Folk took to the chautauqua circuit. In a strenuous summer tour, he spoke before large outdoor gatherings in Iowa, Kansas, Nebraska, Illinois, and New York. His standard speeches were on topics such as "The Duties of Good Citizenship" or "The Reign of Law" and were, by all indications, quite popular. In mid-September he journeyed to Oregon to speak at the Portland Exposition and newspapers throughout the Northwest talked up his presidential possibilities. The following month, the City Club of Philadelphia, looking for an inspiring speaker

16. *St. Louis Republic*, March 29, 1905; *New York Times*, March 29, 1905.

to invigorate its campaign for good government, invited Folk to speak on the topic "Honesty in Municipal Affairs." Billed as the "Western Champion of Reform," Folk spoke before an enthusiastic crowd of 5,000 and "thoroughly aroused the fighting spirit of the anti-graft forces" in that city. Increasingly in demand out of state, Folk never neglected his Missouri audience. He continued to speak at the usual in-state venues such as bridge dedications, Old Settlers' Association reunions, troop encampments, and cornerstone-laying ceremonies, as well as at the state convention of the Missouri Federation of Womens' Clubs.[17]

There were indications that Folk's contacts with other nationally known reformers, his status as a figure in the nationwide reform debate, and his own need to define and project a national message were all growing. In returning from his speech before the Missouri Society of New York, which the New York press covered extensively, Folk stopped briefly in Cleveland to confer with reform Mayor Tom Johnson. The two apparently agreed to arrangements for a larger conference which would include Senator Robert La Follette of Wisconsin and "other leaders before the public mind." Journalist William Allen White, who came to Missouri during the summer of 1905 to gather material for a study of Folk, provided additional national exposure. White's highly complimentary article, "Folk: The Story of a Little Leaven in a Great Commonwealth," in which he referred to Folk as "one of the half-dozen real leaders of civic honesty in America," appeared in the December issue of *McClure's* and served to update the earlier Steffens series.[18]

Indications that Folk's actions were acquiring national attention came from other personalities as well. One such individual was juvenile court Judge Ben Lindsey, who, like Folk, was conducting his own one-man reform crusade in Denver, Colorado. As an ally in the war against "protected lawlessness" (open Sunday saloons and open gambling), Lindsey wrote to Folk offering praise: "the questions agitating the people

17. Geiger, *Joseph W. Folk,* 106; *St. Louis Post-Dispatch,* April 2, May 1, June 20, August 19, 24, September 3, 14, October 1, 16–17, November 5, 1905; *New York Times,* October 17, 1905.
18. *St. Louis Republic,* March 31, 1905; *St. Louis Post-Dispatch,* March 31, 1905; White, "Folk."

in the State [Colorado] now, have received their impetus largely from you and your fight for law and order." Lindsey underscored his admiration for Folk in a postscript to another letter in which he asked the governor for a simple favor: "In my little library at home I have one or two photos of living kicking fellows doing good things. I wish I had yours to add to them."[19]

President Theodore Roosevelt also offered Folk both encouragement and advice by sending him a book of his speeches and essays that had been published as *The Strenuous Life*. Roosevelt evidently called Folk's attention to two of the essays, which Folk found "especially interesting . . . and full of helpful truths." In the first essay, "Latitude and Longitude among Reformers," Roosevelt advised would-be reformers to strive after the ideal but to do so through practical methods accompanied by a sense of moral accountability. He also encouraged reformers to make no compromise with sin. "There can be no meddling with the laws of righteousness, of decency, of morality." In the second essay, "Promise and Performance," he exhorted reformers to promise only what they could perform, but to make good on all that they promised. Roosevelt's correspondence may have been in response to an article by Folk entitled "The Enforcement of Law" in which he defended his recent efforts to enforce the letter of the law in a manner that echoed the President's sentiments. Said Folk:

> A great deal has been said in Missouri in the last few weeks about what is commonly called the "lid." The "land of the lid" means the land of the law. When people talk about taking off the "lid" on Sunday, they mean to let the law be violated with impunity. They mean for officials to violate their oaths of office and to cast away the obligations that they took when they entered office. . . .
>
> The greatest danger to every government lies in the fact that laws that are made are not enforced as they are made. There has been entirely too much making of laws to please the moral element and then allowing the laws to be ignored to please the immoral element.

19. Letters from Ben Lindsey to Folk dated August 1, 1905, and April 4, 1906, Benjamin Barr Lindsey Papers, Library of Congress, Manuscript Division, Washington, D.C.

Encouraged by the likes of Lindsey and Roosevelt and bound by his own imperturbable sense of moral accountability, Folk was determined "to make good on all that he promised."[20]

The governor found, however, that the enforcement of sumptuary laws in communities where resistance to them was united or where officials were reluctant to perform their duties was more problematic than he had anticipated. When the statute repealing the Breeders' Law took effect on June 18, 1905, Folk was shocked to find that betting at the Delmar racetrack went on as usual. Outraged that the sheriff of St. Louis County had apparently yielded to the political influence of the racetrack syndicate and had failed to take immediate steps to enforce the law, Folk issued orders to have bookmakers at the track arrested. If local law enforcement officials remained recalcitrant, Folk threatened to call out the state militia to uphold the law! But St. Louis County Sheriff George Herpel remained obdurate and refused to carry out Folk's order. In a public statement, he informed the governor that "an appeal to bayonets is the first threat of a bigot fired by fanatical zeal to further his personal ambition and ideas against the guaranteed liberties of the people."[21]

In the face of such open defiance and apprehensive as to the impact that the use of excessive force might have on public opinion, Folk ordered President Stewart of the police board and Chief of Police Kiely to assign a delegation of fifty St. Louis policemen to permanent duty in St. Louis County to prevent gambling operations at the Delmar racetrack. Stymied, the owners of the racetrack closed operations on July 28 while they awaited a legal decision from the Missouri Supreme Court. The court handed Governor Folk a setback early in 1906 when it ruled that the St. Louis police had no authority to make arrests in St. Louis County. That became a moot point, however, when the court finally handed down its decision in the Delmar case on June 1, 1906. Deciding in favor of the state, the court fined the club $5,000, revoked its charter, and ordered its officers to settle all outstanding debts. The

20. Letter from Joseph W. Folk to Theodore Roosevelt dated July 29, 1905, Theodore Roosevelt Papers; Theodore Roosevelt, *The Strenuous Life: Essays and Addresses,* 41–62, 143–52; Joseph W. Folk, "The Enforcement of Law."
21. *New York Times,* June 25, 1905.

editors of the *Post-Dispatch* were quick to proclaim the closing of the Delmar track as a victory for law and order and a vindication of state authority, and praised Folk for his firmness and for the vigor with which he confronted "defiant lawlessness."[22]

Within a month after his "victory" over racetrack gambling, Folk expanded his morality crusade to include enforcement of the laws against so-called bucketshops in St. Louis. Bucketshops were places at which the fluctuating prices of stocks, bonds, and various commodities were posted and at which individuals or agents bought or sold shares based on their estimations of future advances or declines. To Folk, this qualified as a form of gambling and lawlessness that was injurious to the public and must be suppressed. Again, in accordance with the governor's instructions, the police board arranged for daily raids of suspected establishments until they, too, suspended operations.[23]

By the fall of 1905 it was obvious to anyone active in the Democratic party in Missouri that Folk was not going to back away from his promise to enforce all the laws. What was not as certain, however, was the effect that Folk's policies were having on voters in Missouri and how attractive the party's platform would be if it remained centered on the single issue of law enforcement. According to one party estimate, Folk's lid policy would cost the Democratic ticket at least 15,000 votes in the next election (1906) and endanger Democratic chances of regaining control of the state legislature. But Folk appeared unconcerned, apparently convinced that his critics were not as adept at perceiving social change or understanding shifting popular attitudes as he was. Blinded by narrow partisanship, they failed to realize that a larger reform impulse was stirring the nation. Part of that propensity was the growing demand from evangelical Protestants to suppress drinking, which reached a peak during Folk's term as governor. Nearly two-thirds of all local temperance elections (where localities decided whether to be "wet" or "dry") that took place in Missouri after the start of local option in 1888 occurred between 1904 and 1908.[24]

22. Ibid., June 19, 25, 1905; *St. Louis Post-Dispatch*, June 21–22, 25–26, 28, July 22–24, 28, 30, 1905, February 27–28, June 1, 1906.

23. *St. Louis Post-Dispatch*, August 21, 26, September 28, 1905.

24. Ibid., October 27, 1905; Thelen, *Paths of Resistance*, 239–40.

Folk increasingly utilized both press and platform to describe the transformation he saw taking place. In his usual evangelical style, the governor told a *Post-Dispatch* correspondent in late October that the nation was in the midst of a moral regeneration: "A moral wave is sweeping over this country that is analogous to the spiritual wave that arose on the coming of Christ and that will not subside until graft in all its forms is swept away. . . . He [Christ] taught the simple truths of morality which are appealing to the hearts and consciences of the American people with so much force today." Recent exposures of grafting and boodling by public officials had awakened a new crusading ideal in the people, and more than a few gave Folk credit for this rejuvenation. Thomas Speed Mosby, Pardon-Attorney for the State of Missouri and a loyal Folk supporter, commented that "the message he brings to the American people is no new gospel. It is as old as Sinai. He electrified the public conscience simply by showing that all was not lost . . . that righteous government . . . was but a matter of honesty and courage." To Folk, the old-time political parties had been slow to acknowledge the change. As a result, they were "losing their hold on the people." A new "Conscience party" had risen in their place and left old-line politicians out of step. "Campaigns," said Folk, "are on in New York, Philadelphia, Ohio and San Francisco. In each of them the issue is graft and in each center the Conscience party is awake. Religion has entered into politics; a new patriotism has been aroused—patriotism of the heart as distinguished from patriotism of the head." In a speech before the Merchant's Association of Boston three months later, Folk expanded his perception of the trend toward national reform to include civic regeneration and boldly asserted to his audience of businessmen that the country was about to "pass from the age of sordid commercialism to the age of high ideals."[25]

Folk's comments went a long way toward explaining his recent law enforcement efforts in St. Louis and elsewhere and why he seemed impervious to criticism. But had his reform vision narrowed in the

25. *St. Louis Post-Dispatch,* November 5, 1905, January 21, 1906; Thomas Speed Mosby, "Governor Joseph W. Folk," 603. Folk later developed this theme into a well-publicized speech entitled "The Era of Conscience," which he presented to the Civic Forum at Carnegie Hall in New York City in February 1908. For details of the speech, see *New York Times,* February 26, 1908.

process? William Marion Reedy, who admitted to being a convert to Henry George's single tax idea, worried about that possibility publicly and concluded that it had. "To my thinking," said Reedy, "Folk as a reformer is only an emotional revivalist. He doesn't get down to the foundations of social wrong." "[He] is all right as far as he goes, but he doesn't get to the guts of reform. . . . Mr. Folk doesn't strike at privilege, but only at the corruption that flows from privilege." And Reedy was not the only one to take Folk to task. The editor of the *Censor*, who had been vilifying the governor for a year over his blue-law crusade, characterized Folk's current conception of reform as "penny-in-the-slot" and had come to the sad conclusion that "his fine work as a boodle 'buster' was . . . exotic to the real character of the man, and that in his proper spirit he was a narrow, bigoted, mistaken fanatic as to the trivial things of life, which he allowed to cut off his view of greater things."[26]

Although Folk had moved away from broader reform issues to concentrate on enforcement of morality statutes, he had not abandoned his reform vision. As the governor entered his second year in office, and as he looked forward to resurrecting Democratic majorities in both houses of the state legislature, he began to prioritize issues that he hoped would serve as the core agenda when the legislature reconvened in 1907. Two such issues were the connected ones of child labor and school attendance. Under Missouri's existing child labor law, children under the age of fourteen were prohibited from working in factories. Enforcement, however, depended largely on the number of factory inspectors in the field. Compounding the problem was the state's school attendance law, which permitted truant officers to grant exemptions if it could be shown that income earned by the labor of a child was necessary to the support of an otherwise indigent family. In such instances, children would be issued a work permit and a waiver from school attendance. As part of a larger national campaign against the employment of children in factories, the Missouri Child Labor League and the National Consumers' League released information that revealed that Missouri engaged only four factory inspectors, spent less than $8,000 on their employment, and restricted their activities to cities with populations of

26. William Marion Reedy, "Folk's Presidential Prospects," 2; William Marion Reedy, "Roosevelt, Folk, Bryan"; *St. Louis Censor,* February 15, 1906.

thirty thousand or more. Appeals to Governor Folk "to lift his hand against the 'New Slavery' " prompted him to visit factories in St. Louis and conduct his own investigation. What he found was that while the child labor law was being enforced, children aged 9–11 were found at work with exemptions that were not legitimate—the result of parental advice rather than economic necessity. Folk's resulting recommendations called for a more comprehensive child labor law and a revised truancy law that would have the state assume the financial support of bona fide indigent parents and eliminate the need for waivers from school attendance.[27]

Other recommendations made by the governor during the spring and summer of 1906 included an election law that would grant St. Louis and other large cities in the state complete home rule over elections. Included in the proposal, couched in terms of antimachine politics rather than nativistic sentiment or ethnic intolerance, was an educational qualification that required that prospective voters be able to read and cast an unassisted ballot. Supplemental to the proposed election law and again aimed at "ending the reign of bosses" was a recommendation for a statewide direct primary law that would require all party primaries to be held on the same day. Expanding his list of priorities even further, Folk proposed that the state organize a road-building system that would include the creation of offices of state and county superintendents. The new roads system, like the public school system, would be financed via a state tax. Governor Folk also outlined a program more radical than any he had previously proposed that would allow for greater public (regulatory) control of public service corporations. The plan, an indication of Folk's broadening governmental philosophy, envisioned the creation of a State Public Service Commission to regulate rates charged by public service corporations—steam and street railways, gas, electric, telephone, and telegraph companies. Supplemental to this last recommendation, and linked to his morality crusade, was a proposal for the creation of the office of State Excise Commissioner with the power to revoke licenses for dramshops in any part of the state and to make it a felony to sell liquor without a license.[28]

27. *St. Louis Post-Dispatch*, March 23, April 29, May 3, 1906.
28. Ibid., April 29, May 6, 13, August 9, 1906; Mosby, "Governor Folk," 605–6.

One view that Folk never articulated as a politician was his position on race. In defending the state party's platform in 1904, Folk had accepted the racial bias of Missouri Democrats at least as it applied to segregated public education. Kicking off his gubernatorial campaign in Springfield, Missouri, in September 1904, Folk had taken time in his hour-and-a-half-long speech to reiterate the party's pledge to "maintain separate schools for white and black children." In supporting the party on this issue, Folk told his listeners: "Instead of throwing the races together in mixed schools, Missouri educates the colored youth better than Republican states and does it without mingling the races." It is not clear whether his statement reflected a deeper racial prejudice or merely a willingness to please old-guard Democrats or his local audience. One would think that if he had personal reservations, he would have simply avoided making any comment whatsoever. Folk rarely touched on the race issue, which still had the potential to irritate old Civil War wounds in the state. As governor, however, he did not hesitate to condemn lynchings. When a mob in Springfield took three black men from a jail and lynched them in 1906, Governor Folk sent the militia to prevent further violence, posted a reward in an effort to catch the perpetrators, and actively supported a grand jury investigation of the incident. Authorities eventually arrested three of the mob's ringleaders, but the ensuing trial resulted in no convictions.[29]

While Folk concentrated on formulating his reform agenda, the Democratic party held its biennial state convention in Jefferson City on June 5–6, 1906, to prepare a platform for the upcoming off-year elections. At issue was Folk's record as governor, specifically his Sunday-closing and antigambling policies. But the "old machine crowd," sensing that a factional debate over the governor's recent policies could only lead to a repeat of the disastrous electoral results of 1904, decided to yield to the call for harmony and party unity. Former Governor Alexander Dockery summed up the sentiment of the opposition best when he appealed to the convention to stand by Folk and what he had done "whether you like it, gentlemen, or not." As a result, the platform as adopted by the convention enthusiastically endorsed the lid and the

29. Missouri *Official Manual, 1905–1906,* 254; *St. Louis Post-Dispatch,* September 1, 1904; Geiger, *Joseph W. Folk,* 81, 105, 128.

suppression of racetrack gambling, and pointedly made it a partisan issue:

> The enforcement of the Sunday dramshop law has made it an issue in this campaign. The Republican party, with characteristic cowardice, evades it.
> The Democratic party meets it boldly, and declares that this is a law, not only in the interest of good morals, but of good government. . . ."
> We endorse the enforcement of the law under which winerooms of the cities have been closed, gambling houses shut and the greatest racetrack syndicate in the world driven from the State, after having enjoyed the special protection of Republican officials in the county where it was located. . . .

Democrats had decided to live or die with the lid in 1906.[30]

The Democratic State Convention took one other action, however, that suggested that Governor Folk's political stock had actually fallen when it formally declared for William Jennings Bryan as the Democratic standard bearer in 1908. The national press had talked up the possibility of a future Folk candidacy for the presidency after his election in 1904, and there was a minor Folk boom in Missouri as well.[31] But that moment now seemed to have passed. Harry Hawes, an ardent Folk opponent, thought so and stated at the time that he favored the party's resolution "not only because it endorsed a great leader for President, but for the further reason that it flattened out the presidential boom of our own Joey." Any explanation seemed to center on Folk's lid policy. A telling political cartoon published in the *Censor* several weeks after the convention captured the essence of Folk's plight. The cartoon, entitled "It [the lid bicycle] Won't Go," humorously depicted Folk trying to repair his broken bicycle with wrench, hammer, and can of "oil of

30. Missouri *Official Manual, 1907–1908,* 366; *St. Louis Post-Dispatch,* June 5–6, 1906.

31. For mention of Folk as a presidential possibility, see "Future of the Democratic Party," 688; "Mr. Folk as an Example"; White, "Folk," 115–32; and "Whom Will the Democrats Next Nominate for President?" See also William Marion Reedy, "Folk for President"; Harvey, "Reform in Missouri"; and *St. Louis Post-Dispatch,* September 3, 1905.

IT WON'T GO.

St. Louis Censor, July 5, 1906, State Historical Society of Missouri, Columbia

piety," while "the people" and Bryan rode off to Washington leaving Folk behind. The editor of the *Censor,* a vocal Folk critic, offered his own assessment of Folk's political dilemma. "When Mr. Folk entered upon his Gubernatorial office, there was much talk of him as a Presidential possibility. He is now no longer seriously considered even as a candidate for second place. Why? It is the realization of the fact that Mr. Folk is not broad, or big, or modern enough that has crowded him from the stage of national attention. . . ." Folk made no comment on the convention's pro-Bryan resolution, nor did he publicly indicate his future plans. When pressed on the subject later in the campaign, Folk would only say that he hoped to secure the approval of his conscience by his actions as governor.[32]

During the summer Folk returned to the chautauqua circuit. But in his speeches in this venue, he increasingly shied away from a discussion of specific political proposals. Instead, he used the opportunity to depict what he perceived as the greater, ongoing moral struggle between the forces of good and evil. In a typical address before an assembly in Clear Lake, Iowa, on July 30, 1906, Folk told his audience: "There is a constant conflict between the forces of right and wrong, the law and the lawless, the true and the false. In every sphere of life the right . . . the law . . . the true must always be fought for; the wrong, the lawless, the false, must always be fought against." Folk also tried to inspire his audiences with idealism. Again, speaking to the crowd at Clear Lake, Folk told them: "If the spirit of civic righteousness now abroad in the land does not die out we shall pass from the age of commercialism into the age of high ideals. . . . The ideal of the young man is not so much to get rich as to get right and stay right. A new standard has been established, new yet old, just plain, common, simple honesty—that is all." And Folk seldom forgot to remind his rural, Protestant, Midwestern listeners that in politics as in life, a moral compass should be one's guide: "We don't want any politics in our religion, but we want all the religion we can get in our politics." In concluding his Clear Lake address, Folk shared a personal story to emphasize that the foundation of his character was religious morality and that it had intensified his own civic activism.

One day, when the outlook seemed especially dreary, I chanced to see a clipping that some one had sent me and the words that I

32. See *St. Louis Post-Dispatch,* June 7, October 10, 1906; and *St. Louis Censor,* July 19, 1906. The cartoon can be found in the *Censor,* July 5, 1906.

read came to me like a benediction. Since then I have made those words my Golden Text. I have used them before juries and before the people of my state, and now, . . . whenever the way seems dark or the task seems hard, . . . when sometimes, in trying to serve the people, it seems that perhaps the people do not care, I think of these words and am . . . encouraged to further endeavor. . . .

> "For right is right, since God is God,
> And right the day must win.
> To doubt would be disloyalty;
> To falter would be sin."[33]

Folk obviously felt comfortable sharing his evangelical values with sympathetic throngs in rural America and he certainly believed passionately in the moral regeneration of man, but he could also abandon moral platitudes to face the political realities that came with leadership of his party. When the state political campaign moved into full swing in early October, Folk undertook an exhaustive speech-making tour during which he focused almost entirely on promoting his previously announced agenda of legislative priorities. Added to the list of proposals for the first time was an antidiscrimination law. Looking to prevent trusts from severely cutting prices with the intention of forcing independent dealers out of business, Folk asked for a law that prescribed criminal penalties for any trust that sold goods at a higher price in one part of the state than in another (transportation charges being factored into any determination).[34]

In the process of promoting his program, however, Folk may have stretched the bounds of propriety. Shortly after the election, rumors circulated in Jefferson City that the governor had maintained a secret press bureau headed by Archie T. Edmondston. Folk had initially appointed Edmondston, a former St. Louis newspaperman, to the position of statistician in the Department of Labor. Somewhere along the way Edmondston began to function as a publicity director who maintained regular contact with many of the state's newspapers. Included in the many informational bulletins mailed by Edmondston to weekly

33. See address by Hon. Joseph W. Folk, Governor of Missouri, at the Clear Lake Chautauqua Assembly, July 30, 1906, in Folk Papers.
34. *St. Louis Post-Dispatch,* October 7, 10, 12–13, 1906.

newspapers were items that dealt solely with promoting Governor Folk and the work he had done. When the press bureau was "exposed," Folk denied any prior knowledge of its existence and terminated its operation. Edmondston, the loyal appointee, publicly stated that he had acted without authorization. Nevertheless, it was an embarrassing incident that made it all the more difficult for Folk to shake the charge that he was an ambitious self-promoter.[35]

The state campaign, waged vigorously by the Democratic party, which invited William Jennings Bryan to the state to tour with Folk aboard a special train, resulted in victory. The Democrats regained control of both houses of the state legislature. Folk loyalists gave him credit for the victory, arguing that the overall increase in the Democratic vote was higher in the counties in which he had spoken than in those in which he had not. But even Folk's faithful supporters had to concede that the governor was more popular among rural voters than urban ones. In St. Louis, where blue-law statutes had been most rigorously enforced, Folk's policies and popularity appeared to be wearing thin. Delegates to the city's Democratic nominating convention actually hissed the mention of his name and refused to endorse him or his lid policy in any specific terms. For his part, Folk made no attempt to heal party wounds in St. Louis. According to the *St. Louis Republic,* after seeing the list of those nominated for representatives and senators from St. Louis, Folk contemptuously categorized most of the nominees as standing for "race tracks, gambling, saloons and lawlessness." In the end, party divisions and voter dissatisfaction contributed to a resounding Democratic defeat in St. Louis in which the Republicans captured ten of fifteen contested seats to the state legislature.[36]

35. Ibid., November 14, 1906.
36. Ibid., October 10, November 8, 14, 1906; *St. Louis Republic,* November 3, 1906.

7

Progressive

D espite his preoccupation with enforcement of sumptuary laws, Folk had, throughout 1906, proposed items of a legislative agenda that suggested that his political thinking was evolving and that his political vision was broadening. He was beginning to sound like a progressive. Confirmation of this intellectual transformation came with the presentation of his first biennial message to the Missouri legislature on January 2, 1907. Confident in his legislative majorities and cognizant of the fact that this was the last opportunity to complete his reform program, Folk presented a staggering list of legislative recommendations along progressive lines. Going beyond his earlier emphasis on law enforcement, Folk centered his attention on three areas: intensified opposition to special interests; greater direct, democratic participation in the political process; and expanding the scope of government regulation.

Folk's opposition to the influence of special interests came forth with surprising intensity. Convinced that the professional lobbyist was an enemy of representative government, and that the free railroad pass was the first step toward bribery, Folk offered two bold preventative proposals. Going beyond his previous efforts to force lobbyists to register and to limit their stay in the state capitol, Folk requested that it be made a crime for anyone to be paid for work as a lobbyist. Private individuals could still appear before legislative forums and present printed briefs or arguments to specific committees, but they would have to file copies of their written information with the secretary of state's office. Once on file, those documents would be available for public scrutiny. Believing that the statute prohibiting railroads from giving free passes to legislators did not entirely eliminate the seductive influence of one of the state's most powerful special interests, Folk asked that the law be made more restrictive and that free travel be denied to everyone (railroad employees being the only possible exceptions).

Folk found it alarming that corporations arrogantly challenged state authority over intrastate commerce and successfully disabled the state's rate-fixing power through use of the court injunction. Equally distressing was the practice by which corporations commonly resorted to price-fixing and price-cutting to invalidate competitive capitalism. To combat these practices, Folk recommended an antirebate law (providing penalties for granting selective discounts on shipments of goods within the state), an antidiscrimination law (prohibiting any business or corporation from gouging consumers or pinching independent dealers by selling its goods at a higher price in one part of the state than in another), and a new maximum freight-rate law (designed to strengthen the 1905 law).

Folk's new anticorporatist stance also included concern for the issues of corporate taxation, the formation of holding companies, and antitrust violations. Having dodged the question of corporate tax reform during his first two years in office, the governor now decided to confront the problem directly. The question, to Folk, was how much corporations should be required to pay for the privilege of routinely doing business in the state. Under existing law corporations paid fees of $50 for the first $50,000 of capital stock and $25 for each $50,000 of capital stock thereafter. Convinced that corporations should be paying more, Folk proposed that the state raise the ante by levying an annual "privilege tax" of one-fifteenth of one percent on the capital stock of each corporation. He also took a dim view of holding companies (ostensibly independent corporations to which had been transferred more than fifty percent of the capital stock of any given number of smaller corporations that it sought to control); he regarded holding companies as inventions to circumvent existing antitrust statutes. As a result, he urged the passage of a law that would prevent any one corporation from owning stock in another and would authorize quo warranto proceedings to be filed to dissolve any corporation that allowed a majority of its stock to be acquired by a holding company. To toughen the state's existing antitrust law, Folk, who believed that antitrust regulation was inadequate without a meaningful deterrent, proposed that the law be amended so that violations would be classified as a felony and penalties include prison punishment in addition to fines.[1]

Vigorous enforcement of the state's antitrust law had not been one of the planks in the Democratic platform of 1904 nor had Folk included it among his list of law enforcement priorities when he took office in 1905. But the willingness of the state's young, Republican attorney general, Herbert S. Hadley, to prosecute corporations who violated the law revitalized the issue.[2] During hearings before the State Board of Railway Commissioners on complaints over railroad rates brought by independent oil dealers in Missouri early in 1905, Hadley learned that two state-chartered corporations, Waters-Pierce Oil and Standard Oil, had allegedly divided the marketing territory in the state between themselves and manipulated oil freight charges to damage the independent trade. He also found evidence to suggest that a third company, Republic Oil, which professed to be an independent and competing company, was in reality a Standard Oil subsidiary. The Republic Oil Company had apparently been created to provide the appearance of competition, but actually sold its oil at prices set by the Standard Oil Company. Hadley concluded that sufficient evidence existed to file suit charging the three companies with having entered into a combination in violation of the state's antitrust law, and on March 29, 1905, asked the state supreme court to annul the charters of the three companies and prevent them from doing business in Missouri.

Hearings in the case began in St. Louis on June 20, 1905, and testimony revealed for the first time the plan of organization and the business methods of the Standard Oil Trust in Missouri. During the summer and fall of 1905 Missourians learned that competition in the sale of petroleum did not exist (suppressed by discriminatory price cutting) and that the accused companies operated in collusion with the railroads (railroads refused to accept shipments from independents and provided Standard Oil with information on its competitors). To those who followed the hearings, the message was clear. The Standard Oil Company possessed the economic power to control the price of oil to

---

1. Guitar and Shoemaker, eds., *Messages and Proclamations,* 298–339.
2. Hadley had made a name for himself as a vigorous prosecuting attorney in Jackson County (Kansas City) prior to winning election in the Republican landslide of 1904.

every town or village in Missouri. Neither consumer nor independent producer could exercise his independent right of bargain. The buyer was at the mercy of the seller, and the seller was a monopoly.

In January 1906 Hadley moved the hearings to New York City. In doing so, he intended to strengthen the evidence of common ownership, and establish the intent of that ownership, by the three companies named in the Missouri suit. He immediately subpoenaed Standard Oil's major officials. But when they refused on "advice of counsel" to answer Hadley's questions, the national press assailed the arrogance of those corporate directors and condemned them for their brazen contempt for the law. Hadley, with the aid of national publicity, had aroused public indignation. Aided by a recent decision of the U.S. Supreme Court, which ruled that immunity from self-incrimination did not apply to testimony by corporate officials that might prevent a corporation from being found guilty of a crime, Hadley was able to force Standard Oil officials to admit to common ownership of all the companies named in the Missouri suit.

Hadley had scored a major victory. He had shown that no combination of money and power was above the law. Like Folk earlier, Hadley was hailed as the valiant young lawman from the West who had the nerve and persistence to demand accountability from lawless corporate directors. In his prosecution of Standard Oil, Hadley reinforced the Missouri Idea and expanded its parameters to include corporate behavior. Viewing Hadley's triumph through Folk's moral prism, the editor of the *Kansas City World* concluded simply that it demonstrated that "the law is the reflection of the moral sense of the people. The way to enforce the moral sense of the people is to enforce the law." Tragically for Folk, however, Hadley had stolen his mantle as the new David smiting malefactors in the political arena. Ironically, the same Missouri editors who scorned Folk's crusade for Sunday closing and ridiculed his intolerance enthusiastically praised Hadley's actions.[3]

Standard Oil delayed the case with appeals, but lost in the end. The Missouri Supreme Court, in 1909, found that the Standard Oil Company, the Waters-Pierce Oil Company, and the Republic Oil Company

3. *Kansas City World*, March 30, 1906; Piott, *Anti-Monopoly Persuasion*, 117–25; Thelen, *Paths of Resistance*, 243.

had illegally conspired to regulate and fix prices, control and limit trade, prevent competition in buying and selling, and deceive the public. The court fined each of the companies $50,000 and ousted them from the state. After payment of its fine, the Waters-Pierce Company reorganized independently of Standard Oil and won back the right to resume business in Missouri. The U.S. Supreme Court finally rejected appeals by Standard Oil and Republic Oil in 1912 and upheld the decision of the Missouri court. Hadley's suit triggered antitrust prosecutions in five other states and served as the basis for the federal prosecution that led the U.S. Supreme Court to dissolve the Standard Oil Trust in 1911. Hadley went on to initiate numerous other antitrust prosecutions during his term as attorney general. Included in the list were suits against the Insurance Trust, the Harvester Trust, the Lumber Trust, and the Beef Trust.[4]

Governor Folk's intensified anticorporatism and Attorney General Hadley's vigorous enforcement of the state's antitrust law suggested that Missouri's two leading state officials shared the same moral imperatives. Both believed that individual moral standards could be applied to the economic system. Though from opposing political parties, Folk and Hadley were natural allies who learned from and assisted each other. Folk helped Hadley to think in political terms and to develop a reform program, while Hadley encouraged Folk to broaden his vision to include expanded state control over corporations.

In adopting strong adversarial positions in regards to Missouri's corporations, Folk and Hadley gained public acclaim but set themselves against conservative commercial elements within their respective parties. In winning national fame as a "trust-buster," Hadley established himself as the leading candidate to succeed Folk as governor in 1908. Running on his tremendous popularity and a progressive reform platform he would, like Folk, win election as the rest of his party's ticket went down to defeat. Once governor, however, Hadley would have to face the economic consequences of his earlier antitrust prosecutions. Under pressure to stimulate the state's economic growth, Hadley would

4. Thelen, *Paths of Resistance*, 243–44. See also Lloyd Edson Worner, "The Public Career of Herbert Spencer Hadley," 93–133; and "Statement Given to the Press During the Campaign of 1908," in Herbert Spencer Hadley Papers, Western Historical Manuscript Collection, Columbia, Mo.

conclude that vigorous antitrust enforcement created an unfavorable climate for business. As a result, he would switch gears, abandon his moral approach to economic questions, and embrace state regulation as a more sensible method of action. Folk, on the other hand, used the popular support generated by his tough anticorporate posture to push for new or tougher corporate legislation—an antidiscrimination law, a revised maximum freight-rate law, an anti–holding company law, and a more punitive antitrust statute. But Folk's anticorporatism angered many conservative Democrats who thought he had gone too far against corporations. David Francis, a leader of this group, regarded Folk as a demagogue whose emotional rhetoric and irresponsible anticorporate demands threatened to harm business and slow economic development in the state. Opposition from this pro-business faction in the Democratic party, which had originally supported Folk for governor on the basis of his anticorruption platform, would later handicap him when he attempted to move to the next political level.[5]

Folk also used his first biennial message to the legislature to express his deepening conviction that representative government would be improved if voters were allowed more direct participation in the political process. As steps in that direction, Folk renewed his request for the enactment of a state primary law and proposed new safeguards for elections. State primary elections would be held on the same day throughout the state with all political parties participating. Voters would, in theory, nominate their party's candidates for elective office. Party bosses would be dispensed with. As part of his primary bill, Folk proposed that Missouri join the growing ranks of states pressing for the direct election of U.S. senators by giving voters the opportunity to register their choice for their party's senatorial nominee. Though the senatorial preference vote would be nonbinding, Folk regarded it to be "the command of the people" that no legislator could "honorably or honestly disobey." For someone like Folk, with limited support within the party but proven popular appeal, the preference primary seemed tailor-made—and Folk was rumored to have senatorial aspirations. To ensure fair elections and an honest ballot, Folk recommended that election commissioners be

5. For Hadley's switch from dissolution to regulation on the trust question, see Piott, *Anti-Monopoly Persuasion*, 131–51. For the reaction of conservative Democrats to Folk's anticorporate policies, see Muraskin, "Missouri Politics," 325–26.

given more authority to supervise the work of judges and clerks and that private citizens be granted more freedom to challenge the legality of any voter so that voter registration lists could be honestly maintained.

Folk's most controversial recommendation for bringing government closer to the people, however, was the recall. With the difficulties encountered in the enforcement of the Sunday Closing Law in places like St. Louis County certainly in mind, Folk argued that voters should have the right to remove elected officials "should they in their public duty forsake the service of the people, or prove incompetent or corrupt." Folk knew that the recall by the direct vote of the people could be obtained by an amendment to the state constitution, but he also realized that such a procedure was protracted and uncertain. Impatient to gain some immediate leverage over recalcitrant local officials, Folk proposed an expedient substitute. His plan authorized the attorney general to file quo warranto proceedings against "any prosecuting attorney, police commissioner, sheriff, mayor, or other official willfully failing to enforce the laws of the state." If the court found the evidence satisfactory, it would order the offending official to be removed from office.

Accompanying the recall was a request for the adoption of a constitutional amendment providing for direct legislation by means of the initiative and referendum. Under the initiative, voters could propose laws or constitutional amendments by petitioning to have those measures placed on the ballot without regard for the legislature. If a majority of those voting approved the measure, it became law. Under the referendum, voters could repeal legislation they thought detrimental to their interests by the same petition method. As mentioned previously, an amendment calling for the initiative and referendum had been rejected by voters in 1904. The decisive negative vote coupled with apparent voter disinterest had convinced Folk to sidestep the issue in 1905 and concentrate his attention on other important topics.[6]

Working to convince the governor that he had made a mistake, and hoping to revitalize the issue of direct legislation, was the Direct Legislation League of Missouri. Organized in 1899 by a group of St. Louis reformers and led by ardent Single-Taxers Silas L. Moser and Dr. William Preston Hill, the league managed to get direct legislation amendments

6. Guitar and Shoemaker, eds., *Messages and Proclamations,* 298–339.

introduced into the 1899 and 1901 sessions of the Missouri legislature, although the measures failed to pass. Undaunted, league officials looked to broaden their political base. During the political campaign of 1902 direct legislationists won support from the Prohibition, Socialist, Public Ownership, and Democratic parties in Missouri as well as the State Federation of Labor and the Missouri Single-Tax League. Realizing that voters and legislators were still not familiar with the merits of initiative and referendum, the league undertook an educational campaign that included hiring speakers, publishing articles, holding conferences, soliciting pledges from prospective political candidates, and disseminating information to editors of small, county newspapers.

Bolstered by their own grassroots efforts and encouraged by Democratic majorities in both houses of the 1903 session of the Missouri legislature, direct legislationists were optimistic that a bill would finally be approved. However, what they got was a much weaker measure than they had envisioned. The final bill allowed for the referendum based on 10 percent of the eligible voters and the initiative based on a 15 percent figure "in each congressional district." In addition, laws relating to the "preservation of the public peace, health and safety" were exempted from the bill as were appropriation items and all laws passed by a two-thirds vote of the legislature. Though the percentages were high and the exclusions broad (Republicans attacked the proposal as "so cumbrous as to make its application impracticable"),[7] most proponents accepted the amendment as written as better than nothing.

Voters had an opportunity to cast their ballots for the proposed amendment to the state constitution at the general election of 1904. To encourage support, the Direct Legislation League mailed over 150,000 publicity circulars stressing the merits and importance of the initiative and referendum, published an article entitled "The Initiative and Referendum [and] What These Legislative Reforms Might Accomplish for Missouri" in 545 Missouri newspapers, and distributed statewide a popular political cartoon that depicted the "Honest Citizen" standing atop the capitol steps at Jefferson City using his whip (the initiative and referendum) to drive boodlers and franchise grafters from the capitol. The league also gained valuable assistance from the State Federation of

7. Missouri *Official Manual, 1905–1906,* 229.

Labor, which sent out thousands of direct legislation leaflets to every union in the state. But despite these efforts, the amendment lost. While the proposal received a 53 percent majority from Missouri's five most urbanized counties, it gained only a 33 percent vote from the remaining counties in the state. Dr. William Preston Hill placed blame for the amendment's defeat on rural Missourians who were, in his mind, still too uninformed about the merits of direct legislation to rally for its adoption.[8]

The defeat in 1904 so devastated the leaders of the direct legislation movement in Missouri that they did not even attempt to have another amendment submitted during the 1905 session of the legislature. When Governor Folk focused attention on the issue during his biennial message and made it a part of his Missouri Idea their hopes revived. In lending his support to direct legislation, Folk stated that he regarded the initiative and referendum "as of much importance in the final elimination of corruption and the establishment of true representative government." "It puts an effective stop to bribery in legislative halls, for bribery of legislators would be useless where the people are the final arbiter of a measure."[9] But adoption of the initiative and referendum could also yield immediate practical benefits. Bills vetoed by the governor, or (more important for Folk) measures proposed by the governor and either ignored or defeated by the legislature, could be resurrected by popular petition and put to popular vote.

Along with Folk's growing opposition to the influence of special interests and his new appreciation for the power of direct democracy was his desire to see the state's regulatory powers expanded. As part of his ongoing struggle to gain control over the unrestricted liquor traffic in the state, and as proof that he had not abandoned his morality crusade, Folk recommended the creation of the appointive office of state excise commissioner. Although the governor already had the authority to regulate dramshops in St. Louis, Kansas City, and St. Joseph, he had little control over the rest of the state. Under the strict control of a new excise commissioner, liquor dealers would be required to obtain a state license

8. Piott, "Giving Voters a Voice"; Missouri *Official Manual, 1905–1906,* 255; Thelen, *Paths of Resistance,* 231.
9. Guitar and Shoemaker, eds., *Messages and Proclamations,* 336.

in addition to any existing municipal and county licensing requirements. Dealers who attempted to operate without proper certification would be subject to both fine and imprisonment. To guarantee that the new law would be enforced, Folk recommended that the governor be authorized to appoint a special prosecutor to enforce the law when local officials, by his determination, failed to do so.

Folk also regarded state regulation as a necessary protection for consumers. Central to this idea was his proposal for the creation of a department of corporations. The department would have authority to examine all applications for corporate charters, monitor all existing charters for abuses, and collect the proposed corporate privilege tax. But because of the rapid growth of public service corporations in the state, the governor felt it was also necessary to regulate rate charges "in order to prevent extortion from the public." Either the department of corporations or possibly a new public service commission would be empowered to examine corporate books and to set rates that would be reasonable to consumers and yet allow a fair return on invested capital. He also recommended that the state set passenger rates for rail travel at two cents per mile (the current rate was three cents), enact a pure food law, and greatly enlarge the regulatory powers of the State Insurance Department to protect policyholders.[10]

Convinced that abuses existed in the selling of insurance in Missouri, Folk had appointed Willard D. Vandiver, his former campaign manager, as the new Superintendent of Insurance shortly after taking office in 1905. But before Vandiver could begin a probe of the industry in Missouri, the nation was shocked by the Equitable life insurance scandal in New York. As policyholders grew alarmed over disclosures of corruption in the Equitable Company, the New York legislature created a special body (the Armstrong Committee) to examine all life insurance companies operating in New York. The subsequent hearings, under the legal direction of brilliant general counsel Charles Evans Hughes, revealed that New York Life president John A. McCall had misused policyholder's money for the purpose of making political campaign contributions, lobbying, and paying exorbitant salaries for company officials.

10. Ibid., 298–339.

Morally outraged, yet ever the political pragmatist, Vandiver seized the opportunity to attract public attention and trigger his own reform campaign with a sensational application of the Missouri Idea. On October 7, 1905, he notified New York Life that unless the company repaid to its policyholders an amount equal to its campaign contributions ($148,702), and unless McCall and other top officials resigned within thirty days, he would revoke the license of the firm to do business in Missouri. When New York Life failed to meet Vandiver's ultimatum, he suspended the company's license. New York Life immediately obtained a temporary restraining order against the Missouri Insurance Department until a hearing could be held. But before the hearing date, the company's two top officers, Vice President and Chief Fiscal Officer George W. Perkins and President McCall, abruptly resigned. When that happened, Vandiver looked like a conquering hero. Not long afterward, company officials announced that the misused funds would be restored to the company treasury and that new safeguards would be implemented to protect policyholders.[11]

The New York Life scandal emphasized the need for greater vigilance over the insurance industry in Missouri. In assessing insurance practices at the end of his first year in office, Vandiver emphasized that fact by warning that problems (offering rebates to special policyholders, issuing side-contracts as special incentives to take out policies, making extravagant use of statistics to mislead policyholders as to the amount of projected profits and dividends) existed. But if Vandiver had pointed out the need for greater regulation and expanded insurance protection, Folk added a sense of urgency by making specific recommendations in his biennial message, including a standard policy act for all insurance companies; an annual apportionment law that would require life insurance companies to pay annual dividends or offer credits to policyholders; an act prohibiting rebating; an act prohibiting the publication of figures that misrepresented the terms of any policy or the amount of projected profits or dividends; an act prohibiting life insurance companies from making any political campaign contribution; an act limiting salaries of life insurance officials to $50,000 a year; and an act requiring

11. H. Roger Grant, *Insurance Reform: Consumer Action in the Progressive Era*, 37–43, 144–50; Vandiver, "What Governor Folk Has Done," 260.

nonresident life insurance companies to set aside a financial reserve for the protection of Missouri policyholders.[12]

Seemingly unconcerned about the number of proposals he thought the legislature might adequately deal with in a sixty-day session, Folk rounded out his legislative wish list with calls for a law that would close loopholes in racetrack gambling by extending the existing law against bookmaking to include those who telephoned bets out of state, a law making bucketshop wagering a felony, an antibribery law that would compel witnesses in bribery cases to testify but grant them immunity from prosecution for their testimony, a tougher child-labor law, the creation of a juvenile court, a good roads bill, authorization for cities and towns to own and operate public utilities as well as for cities to have the right to establish their own municipal police departments (home rule), and a revised tax law that would separate the sources of state and local revenue and exempt real and personal property in the counties from any state taxes.[13]

Overall, Folk's recommendations to the legislature were farther reaching than those made by any of his predecessors. The progressive *Arena* regarded the governor's address as one of the most remarkable state papers to appear in years. "In its simplicity and directness, its lofty note of patriotism, its evident sincerity and its fidelity to basic principles . . . ," said the editors, "this message suggests the State papers of Washington, Jefferson and Lincoln." William Marion Reedy agreed, calling Folk's message "the most statesmanlike document that the assembly has listened to in more than a quarter of a century. It shows thought for the public weal."[14]

What appeared as enlightened statesmanship to the editors of the *Arena* and the *Mirror*, however, seemed to Folk's critics to be a grand scheme for centralization (even the friendly Reedy found "a suggestion of too much government" in parts of Folk's address) and a serious threat to local self-government. They grumbled that the governor, despite his sincere tone, sought "Czar-like" domination over all saloons

12. Vandiver, "What Governor Folk Has Done," 260–61; Guitar and Shoemaker, eds., *Messages and Proclamations*, 300–302.

13. Guitar and Shoemaker, eds., *Messages and Proclamations*, 298–339.

14. "The Biennial Message of Governor Joseph W. Folk," 293; William Marion Reedy, "Chances of Folk's Programme."

and corporations, and complete control over county and municipal officials. Using charges of excessive centralization and abuse of executive authority to good effect, the governor's opponents were able to modify or defeat measures that he desperately wanted. The debate over the bill requesting a state excise commissioner is a good example. Arguing that the creation of the office of state excise commissioner with deputies in the counties would threaten their way of life, deny them local self-government, discredit their own county courts that had previously controlled saloon licensing, and provide a new basis for the development of a statewide political machine, Folk's opponents were able to persuade rural Missourians to help defeat the measure. Ironically, the same people who supported Folk on the question of law enforcement and Sunday closing and applauded his use of the excise commissioner to control the liquor menace in the big cities refused to grant him that prerogative in their own rural enclaves.[15]

Folk did what he could to preserve his program. In an unsuccessful attempt to save the excise commissioner, he tried to counter charges of excessive centralization. He told a *Post-Dispatch* reporter that "if it takes much power to some official to compel the lawless liquor sellers to obey the law, it is because their insolent disregard and defiance of law render such power necessary. . . ." He regarded accusations that creation of an excise commissioner would pose a threat to local self-government just as groundless, "for manifestly where there is local government the Excise Commissioner would not be called upon." On this and other critical questions, Folk demanded party allegiance, held private conferences with individual legislators, and presented several special messages to the legislature to encourage support for important projects. But there was only so much Folk could, or would, do. Opponents took advantage of what historian Louis Geiger has correctly described as a "strong current of personal hostility to Folk" to make his way difficult. Fascinated by the apparent paradox by which a politician was both idolized by the masses yet scorned by many of their representatives, William Reedy asked one veteran lobbyist why Folk had so much trouble with the legislature. "Folk has no friends," said the lobbyist. "He does nothing for anybody. . . . He expects votes when he won't make any concessions. . . . The trouble

15. *St. Louis Post-Dispatch,* January 27, 1907; William Marion Reedy, "The Burning Liquor Question."

with Folk is simply Folk. He is no ingratiator." In the end, a prisoner to his principles, Folk was able to score only a limited victory.[16]

The final legislative tally, though impressive, was a disappointment to Folk. The legislature modified or defeated almost every one of his recommendations that appeared to them to be either self-serving or aggrandizing or that severely threatened special interests. Defeated measures included those that would have expanded the law against racetrack gambling, prohibited free railroad passes, granted municipalities the power to regulate the rates charged by public service corporations, authorized municipalities to own and operate public utilities, provided for the office of state excise commissioner, outlawed holding companies, allowed for the recall of public officials, exempted witnesses for the state from prosecution in bribery cases, provided for the department of corporations, authorized the imposition of a corporate privilege tax, and allowed the cities of St. Louis, Kansas City, and St. Joseph to establish their own municipal police departments.[17]

Even some apparent victories were, in reality, defeats. The legislature did approve the senatorial preference primary, but removed Folk's advantage by scheduling it with the general election rather than the state primary. As passed, the bill decreased the likelihood of Republican crossover voting. Also modified by the legislature was Folk's prohibitory antilobby law, which was weakened to a registration requirement and imposed rather modest penalties. Under the new law, violations would be deemed a misdemeanor. Conviction entailed imprisonment (ranging from ten days to twelve months) in the county jail and a fine (from $100 to $500). The forty-fourth General Assembly also made little change in the dramshop laws, limiting new legislation to a $100 increase in the license fee and a requirement that saloons close at one o'clock in the morning.[18]

16. *St. Louis Post-Dispatch*, February 20, 1907; Geiger, *Joseph W. Folk*, 113; William Marion Reedy, "Why the Governor Isn't Liked."

17. *St. Louis Post-Dispatch*, March 10, 17, 1907. The administration made no real effort to gain home rule in the conduct of police departments for the state's major cities. William Reedy suggested that Folk's initial proposal was always conditioned on securing a state excise commissioner and the power to recall public officials. Reedy, "Chances of Folk's Programme," 4.

18. Geiger, *Joseph W. Folk*, 113–14; *Laws of Missouri Passed at the Forty-fourth General Assembly*, 253–54, 258–59, 351–53.

The proposals that did pass, and there were many, were more in keeping with the national reform trend and probably gained approval as much on their own merits and perceived popularity as anything else. Included in this list were measures that reduced passenger rates on railroads from 2 to 3 cents a mile, removed defects in the maximum freight-rate law passed in 1905, prohibited any corporation from intentionally cutting prices to ruin competition (antidiscrimination), granted numerous protections to insurance policyholders, amended the antitrust law to make violations a felony, established a state primary, made the operation of bucketshops a felony, prohibited the mislabeling and adulteration of foods and drugs, toughened the child labor law, and took the first steps toward obtaining good roads in the state. Also gaining approval were measures that provided for the submission of the initiative and referendum and reform of the state tax system as amendments to the state constitution to be voted on in the next general election.[19]

Shortly after the close of the regular session of the General Assembly on March 16, 1907, Folk announced that he would call the legislature back into special session. Obviously smarting from recent legislative defeats, the governor hoped that by focusing attention and effort on a short list of key measures he could still salvage major elements of his reform program. When legislators returned to the state capitol on April 9, Folk asked them to take immediate action on five recommendations: allow municipalities to regulate the rates charged by public service corporations, amend the racetrack gambling law to prohibit the telegraphing or telephoning of bets, grant the governor the power to direct the attorney general to initiate proceedings to have negligent county officials removed from office, establish home rule in the control of police for the state's three largest cities, and create the office of state excise commissioner.[20]

Folk eventually added one other item to his legislative request list. After receiving pressure from the *St. Louis Post-Dispatch*, the Missouri

19. *St. Louis Post-Dispatch*, March 17, 1907; Geiger, *Joseph W. Folk*, 115–16. Petition requirements were set at 5 percent for the referendum and 8 percent for the initiative, but these percentages had to be obtained in at least two-thirds of the state's congressional districts. See *Laws of Missouri Passed at the Forty-fourth General Assembly*, 452–53.

20. *St. Louis Post-Dispatch*, March 17, 20–21, April 9, 1907; Guitar and Shoemaker, eds., *Messages and Proclamations*, 340–54.

branch of the United Mine Workers of America, and numerous St. Louis labor organizations, the governor requested an amendment to the state's twelve-year-old Fellow-Servant Law. The new law would allow Missouri's forty thousand coal, lead, and zinc miners to recover damages from accidents that occurred through the negligence of a fellow workman in the same manner that railroad and street railway employees could. The demand for a fellow-servant law was a reminder that Folk's interest in labor reform was always secondary to his other reform interests. Aside from a concern for the legal rights of parents of unmarried adults in negligent death cases and a genuine interest in child labor legislation and in effective factory inspection to enforce that legislation, Folk paid little attention to labor issues. Laws passed in 1905 (a maximum hours law for railroad workers and an eight-hour law for workers in mines and smelters) and 1907 (the creation of a Bureau of Labor Statistics and an eight-hour law for telegraph operators and train dispatchers) had not been mentioned in either his inaugural or biennial messages to the legislature. Leadership behind passage of those measures came from others. His belated support for a miner's fellow-servant law suggested that, at best, he had a blind spot in his reform thinking.[21]

By the time the special session finally completed its work, Folk had recouped some of his previous losses. Although he again failed to obtain a home rule bill for police departments in St. Louis, Kansas City, and St. Joseph, and his bill for a state excise commissioner suffered another crushing defeat, he gained everything else. Victories included a fellow-servant law for miners, an amendment to the antigambling act prohibiting out-of-state betting, and an act enabling the governor to proceed against county officials who failed to perform the duties of their office (recall). The legislature also expanded dramshop regulation. New laws prevented brewers and distillers from obtaining a license to operate a dramshop, allowed citizens to sue in court if dramshop laws were violated, and prohibited the operation of any dramshop within five miles of any state university. To those concerned about public control over public service corporations, the passage of a bill allowing cities to regulate the rates that public utilities charged for gas, electricity,

---

21. *St. Louis Post-Dispatch,* April 10, 24, May 9, 1907; *Laws of Missouri Passed at the Forty-fourth General Assembly,* 326–33.

telephone service, and fares on street railways had special significance. Understating his enthusiasm, Folk complimented the legislature on having "given to the people . . . a number of measures of incalculable value to the public welfare." With the special session, Folk had managed to redeem his once-floundering reform program and recapture much of his lost prestige. But in aggressively pursuing additional executive control outside the major cities, Folk alienated rural party stalwarts that comprised Missouri's local courthouse rings.[22]

By every indication, Folk was as busy as governor as he had been as circuit attorney. As a result, he had little time for recreation or social activities. Gertrude Folk has described her husband as being "quite inflexible when it came to doing things for pleasure alone." Aside from an occasional excursion with a group of political associates for a few days of fishing or quail shooting in the Ozarks, Folk was rarely seen outside his office or the Governor's Mansion. Joe and Gertrude Folk seemed to keep to themselves, much as they had in St. Louis. Interestingly, Folk apparently left his work at the office. Gertrude Folk recalled that her husband never discussed his "political prejudices" with her and that although she knew he had "enemies," he never mentioned them.

Gertrude Folk did bother to jot down a few recollections of her time as "First Lady of the State." Although she noted that the "publicity of politics" never appealed to her, she remembered the period as a "delightful four years." Only thirty-two years old at the time of her husband's inauguration, she recalled being "deeply touched by the magnitude" of her new position. In defining her role, she designated Mondays as "at home" days and opened the executive mansion to visitors. Public receptions at the mansion were "simple, informal affairs" and were intended to give visitors the opportunity to meet the governor and his wife and to visit the executive residence. On friendly terms with the wives of the members of the legislature, Gertrude Folk made her social calls in person and accepted all invitations. She also joined several clubs and organized her own successful music club. Later, when living again in St. Louis, she would continue to pursue her long-standing interest in music and serve as president of the Choral

22. *St. Louis Post-Dispatch,* May 12–13, 1907; *Laws of Missouri Passed at the Forty-fourth General Assembly,* 254–57.

Society, a large singing organization for women. As the wife of the governor, she also organized a very popular Christmas festival for the children of the poor in Jefferson City. Although the Folks never had any children, Gertrude Folk's cousin, Bess Thomas, spent a large part of her life living with the couple and was regarded as a daughter by them.[23]

The scant record of Folk's social life only seems to underscore the obvious conclusion that his all-consuming interest was politics. Young, eager, and ambitious, Folk had already done a notable job as both circuit attorney and governor and had won a national reputation. And early success seems to have intensified his desire for further accomplishment. Hal Woodside, Folk's secretary, recalled that early in his term as governor Folk admitted to being seduced by the lure of politics and believed he was on a trajectory to national office.[24]

After his bruising but successful battle with the legislature over his reform program, Folk looked forward to another summer of speechmaking and travel on the chautauqua circuit. Unlike his earlier speeches in that venue where he had shied away from a discussion of specific political proposals and avoided national political issues entirely, the governor now looked to catch the breeze of national politics and joined the national political debate for the first time. In doing so, he set an unannounced course for national political office. On route to deliver an address to a chautauqua meeting in Oklahoma City in late June, Folk told a newspaper reporter that he would like to see the national Democratic party become the party of "positive, aggressive ideas," and not merely the party of opposition to the ideas of others. "If I were asked today," said Folk, "to suggest a platform, I would have it declare for tariff for revenue only; for protection for the people against monopolies . . . ; for an income tax and inheritance tax; for strict regulation of railroads and public utilities . . . ; [and] for the right of the states for self-government as to all matters not delegated to the Federal Government."[25]

23. Park and Morrow, *Women of the Mansion*, 292–307; Jerena East Giffen, *First Ladies of Missouri: Their Homes and Their Families*, 150–55; "Wife of Former Governor of Missouri Homesick for Friends in St. Louis," article dated October 24, 1915, in Mrs. Joseph W. Folk vertical file; Geiger, *Joseph W. Folk*, 105–6.

24. Geiger, *Joseph W. Folk*, 94.

25. *St. Louis Post-Dispatch*, June 26, 1907.

Folk expanded his discussion of state sovereignty in a speech before a crowd of ten thousand people gathered at a Fourth of July chautauqua celebration in Evansville, Indiana. What particularly irked the governor was the manner by which the federal courts allowed for the nullification of state laws by issuing injunctions without a hearing and before trial. Folk argued that state statutes (like Missouri's suspended maximum freight-rate law) should be presumed to be good until, in court, they could be shown to be bad. To Folk, the modern injunctive process allowed for abuses and encroached upon the rights of states by arbitrarily suspending statutes and preventing state officers from enforcing the law. Railroads, said Folk, were the primary beneficiaries of this practice as they were able, through the court injunction, to veto any legislation they did not like. Folk would continue to be an advocate for the protection of state's rights from encroachment by federal courts throughout his remaining term as governor. He achieved national notoriety for his position as a result of remarks he made at a White House conference on the conservation of natural resources in the spring of 1908. By that time, Folk had come to the conclusion that the "dignity of the states" could be preserved only if Congress enacted a law rescinding federal jurisdiction in cases where corporations attempted to obtain an injunction to prevent the enforcement of state laws.[26]

Folk continued to define his position on national issues in an interview with reporters from the *Post-Dispatch* and the *New York World* on September 1. In answer to questions posed to him, the governor suggested that the regulation of railroads and public utilities, a just inheritance tax, the direct election of U.S. senators, and the protection of state laws from federal encroachment were causes the Democratic party should champion. But the paramount issue before the people, said Folk, was the eradication of all special privileges. And in his reform philosophy, the elimination of unjust privilege was a moral question. The tariff was a case in point. "A tariff schedule," said Folk, "deliberately designed to give a special class a protected privilege, and to enable the few to prey upon the many, was prohibited when the tables of stone came from the thunders of Sinai in the commandment, 'Thou shalt not steal.' " Folk also argued, as many Democratic reformers did, that the

26. Ibid., July 4, 1907; *New York Times,* July 5, 1907; *Washington Post,* May 15, 1908.

tariff question and the trust problem were directly connected. "It is well enough," said the governor, "to prosecute trusts, and it is better still to put some of the heads of trusts in stripes for violating the law, but it is hardly practicable to attempt to suppress the trusts with one hand while the other is feeding them with the milk of protection on which they become fat and arrogant."[27]

In a speech delivered three weeks later at the Jamestown, Virginia, Tri-Centennial Exposition, Folk further refined his thinking on the tariff and argued that a "monopoly-creating" tariff could no longer be defended on economic or moral grounds. As an emerging internationalist, Folk argued that it was time for statesmanship. "International commerce," said Folk, "can never be a one-sided transaction. Mutuality is the primary law of trade. Trade restrictions breed trade retaliations, and so long as we pursue a policy of hostile exclusiveness we can never hope to dominate the commercial markets of the world. This can only be done by reciprocal trade relations with the leading nations."[28] But it was not just the liberal/progressive stance that Folk was assuming on the issues that was important. He was acting and sounding like a politician with the potential to be a national leader.

Having used the summer as a testing ground for his viability as a candidate for national office, Folk confided to friends on November 1 that he had decided to enter the race for U.S. Senator in 1908. The decision certainly came after a great deal of deliberation as it required Folk to challenge incumbent Democratic Senator William J. Stone for the office. Stone and Folk were the leaders of the two factions that divided Missouri Democrats, and the popular Stone had an army of anti-Folk loyalists at his command. But Folk had an advantage of his own. Popular with the people if not the politicians, Folk knew that the next senatorial contest in Missouri would be decided in the newly created senatorial preference primary where popular appeal again had a chance to triumph over party organization. One week after his "announcement," and at the invitation of William Jennings Bryan, Folk traveled to Lincoln, Nebraska, to confer with the probable Democratic presidential nominee in 1908. Though they did not reveal the details

27. *St. Louis Post-Dispatch,* September 1, 1907.
28. Ibid., September 21–22, 1907; *New York Times,* September 22, 1907.

of their conversation, they had much to talk about—the approaching presidential campaign, the Democratic platform for 1908, and, in particular, the senatorial campaign in Missouri that promised to be as bitterly contested as the 1904 gubernatorial race.[29]

29. *St. Louis Post-Dispatch,* November 2, 9, 11, 1907.

8

Disappointment

Governor Folk publicly announced that he would oppose William J. Stone for the Democratic nomination for the U.S. Senate on January 23, 1908. Folk and Stone had been rivals for some time, and they represented distinct factions within the State Democratic party. Stone, along with Harry Hawes, Rolla Wells, Alexander Dockery, James A. Reed, and David R. Francis, headed the list of Missouri Democrats who had become associated in the public mind with the anti-Folk wing of the party. He was also the acknowledged leader of the "old guard" in the party, an organizational Democrat, and the consummate party man. His loyalty to party, however, included embracing fellow Democrats who had been tarred with the brush of corruption. His close association with various special interests and his slick and noiseless methods had earned him the sobriquet "Gumshoe Bill."

Folk, in contrast, stood as the accredited leader of the reform wing of Missouri Democracy. He could count lesser-known progressive Democrats like W. D. Vandiver of Columbia, Frank P. Walsh of Kansas City, and Ewing Y. Mitchell of Springfield as his closest advisers. As a candidate for governor, he had denigrated partisanship and denounced Democratic candidates tainted by corruption. He had also violated party loyalty by appealing to reform-minded Republicans for support. As governor, he had refused to accept party counsel or to gratify demands for preferment. His moral fervor and his unyielding enforcement of Sunday Closing Laws had made him appear zealous and puritanical. Both friends and enemies knew him as "Holy Joe."

Folk's announcement triggered a discussion of the relative strengths and weaknesses of the two contestants. Folk's friends argued that his record as governor made him the logical successor to Stone and that his importance to the cause of progressive reform necessitated that he seek advancement in 1908 rather than later. They felt confident that his strength in the country districts would more than offset the losses he might suffer in St. Louis, Kansas City, and St. Joseph due to his lid policy and opposition from gambling and liquor interests. They speculated that Folk would challenge Stone's public record and draw attention once again to his role in the infamous Baking Powder Trust scandal. Folk's supporters also thought that the governor might press Stone on the liquor question. They noted that during the previous special session of the legislature Stone had publicly opposed Folk's requests for a state excise commissioner and for the recall of negligent county officials, and implied that Stone acted as an unpaid lobbyist for the liquor interests.

Stone's friends, on the other hand, anticipated a campaign that would stress the senator's experience and his reputation for party loyalty, and exploit Folk's weaknesses. Conceding Folk's popularity with evangelical Protestants and his strength in the rural districts, they felt confident that the cities would give Stone "top-heavy" majorities as a result of Folk's Sunday closing campaign. Admitting that Stone had worked against at least two of Folk's pet measures, his friends found his actions justified. Folk's attempt to establish a state excise commissioner had provoked Stone and many courthouse politicians to label such action "unnecessary, dangerous, and undemocratic." They also regarded his plan to recall negligent public officials as a blatant attempt to place too much arbitrary authority in the hands of the governor. Stone's supporters also found Folk vulnerable because of his unpopularity with the politicians. They contended that Folk had no political organization worth mentioning in either St. Louis or St. Joseph and expected the local courthouse rings to go after Folk with "savage vindictiveness." Stone's friends speculated that the senator would make an issue of Folk's political independence and that influential Democrats in every county would line up behind Stone when the time came. It was rumored that Stone had maintained communication with his "lieutenants" in the counties and had encouraged them to raise the cry that Folk's entry into the race would throw the Democratic party in Missouri into disorder. Last, Stone's supporters charged that Folk was overly ambitious, because otherwise he would have waited until 1910 and contested the senate seat held by Republican William Warner.[1]

1. *St. Louis Post-Dispatch,* May 26, 1907, January 12, 23, March 27, 1908.

On April 4, 1908, the *St. Louis Republic* published preliminary statements from each of the candidates. As expected, Stone stood on his record and his service to the party. He told voters that his "experience" and "acquaintance with public men and national affairs" made him especially suited for the position. He reminded voters that the senators with the greatest influence and power were those with the most seniority. Defending his reputation against charges that questioned his integrity, he referred to such allegations as having been "so distorted as to constitute in the substance nothing short of gross mendacity." Underscoring his party loyalty, Stone asserted that no one had ever "discredited my Democracy, or questioned my party fidelity." Arguing that there was still value in old-line party Democrats like himself as opposed to the new breed of independent reform Democrats like Folk, Stone reassured Missourians that he was an "old-fashioned Jeffersonian-Jacksonian Democrat," that he had no platform other than that of his party, and that he had never sought public office by courting favor among Republicans.

Just as predictably, Folk stood on his record as governor and on his uncompromising commitment to principle. "I want the people of Missouri to approve or disapprove what has been accomplished, for the guidance of those who will follow in official position. This fight is not merely to win a political fight; it is to establish a vital principle that this State belongs to the people, not to special interests." He told voters he wanted to "win on the strength of my own cause, not on the weakness of my opponent. I want votes that are for me because they think I am right." He implied that his platform would be his own more than his party's. It would rest on the record of his accomplishments and the Democratic policies he believed should be carried into the governmental affairs of the nation. He assured voters that he would continue to defend the law: "I believe lawlessness is anarchy, whether at the top of society or the bottom of society, and that contempt for the law is no less reprehensible when wantonly flaunted by saloonkeepers or gamblers than when plotted over a directors' table or shouted under a red flag at an anarchist meeting." Folk told voters he was proud of the enemies he had made. He included in this list grafters, gamblers, and liquor dealers who had been stung by his persistent enforcement of the law against them, corporate interests made bitter by laws enacted during his administration to regulate and restrict them, and professional politicians who were angry that he had looked to the people and not to them for support. In closing, Folk assumed the moral high ground: "It may not be essential that I win, but it is essential that I be true. It may not be essential that I succeed, but it is essential that I keep the faith."[2]

Folk opened his campaign with a speech at the Tootle Opera House in St. Joseph on April 24. With a "fighting quality in his voice," Folk used the occasion to rekindle the passion that had propelled his successful 1904 campaign. He began his address by reminding his listeners of the conditions in Missouri when he became governor:

> Laws were bought and sold like merchandise; . . . the trail of the unclean dollar was everywhere apparent; gambling houses ran wide open in the cities; saloons made no pretense of obeying the law . . . ; winerooms operated with wanton boldness; the State was in partnership with racetrack gambling; a powerful lobby prevented the passage of laws in the interest of the people; elections in the cities were often the scenes of thuggery and ruffianism; the police departments of the cities were political machines.

And though the Democratic party had not caused those conditions to occur, said Folk, it assumed the responsibility for bringing them to an end. As a result, corruption in the state legislature had been eliminated, and the pledges of the party in its platform and of its gubernatorial nominee had been "redeemed." And Folk reminded his listeners that the last General Assembly had continued that effort, enacting more good laws than any other in the state's history. That accomplishment alone, argued Folk, suggested that the prospect for the triumph of democratic ideals was never brighter. Defining "democratic ideals" as those principles included in the expression "equal rights to all, special privileges to none," Folk proposed that Americans adopt that principle as their motto. "With this rule for our guidance we can not lose our course, or be led into the quicksands of dishonor and despair. With this maxim as our chart, the infamies of privilege in every form can be destroyed and unto all men there be restored the equal right that belongs to each, the fair and equal opportunity for every man to live and labor upon the earth . . . and enjoy untrammelled

2. *St. Louis Republic,* April 5, 1908.

the gains of honest toil." In concluding his speech, Folk chose words characteristic of his notion of progressive reform: "Let us seek as a remedy for existing evils, not less democracy, but more democracy; not more money, but more manhood, not more cunning, but more conscience."[3]

While Folk stormed the state with speeches at Chillicothe, Rolla, Lebanon, Aurora, Monett, Neosho, Joplin, Lamar, Nevada, Mexico, Montgomery City, Farmington, Ste. Genevieve, and Flat River during the eight weeks following his St. Joseph address, Senator Stone remained silent. Confident that his state organization was in place, Stone delayed his opening speech until July 16, nearly three months after Folk's start. In his address, spoken from a platform on the courthouse lawn in Marshall, Stone focused attention on his firm grasp of national issues and virtually ignored Folk's candidacy entirely. But Stone did lay the foundation for his political defense. Responding to charges that he was strong in the cities but not in the country, Stone maintained that by birth, marriage, and personal associations he qualified as a rural Missourian. And he had, he said, been their champion. "For thirty years, in office and out of office, I have been fighting their battles, and they know it." He contrasted perceptions of Folk as arrogant and aloof with professions of his own modesty and humility. "To me the thought is repulsive of painting myself as a shining light, as a colossal Ego. . . ." "I am . . . a plain, blunt man—an average citizen—neither better nor worse than any other man. . . ." He countered Folk's individualism with his own loyalty to party. "I am not here to speak for myself, but for the Democratic party." And he resisted any attempts on the part of the Folk camp to resurrect allegations of past improprieties by pleading for courtesy and harmony in the senatorial fight. "Let us fight Republicans, not each other."[4]

Stone's biographer has suggested that the watchwords of his campaign against Folk were "organization" and "exposure." As a masterful campaigner, Stone had demonstrated talents as a dramatic orator and possessed both an infallible memory and a thoroughly informed

3. *St. Louis Post-Dispatch,* April 25, 1908.

4. Ibid., April 25, 30, May 9–10, June 21, 1908; *Palmyra (Mo.) Spectator,* July 16, 1908.

knowledge of national issues. His straightforward personality had won him many loyal friends. Despite the fact that he was over the age of sixty, Stone traveled to every county in the state, attending picnics, fairs, and old-settlers reunions. He could easily speak for over an hour at a time, often spoke two or three times a day, and, during three months of campaigning, gave some 250 public addresses. And he could strike back when provoked. When Folk challenged his public record and his integrity, Stone harangued Folk for his holier-than-thou morality that allowed him to claim "to typify whatever is good in public and political life" and to assail him [Stone] as representing "only evil influences." Stone found Folk's charges "brazen, shameful and intolerable." But Stone could stretch the bounds of decency as well. As the campaign neared its close, Stone accused Folk of plotting with the Republicans to throw his support to Herbert Hadley, the Republican candidate for governor, in return for Republican votes. "I charge boldly," said Stone, "that Joseph W. Folk is . . . plotting treason to the party to promote his own selfish interest."[5]

In contrast to Stone, Folk counted on "principle" and "exposure" to carry him to victory. He told voters that he had kept his promises. "I said . . . that if you elected me Governor I would keep up the work I began as Circuit Attorney. I believe I have kept the faith. I have enforced the laws as I found, without fear or favor. . . ." And he promised to do the same as senator. "There is no place in the world where there is more to be done for the people against graft, greed and lawlessness than [in the United States Senate]." And although he admitted there were good men in the Senate:

> there is undoubtedly more rottenness there than there ever was in the Legislature of Missouri, or even in the Municipal Assembly of St. Louis. . . . Instead of being senators of the people, too many of them [a possible reference to Stone?] have been subsidized by special interests to represent them instead of the people. . . . The reforms that I have worked for in St. Louis and in Missouri must be fought for in the United States Senate, if the reform work is to continue.

5. Towne, *William J. Stone*, 77–80.

Folk was convinced that a reform sentiment was sweeping the country and that the people were behind him. "The people want a change everywhere and are saying so."[6]

Folk campaigned almost without pause after he took the field in April, and demonstrated that he could match Stone as a seasoned campaigner. The *St. Louis Post-Dispatch* estimated that by mid-October Folk had made nearly 200 speeches, spoken to more than 300,000 people, and traveled more than 20,000 miles in crisscrossing the state. He rarely spoke fewer than three times a day and sometimes gave as many as six speeches in one long day of stumping. He lacked Stone's expertise on national issues, but could speak with authority on the need for election and ballot reform, on the need to regulate railroads and public service corporations, on the need to prosecute monopolistic trusts, and on the need to fight graft and boodle at all levels of government. And he could, like Stone, sling mud if necessary. When Stone accused him, in the closing days of the campaign, of plotting a "corrupt bargain" with the Republicans for personal advantage, he responded by characterizing the Stone camp as a "gang of political pirates utterly devoid of all scruples; there is . . . no lie too malicious for them to utter."[7]

When voters finally registered their preference in the November senatorial primary, they gave Stone 159,512 votes to 144,718 votes for Folk. "Gumshoe Bill" had defeated "Holy Joe." Folk carried seventy-five counties to Stone's thirty-nine and had a plurality of almost 9,000 votes outside the state's major urban centers, but lost. Why? How could that happen? Folk's supporters cried fraud. They charged that Stone's strong showing in rural Missouri resulted from the actions of partisan election commissioners (appointed by members of the county courts who took their orders from "old guard," anti-Folk Democrats) who had thrown out ballots for Folk. Voting results, however, offered another explanation. Folk won far more rural counties than Stone, but they tended to be the ones in the less populated regions of the state—in Missouri's "Bible-belt" (southeastern Missouri and the eastern Ozarks). Stone, on the other hand, showed strength in the more populous counties of western Missouri and in the traditional Democratic stronghold known as "Little

6. *St. Louis Post-Dispatch,* October 25, 28, 30, 1908.
7. Ibid., October 25, 1908; Stone quoted in Towne, *William J. Stone,* 80.

Dixie" (north-central Missouri). As Stone's biographer has noted, these had always been the areas where Stone ran strongest.

Stone also won big in the cities, defeating Folk by close to 15,000 votes in St. Louis and almost 9,000 votes in Jackson County (Kansas City). Here too, Folk's supporters charged that vote frauds in the machine-dominated urban wards had allowed Stone to steal the election. Republican Governor-elect Herbert Hadley agreed that vote fraud in St. Louis "doubtless contributed to Stone's election," but thought it "probable that Stone had a majority even after the elimination of the votes that were dishonestly cast and counted." William Reedy added credence to the charges of conspiracy by asserting that Folk was "slaughtered by the railroads . . . the brewers, the gambling interests, the saloonkeepers, and the politicians." But theories that focused on the corruption of election commissioners, the manipulations of the machine, and the influences of various special interest groups offered only a partial explanation for Folk's defeat.[8]

In a very real sense, Folk's lid policy had come back to haunt him. As William Reedy harshly concluded, [Folk] "attempted to squeeze the two great cosmopolitan cities into the narrow limits suitable only to the New England village, to shape many thousands of men of many customs, diverse habits and ways of thought to one common, narrow, bigoted Pharisaic ideal—his own. . . ." And Folk made his poorest showing in areas where his zealous enforcement of the Sunday Closing Law had caused the most dismay—amongst German-American and working-class voters. As Reedy noted: "The average St. Louisan did not know much of the viciousness of the principle whereby Mr. Folk . . . arrogate[d] to himself the right to say what a man shall or shall not do on Sunday, but he did know that Mr. Folk prevented him getting his glass of beer on Sunday, and that was enough for him."[9]

Folk was also out-organized and, in a manner, outfoxed. Unlike Stone, who had maintained his party connections and demonstrated tact in dealing with party regulars, Folk all but divorced himself from his party

8. Letter from Herbert Hadley to Mark Sullivan dated October 30, 1911, Hadley Papers; William Marion Reedy, "How and Why in Missouri"; Towne, *William J. Stone,* 80. For election results, see Missouri *Official Manual, 1909–1910,* 664–66.

9. William Marion Reedy, "The Finish of Pharisee Folk"; Towne, *William J. Stone,* 81–82.

and openly flaunted his independence. Rebuffing the state machine
had worked as a tactic to get himself elected in 1904, but proved a
handicap once he became governor. As Herbert Hadley commented to
journalist Mark Sullivan several years later: "Folk was never popular
with the political leaders of the party. During his term as Governor
he did not succeed in binding men to him personally and lost the
support of men of prominence throughout the State who had actively
favored him for Governor." The 1908 campaign was also much different
from the one in 1904. In 1908 Folk was no longer the "independent"
running for governor, first against the likes of Hawes, Reed, and Gantt
and then against the hopelessly handicapped Walbridge. Against Stone
he challenged incumbency, party loyalty, and personal popularity. In
pushing himself or allowing himself to be pushed into the senate race
against Stone, he jeopardized the success of the entire party ticket. As
Stone's biographer has noted, in running against Stone "Folk challenged
the man who had the right to the organizational support [of his party]."
He might have had a chance to defeat Stone in an emotionally charged,
no-holds-barred campaign in which he relentlessly hammered Stone's
political record and his questionable political integrity, but to do so
in 1908 was to risk party chaos and, ultimately, party defeat. Such a
tactic would have had to have been premised on the assumption that
he could attract Republican crossover voters, which the new primary
set-up precluded.[10] Stone had pleaded for courtesy and harmony in
the senatorial contest, and Folk, without much choice, had largely
complied.[11]

Folk might well have gone to the Senate if he had compromised
principle for success or if he had been more endearing. But he would
not and could not. He steadfastly refused to build a political machine,
appease his most severe critics by backing away from his law enforcement
program, or seek any kind of peace with special interests. Folk was an
effective speaker, a diligent prosecutor, a capable administrator, and an
indefatigable campaigner, but he was too cool, too formal, too aloof, too

10. Only those who voted the Democratic ballot had the right to vote for Stone
or Folk.
11. Letter from Herbert Hadley to Mark Sullivan dated October 30, 1911, Hadley
Papers; Towne, *William J. Stone*, 83.

humorless, too self-centered, too didactic, and too self-righteous to ever qualify as a La Follette–like vote getter. One might argue that Folk was a victim of his own success—that by eliminating state-level corruption and fulfilling legislative promises, he had accomplished his political mission. In eliminating his theme (anticorruption), he had diffused the popular passion behind his original candidacy. But in reality, Folk should have been even more popular in 1908 than in 1904. The passage of his legislative agenda was a remarkable accomplishment that stood as a model of progressive reform. But Folk never received the credit he deserved. He should have been proclaimed a hero, a champion of the people. But he was not. His inability to triumph over partisanship and party organization in 1908 rested with his inability to evoke charisma or to generate enduring popular loyalty. As a friend of Folk's once commented: "few people ever threw their hats in the air [for Joe Folk]."[12] The perceptive William Reedy concurred: "He [Folk] was not popular, but he was right—too rigidly so for a generation that capitulates to personal expediency and has made principle elastic."[13]

Despite Folk's defeat, the state election returns of 1908 offered some encouragement to reformers in general. Missouri voters had, as Folk informed William Jennings Bryan, done one "good thing." They had expanded the bounds of popular democracy by adopting the proposed initiative and referendum amendment, making those forms of direct democracy part of the state's constitution. They had also elected Herbert Hadley as Missouri's new governor. As noted, Folk and Hadley had worked closely together as governor and attorney general. They held sympathetic views on most issues and shared a similar reform spirit. Hadley had, in fact, campaigned on a Folk platform. He promised strict enforcement of the law and the enactment of "such new laws as experience may show to be necessary and advisable for the further suppression of the evils of the liquor traffic." He supported state regulation of the charges levied by public service corporations to ensure fair rates to consumers, and favored a law making it a criminal offense for railroad companies to discriminate in freight charges or to give free passes to individuals (some exceptions noted). He also supported a

12. Quoted in Geiger, *Joseph W. Folk,* 130.
13. William Marion Reedy, "Exit Folk."

change in court procedure that would prevent a judgment in a civil or criminal suit from being reversed unless the court could "affirmatively say upon the entire record that the judgment was for the wrong party, and that but for the error complained of a different judgment would have been rendered." Folk had advocated such a change ever since the Missouri Supreme Court had overturned many of his boodle convictions on technicalities.[14]

In presenting his farewell message to the Missouri General Assembly on January 7, 1909, Folk indicated that he hoped the new governor and legislature would continue to press for progressive reforms and offered them no fewer than seventeen recommendations. His list of suggestions included compulsory voting; home rule for police departments in St. Louis, Kansas City, and St. Joseph; changing the date of the state primary; tax equalization; elimination of the prison contract labor system; creation of a special juvenile court judge; extension of the law against child labor; application of the eight-hour law to all state and municipal employees; a good roads system; and appointment of waterway and forestry commissions.[15]

Immediately after leaving office Folk transferred his residence to St. Louis, ostensibly to resume his law practice. But in a letter to William Jennings Bryan (who had himself just been defeated by William Howard Taft in his third bid for the presidency) in mid-December 1908, Folk more accurately revealed his plans for the future. He confided to Bryan that he did not mind his own defeat "at all." His exit from public office would provide him with more time for purposeful writing and speaking. "My idea is the fight for reform should continue even more aggressively. The people will do right when they know right and the effort should be to teach them." Apparently, his reform passion had not diminished. Not yet forty years old, Folk had ample time to reflect and plan his political future.[16]

14. Letter from Joseph W. Folk to William Jennings Bryan dated December 18, 1908, William Jennings Bryan Papers, Library of Congress, Manuscript Division, Washington, D.C.; Missouri *Official Manual, 1909–1910,* 419–25.

15. See Guitar and Shoemaker, eds., *Messages and Proclamations,* 355–96; and *St. Louis Post-Dispatch,* January 7, 1909.

16. Letter from Joseph W. Folk to William Jennings Bryan dated December 18, 1908, Bryan Papers.

How to keep his name before the public, however, would be a concern. In early February 1909, Folk traveled to Hodgenville, Kentucky, to participate in the laying of the cornerstone at the site commemorating Abraham Lincoln's birthplace. As president of the Lincoln National Farm Association, Folk presided over the highly publicized ceremonies that included speeches by President Theodore Roosevelt and William Jennings Bryan. Early that same year Folk announced that he planned to begin a national lecture tour with stops in selected eastern cities. The tour, sponsored by the Redpath-Slayton Lyceum Bureau, would be extended off-and-on for the next four years. It provided an opportunity for Folk to test the extent of his popularity and perhaps begin to make a bid for a national following. The venture also promised to be a lucrative source of income (Folk was reportedly broke when he left office). By late September Folk had delivered more than 200 speeches and, at an estimated $200–$250 per address, had earned well over $40,000 (more than eight times his annual salary as governor).[17]

The speeches themselves tended to be expressions of Folk's political philosophy rather than outlines of any specific political program. His topic was usually citizenship or civic righteousness and his talks seemed aimed at inspiration as much as anything else. One address, "The Era of Conscience," was typical of the type. Folk believed that an ethical awakening had brought about the "birth of a new epoch" in national life. He hoped to convince his listeners that morality could be applied to politics and that an aroused public conscience could be a powerful force for civic betterment. The recent tendency toward reform at all levels of government, argued Folk, proved that bribery, corruption and special privilege could be resisted. The public now recognized that the government belonged to them and that it had rights that must be respected. After hearing Folk speak at a Boise Democratic Club banquet, an editor for the *Idaho Statesman* recounted that he found the Folk style captivating:

> Gov. Folk proved to be an uncommon orator, and his methods were distinctively individual. He possesses a voice of varied range,

17. Geiger, *Joseph W. Folk,* 134–35; *St. Louis Post-Dispatch,* January 17, February 12, September 24, 1909, January 22, 1910.

which can either thunder like Juvenal or plead like Cicero. . . .
His eyes glowed with Southern fires holding the vision of a martyr
of ancient days. At times, when he reached the higher flights of
mingled denunciation of the criminal rich and ecstatic picturing of
what the republic should be, his gaze gleamed like that of Giordano
Bruno at the stake . . . here was a man who knew what he was
talking about, believed what he spoke, and desired with a self-
consuming desire to make others believe what he believed.

Fearlessness, aggressiveness, the uncompromising traits of the
Puritan blended with the softer gallantry of the cavalier, a sparkling
of true Southern humor, a tang of native dialect, an attitude of
defiance to the strong and protection for the weak—these were
the characteristics that impressed his hearers.

Whatever their effect, Folk's speeches allowed him to validate his credentials as a spokesman for a progressive ideal. And as one writer
observed, Folk's pronouncements had "the achievements of the man
behind them. While many men have been hearers and sayers of the
words civic righteousness, here has been a doer of them."[18]

At no time, however, during 1909 did Folk articulate what his future
political plans might be. Most political observers assumed that he would
make a run for the U.S. Senate seat held by Republican William Warner
in 1910. Others thought he had an outside chance to capture the
Democratic presidential nomination in 1912, especially if no other
strong candidate emerged. The decision was complicated by financial
considerations. If Folk decided on the senate race, he would have to
stop lecturing and start campaigning. But if he declined to run for the
Senate and made a bid for the presidency instead, he could continue
to prosper as a lecturer. In fact, an announcement of his candidacy for
the nation's highest office would most certainly enhance his prestige on
the lecture platform. In September of 1909 the *St. Louis Post-Dispatch*
reported that the latest "tip" from the inner circles of the Democratic
State Committee was that Folk would be "induced" to stay out of next
year's Senate race with the assurance that he would be given the support
of the Missouri delegation for the Democratic presidential nomination

18. *Idaho Statesman* quoted in *St. Louis Post-Dispatch,* July 14, 1910; Geiger,
Joseph W. Folk, 135. See "The Era of Conscience," typed manuscript, in Folk Papers.

in 1912. In January of 1910, R. W. Napier, former secretary of the Democratic State Committee, advanced a rumor that an Eastern lecture bureau had offered Folk a $40,000 speaking contract for the remainder of the year.[19]

Talk of Folk as a candidate for the Senate revived, however, during the early months of 1910. Both James A. Reed, former mayor of Kansas City, and David R. Francis, former governor, had already announced their intentions to seek the nomination. Despite statements from Folk that the senatorial race was not "attractive" to him, many of his supporters pushed him to enter the contest. Reports indicated that Folk's state organization had strengthened itself and that it could claim 20,000 members. In February Folk admitted that he had written letters to Democratic leaders in different parts of the state asking them to assess the strength of his support. The country districts and "dry" counties (Folk had captured more than three-fourths of the local option counties in Missouri in his 1908 campaign) appeared most favorable to his candidacy, but there were doubts whether Folk had either sufficient urban support or adequate financial backing to win his party's nomination.[20]

Folk finally put an end to the speculation by privately announcing in late May that he would allow his friends to launch his candidacy for the presidential nomination. When it became apparent that Folk had made his decision, James A. Reed declared that he would lend Folk his support. Coming from one of Folk's political adversaries, Reed's announcement had the appearance of a "corrupt bargain" by which he would publicly pledge his support to Folk in return for Folk's endorsement of his candidacy against David R. Francis. Folk formally announced that he would skip the Senate race and concentrate, instead, on winning the Democratic presidential nomination at a banquet given in his honor at the Southern Hotel in St. Louis on June 2. Six hundred Democrats representing every county in the state attended the banquet organized by the Missouri Democratic League. Lon Sanders (St. Louis) served as president of the new organization with William J. Cochran (St. Louis) as secretary and E. S. Lewis (St. Louis) as treasurer. The executive committee included Nelson W. McLeod (St. Louis), M. E. Benton

19. *St. Louis Post-Dispatch,* September 17, 1909, January 28, 1910.
20. Ibid., September 26, 1909, January 19, 29, February 4, 13, 1910.

(Neosho), John C. Roberts (St. Louis), W. D. Vandiver (Columbia), J. H. McCord (St. Joseph), and J. M. Lowe (Kansas City). Those in attendance adopted resolutions in which they pledged themselves to work for the Folk-for-President program, and called upon Democrats in other states to join the Folk-for-President movement.[21] The leadership of the Missouri Democratic League proclaimed that they would seek to have the Missouri State Democratic Convention endorse Folk's candidacy at its September meeting. Not surprisingly, the one most miffed by the turn of events was David R. Francis. He refused to attend the St. Louis dinner, and used his newspaper, the *St. Louis Republic,* to argue against the plan to have the Missouri convention pledge its support to Folk.[22]

During the spring and summer of 1910 Folk began to sketch the outlines of his political program. Portraying himself as an antimonopolist, a tariff reformer, and an enemy of special privilege, Folk characterized the trusts and the tariff as the two most corrupting influences in American life. "The trust magnate," said Folk, "who secured a monopoly on some necessity is robbing the public through a graft enabling him to demand and receive more than a natural price. It is this form of graft, coupled with a high protective tariff, that is responsible for the present extortionately high cost of living." And the way to "exterminate" the evil was, as always with Folk, through the enforcement of the law. "There is law enough now . . . to suppress all of the great trusts. . . . We do not need new laws so much, however, as we need the sincere enforcement of the laws we have." The slogan of his campaign would be "equal rights to all, special privileges to none." And he would demand that the Democratic party adamantly insist on stamping out graft and corruption in government; eradicating all special favors, bounties, and subsidies; opposing any tariff for any purpose other than revenue; enforcing the laws; regulating the rates of public utility corporations; preserving the rights of states to self-government; restricting American territory to the Western Hemisphere; enacting a Federal income tax; and electing U.S. Senators by direct vote.

21. By late August formal steps had been taken to organize Folk Progressive Democratic Leagues in the New England states, New Jersey, Maryland, Pennsylvania, and Delaware. *New York Times,* August 21, 1910.
22. *St. Louis Post-Dispatch,* May 21, 26, June 1, 3, 1910; Muraskin, "Missouri Politics," 328–29.

Although the emphasis was his own, the platform itself was one that most Bryan Democrats could readily support.[23]

At the Democratic State Platform Convention, held in Jefferson City on September 13–14, 1910, Folk's supporters in the Missouri Democratic League succeeded in gaining the unanimous endorsement of Folk for president in 1912. A precedent for this action had been established in 1906 when a similar convention formally declared for William Jennings Bryan for president. As a result, the State Democratic platform included the following statement:

> In the battle for good government we commend to the Democracy of the country the leadership of one who has been at all times foremost in the fight, and whose work as circuit attorney of St. Louis and Governor of Missouri accomplished so much for political and practical reform, which like a tidal wave is now sweeping over the whole country. Conservative as an administrative officer and progressive in his legislative policy, he is the foe of all grafters, the friend of honest toilers, and will make the doctrine of equal rights a living force in government. Therefore the Democracy of Missouri presents for nomination for President in 1912 Joseph W. Folk, and pledges to him our hearty support.[24]

James Reed and Congressman Champ Clark, temporary chairman of the convention, at least acquiesced in the endorsement.

On the surface, it appeared as if the Folk campaign had taken a great leap forward. But the endorsement was technically nonbinding. The *St. Louis Post-Dispatch* sharply underscored this point in an editorial in which it referred to the convention's action as "at best a perfunctory proceeding which neither increases nor decreases the chances of the St. Louis man [Folk] for the nomination and does not in any way commit Missouri Democrats to his candidacy." While Folk's backers certainly viewed the home-state endorsement as a necessary hurdle to be gotten over if Folk were to be a viable candidate, and undoubtedly planned to use it to leverage support nationally, others saw it as masking reality and

23. *New York Times,* April 25, May 1, 1910; *St. Louis Post-Dispatch,* April 25, May 1, June 3, 1910.
24. Missouri *Official Manual, 1911–1912,* 368.

misrepresenting Folk's true popularity in the state. Governor Herbert Hadley remembered the statement "purely as a strategic proposition, in order to hold for the Democratic party the independent vote of the State," while the *Post-Dispatch* regarded the convention's action as "the product of a desire for party harmony, designed to attract to other candidates the support of the supporters of Folk."[25]

A key element of Folk's strategy throughout 1910 and 1911 was to try to win the support of Democratic icon William Jennings Bryan. The two had been friendly admirers for years. Folk had been a Bryan supporter since 1896, and Bryan had publicly praised Folk after his victory in the Missouri governor's race in 1904. Bryan had traveled to Missouri on several occasions to speak for the Democratic party in general or on behalf of Folk in particular, and Folk had conferred with him prior to entering the Senate race in 1908. They also had much in common: a fervent evangelical Protestantism, and a belief that every civic and social question was in fact a moral question and that its solution should be found in the moral law; a view of progressive reform that favored an activist, interventionist government with an overriding obligation to protect the weak and restrain the strong; and a firm commitment to a democratic ideology that placed its faith in the people and favored modifications to representative government that would further empower them. When constructing a political platform from which to launch his presidential bid, Folk took planks from Bryan's own. While Folk kept busy lecturing on the chautauqua circuit and speaking at Democratic party banquets around the country, his followers continued to work to line up support outside Missouri, primarily among former Bryan men.[26]

Although Bryan refrained from overtly praising any candidate at this early date, there were indications that he liked what Folk was saying. In January 1911, Bryan featured an article by Folk entitled "The Religion of Democracy" on the front page of *The Commoner*. In the article, really a political speech, Folk again tied religion to politics. "Democracy," he said, "is more than a name, it is a religion, the religion of brotherhood

25. Letter from Herbert Hadley to Mark Sullivan dated October 30, 1911, Hadley Papers; *St. Louis Post-Dispatch*, September 14, 1910; Geiger, *Joseph W. Folk*, 140.
26. Geiger, *Joseph W. Folk*, 139.

among men, the religion of equal opportunity for all mankind. It is the religion that demands more of the golden rule and less of the rule of gold in government." In its ongoing war against the Republican party, Folk urged the Democratic party to fight aggressively for progressive democratic principles and flattered Bryan in the process.

> It is not essential that we always win, but it is essential that we be true to democratic ideals. . . . More was gained for the people in the Bryan campaigns that ended in apparent defeat than would have been accomplished by the barren victory of leaders controlled by the powers that prey. These campaigns wrought a revolution in the public conscience, and aroused the people to the need of reform.[27]

Underlying each of the Bryan campaigns, however, "and greater than any specific issue," said Folk, "was the struggle of humanity against the oppression of plutocracy, of men against dollars and of conscience against greed." And it was special privilege that threatened the doctrine of equal rights. "We ought not to permit the party to be prostituted to the service of selfish interests, or to be made the tail to the kite of monopoly." "As privilege increases opportunity must diminish, and as opportunity diminishes the rights of the individual are destroyed." But an active government could redress the socio-economic imbalances in society. "We cannot bring about a forced equality of conditions, but there may be an equalization of burdens and opportunities." And Folk knew where to begin. "Watered stocks, fictitious bond issues and the tariff graft should be done away with, and holding companies . . . should be placed under the ban of the law." Likewise, said Folk, the rates of public utility corporations should be regulated, the laws vigorously enforced (corporate directors should be held criminally responsible for lawless corporate acts), and a progressive income tax should be enacted to distribute more equitably "the burdens of government." And if government by privilege should be discouraged, democracy should be encouraged. Senators should be elected directly by the people. Initiative and referendum laws should be enacted to check corruption and ensure that government is representative of the people. And a national antilobby

27. Joseph W. Folk, "The Religion of Democracy," 1.

law should be passed where failure to "register in a public record" would be regarded as a felony.[28]

In July 1911 *The Commoner* ran another front page feature, "Ask The Candidate," in which the editors proposed that every candidate for the Democratic presidential nomination respond to a series of public questions. Included in their list of questions were the following: "Do you believe in the publicity of campaign contributions?" "Do you believe in the support of state governments in all their rights?" "Do you endorse the labor planks of the 1908 platform?" "Do you believe in the strict regulation of railroads?" "Do you favor legislation compelling banks to insure depositors?" The editors sent the questionnaire to Folk, Governor Woodrow Wilson of New Jersey, Congressman Champ Clark of Missouri, Governor Thomas Marshall of Indiana, and Congressman Oscar Underwood of Alabama. Evidently only Folk and Marshall bothered to respond, and only Folk did so in a forthright manner. As a result, the editors rewarded Folk by printing his responses on the front page of the August 4 issue. To no great surprise, Folk's answers (which were all in the affirmative) were ones that Bryan would have applauded. A follow-up article in the *Literary Digest* suggested that Bryan was certainly pleased with Folk's responses and reprinted a cartoon from the *Seattle Post-Intelligencer* that showed Folk at the top of Bryan's list of presidential favorites (Woodrow Wilson and Champ Clark were the other names on the list).[29]

A final indication that Bryan might be warming to Folk as a candidate came with the September 15 issue of *The Commoner*. This time the publication devoted a full page to "The Political Career of Joseph W. Folk." The editors referred to Folk as a "pioneer" in his work for reform, gave him credit as the man who made reforms popular when they were unpopular, and reminded readers that it was Folk who first proclaimed the doctrine known as the "Missouri Idea," "which is familiar in every part of the earth today." The article listed all of Folk's many accomplishments as governor and included, as a boxed insert, the Democratic State Convention's endorsement of him for president.[30]

28. Ibid., 1–2.

29. "Ask the Candidate," 1, 4; "Where Former Governor Joseph W. Folk Stands"; "Mr. Bryan's List"; *St. Louis Post-Dispatch,* July 19, August 1, 1911.

30. "The Political Career of Joseph W. Folk."

The truth of the matter, however, was that Folk's chances of gaining the nomination had steadily diminished since the 1910 elections.
Included in that Democratic triumph (the party won control of both
houses of Congress) was the election of Woodrow Wilson, a political
newcomer, as governor of New Jersey. Wilson quickly seized control of
the Democratic party from the bosses and established a reputation as
a progressive reformer in a state known for its corruption and lax laws
governing corporations. His success at pushing major reform measures
through the state legislature early in 1911—a program that included a direct primary law, regulation of public utilities, workman's compensation,
and a corrupt practices act—catapulted him to national prominence and
made him a player in the presidential sweepstakes.[31]

Just as significant for Folk's future was the emergence of other
Democrats as national political figures. Most notable in this group was
Congressman Champ Clark of Missouri. Clark's election to the powerful
and prestigious position of Speaker of the House of Representatives early
in 1911 triggered talk about him as a presidential possibility as well.
And there were others—Democratic majority leader Oscar Underwood
of Alabama, and Governors Thomas Marshall of Indiana and Judson
Harmon of Ohio. In fact, the only candidate not currently holding
elective office was Folk, who by January 1912 had been out of office for
three years. The once-loyal *St. Louis Post-Dispatch* found Folk vulnerable
on just that point. "Mr. Folk is identified with the Chautauqua circuit
rather than the political arena. . . . Since Mr. Folk's affiliation with the
forces of intolerance and his defeat for the Senate, his political strength
has waned steadily." In July 1911 the same editors harshly, and perhaps
unfairly, commented: "One of the mysteries of the day is Mr. Folk's views
on the things that have happened in public affairs since 1908. . . ." The
implication seemed to be that Folk had been left behind in the recent
Democratic resurgence.[32]

William Reedy, an ardent supporter of Folk as a presidential aspirant,
agreed that his popularity had dropped, but found an explanation for
that in what Folk had done rather than in what he had failed to do.
To Reedy, one needed to look to the changes that had taken place in
the business of print journalism, to the general decline of muckraking

31. Kendrick A. Clements, *Woodrow Wilson: World Statesman,* 50–73.
32. *St. Louis Post-Dispatch,* June 14, July 12, 1911.

by 1911, and to the common association of Folk with Bryanism. "Magazines that once praised him," said Reedy, "have fallen silent since they were consolidated and trustified. All because he stopped ring rule in Missouri, because he made saloons obey the law, . . . because he did something to stop corporation supremacy in this State, because, finally, as I believe, he is too close in thought and spirit to Mr. Bryan."[33]

As the presidential campaign moved into 1912, Folk's fortunes worsened. Bryan, who had periodically teased Folk with the possibility of his support during 1911, told his brother Charles early in the new year that he had not made up his mind between Woodrow Wilson and Champ Clark! Although Bryan never publicly admitted to having made such a decision, Folk's days as a viable candidate were all but numbered. He had already lost the support of many "new" Democrats for being linked in the public mind with "old" Bryanism, and now he could count on none of Bryan's support.

Just as damaging to Folk's campaign was Clark's decision to stop posturing and mount a serious presidential bid. That decision created a dilemma for all Missouri Democrats. If Clark were to win the nomination, he would have to have the support of the Missouri delegation to the national convention. To obtain that endorsement, Missouri's Democrats would have to repudiate the promise they had made to Folk in 1910. Folk and Clark had been on friendly terms. In fact, Clark had supported Folk for the Senate in 1908. But when Clark's supporters pressed the issue, an acrimonious debate ensued that once again threatened to divide the party. Folk's supporters insisted that Clark, as temporary chairman of the 1910 convention, was bound to support his party's platform pledge. At that point, two prominent Missouri politicians sought to tip the balance by adding their political influence to the fight. Regarding Clark as the more acceptable candidate, David R. Francis and Senator William J. Stone both worked to undermine Folk's presidential bid by blocking the election of Folk men to state party positions.[34]

In an attempt to settle the dispute and restore party harmony, William Jennings Bryan stepped in to act as peacemaker. He proposed that Folk and Clark agree to let the voters decide the question in a primary election. But Folk evidently objected to the idea because he feared such

33. William Marion Reedy, "The Status of Mr. Folk."
34. Muraskin, "Missouri Politics," 330–32.

an impromptu primary could be "fixed" by the Democratic State Committee where Clark had more support.[35] His initial proposal rejected, Bryan offered a compromise. If both candidates agreed, the Democratic State Convention would be instructed to divide the delegate vote evenly between the two "favorite sons" when it convened in Joplin on February 20. After the first ballot at the national convention, the candidate showing the greatest strength would receive the entire vote. Folk agreed to the proposal, but Clark refused. The impasse placed Folk in an awkward position. He could cling to his endorsement, continue to run as a weakening candidate, and risk having the state convention rescind its pledge anyway. The result would be embarrassing and certainly lead to accusations that he once again placed himself above his party. The other option was to drop out of the race entirely. Folk chose the latter. As a face-saving arrangement, Clark publicly agreed to accept Bryan's proposal to split the delegates, which Folk then negated by announcing that he was no longer a candidate.[36]

Between his withdrawal on February 10 and the national convention in Baltimore in late June, Folk dropped out of public view. He attended the convention, heard his name idly mentioned along with a dozen other "dark horse" candidates, and gave one minor speech to a restless, inattentive audience. He had hoped for so much more. Appointed to the Democratic National Campaign Committee after the convention, Folk campaigned for Woodrow Wilson (who won the nomination over Champ Clark after forty-six ballots). It remained to be seen whether a victorious president would find a place in his administration for a fellow progressive.[37]

35. The Democratic State Committee did adopt a scheme that permitted St. Louis and Kansas City to hold primaries to elect their delegates to the state convention, but allowed each county central committee to select their delegates in any way they chose. See Thomas Ralph Yancey, "The Election of 1912 in Missouri," 18.

36. Ibid., 10–26; William Marion Reedy, "The Folk-Clark Row"; LeRoy Ashby, *William Jennings Bryan: Champion of Democracy,* 137; Geiger, *Joseph W. Folk,* 146–52; Estal E. Sparlin, "Bryan and the 1912 Democratic Convention"; Mark Sullivan, "Credentials from the People." For coverage of the Folk-Clark controversy in the press, see *St. Louis Post-Dispatch,* October 19–20, November 12, December 17, 28, 1911, January 14, 26, February 3, 10–12, 1912.

37. Geiger, *Joseph W. Folk,* 152–53; *St. Louis Post-Dispatch,* June 26, 1912.

9

Wilsonian

J oe Folk must have found 1912 to be a time for soul searching. His acclaim as a crusading circuit attorney and praise as a reform governor had grown distant with time from the public consciousness. Defeated as a senatorial candidate, he had been denied as a presidential aspirant and disowned as a "favorite son." Without a recent victory to his credit, he faced declining demand as a chautauqua speaker, financial insecurity, and an uncertain political future. He could resume his law practice, secure his financial future, and join St. Louis's professional elite. But he had a passion for politics and a commitment to public service. Just as important, he enjoyed the life of a public figure and relished being near the center of power. And there was still plenty of time to turn his career around. He was only in his early forties and had an impressive record of service and accomplishment. And he was still ambitious. He just needed a place to start.

With the Democratic victory in 1912 it seemed almost a certainty that there would be a place for Folk in the new Wilson administration. Immediately after the election the *St. Louis Post-Dispatch* reported that "Democratic leaders" felt confident that Folk would be offered a place in President Wilson's cabinet. When Wilson asked his newly appointed Secretary of State William Jennings Bryan for his advice on filling positions in December, Bryan informed Wilson that he had received "a number [of letters] . . . recommending Folk for Atty Gen." But Wilson found Folk unacceptable to the dominant Democratic faction in Missouri and too radical for attorney general. "The people," he explained "must have confidence in the Department of Justice—they must have confidence in the Attorney General. He can not be a person of the crusader type in public life." Wilson, instead, chose James C. McReynolds.

159

McReynolds had previously served as assistant attorney general during the Roosevelt administration. His return to Washington in 1910 to assist the Justice Department in its prosecution of the American Tobacco Company had gained him an unwarranted reputation as an opponent of monopoly. In contrast to Folk, McReynolds was "at heart an extreme conservative with a narrow view of the proper role that government should play in economic affairs."[1]

When six months had passed and Wilson still had not found a place for Folk, Bryan again took up his friend's cause. This time he requested that Wilson consider Folk for appointment as Minister to China. In an interesting summation of Folk's qualifications for the position, Bryan stated: "He [Folk] has had official prominence, he has a national reputation, he is progressive and was friendly to you before the convention. He would be a valuable adviser to the Chinese leaders in matters relating to the fundamental principles of popular government, and he is identified with the religious life of the nation, and would, I am sure, be acceptable to the missionaries." Despite Bryan's pleadings, Wilson decided instead on Paul S. Reinsch, a professor at the University of Wisconsin and an authority on the Far East. Finally, and again on Bryan's recommendation, Wilson appointed Folk to the position of solicitor general (chief legal adviser) in Bryan's own State Department at a salary of $4,500 a year.[2]

Folk quickly became an avid admirer of Woodrow Wilson and a consistent supporter of his domestic policies. On a personal level, the new president's style, focus, and message mirrored Folk's. Many people found Wilson "cold and aloof." "[His] austere facade prevented him from getting the public affection he craved and made it hard for him to influence politicians and the press." He also had a reputation for valuing principle over policy or expediency. And when he presented his case to

1. Letter from William Jennings Bryan to Woodrow Wilson dated December 30, 1912, in Woodrow Wilson Papers, Library of Congress, Manuscript Division, Washington, D.C.; Arthur S. Link, *Wilson: The New Freedom,* 116–17.

2. Letter from William Jennings Bryan to Woodrow Wilson dated June 2, 1913, in Wilson Papers. The offer of the State Department position was made in July 1912. Folk's appointment became official in September. *St. Louis Post-Dispatch,* November 6, 1912; Paolo E. Coletta, *William Jennings Bryan,* vol. 2, *Progressive Politician and Moral Statesman, 1909–1915,* 111.

the people, he did so "in powerful speeches that set the issue as a choice between good and evil."[3]

Folk found the major pieces of Wilson's New Freedom—tariff, banking, and antitrust reform—to his liking. He also showed special interest in Wilsonian reforms that attempted to expand the scope of popular democracy. When the President addressed Congress on December 2, 1913, and requested passage of legislation creating a presidential preference primary, Folk was quick to offer his support. At the First National Conference on Popular Government held in Washington, D.C., on December 6, Folk appeared as one of the featured speakers and used the occasion to promote the idea. A month later Folk found himself the administration's point-man leading the agitation for a plan that would allow voters to select their own presidential nominees without the intervention of nominating conventions. At a luncheon for prominent Democrats given by the Common Counsel Club in Washington, D.C., on January 6, Solicitor General Folk proposed a plan that would have protected the rights of the states to regulate and conduct their own elections by creating state primaries for determining the party's presidential nominee. Party conventions would be maintained only for the purpose of confirming the results of the primaries and formulating party platforms. The Wilson administration, however, was unable to make any immediate progress with the idea.[4]

Folk, soon to be a member of the Committee on Legislative Forms of the National Popular Government League, also favored "with slight changes" the so-called gateway amendment introduced in Congress by Senator Robert La Follette of Wisconsin as a joint resolution in August 1912. The proposal would have allowed voters, in a popular referendum, to decide the fate of any proposed Constitutional amendment whenever a majority of the members of both houses of Congress or whenever ten states, either by popular vote or action by the state legislature, should propose such an amendment. The La Follette resolution died in the Judiciary Committee. La Follette resubmitted his proposal in 1913, while Senator Robert Owen of Oklahoma, Senator Albert Cummins of

3. Clements, *Woodrow Wilson*, 103–4.

4. *Congressional Record*, 63d Cong., 2d sess., 44; *New York Times*, December 7, 1913, January 7, 1914; *St. Louis Republic*, February 16, 1914.

Iowa, and Representative Walter Chandler of New York all submitted
modified gateway amendments of their own. None of the proposals,
however, ever made it out of committee. In taking a public position in
support of proposals aimed at expanding popular democracy, however,
Folk established a reputation as an advocate of such reforms and carved
out a niche for himself as a useful servant of the administration.[5]

In March 1914 Folk left the State Department to accept a more lucra-
tive position ($10,000 year) as chief counsel of the Interstate Commerce
Commission (I.C.C.). Shortly after assuming his new position, Folk
instituted hearings in the third I.C.C. investigation of the New York,
New Haven & Hartford Railroad. The financial manipulations of the
New Haven Railroad had been a national scandal ever since attorney
Louis D. Brandeis agreed to act as legal counsel for stockholders of the
Boston & Maine Railroad in a suit against the New Haven in 1905.
Both the stockholders and Brandeis feared that aggressive purchases of
stock in the Boston & Maine by the New Haven was the beginning
of a hostile takeover aimed at monopolizing the railroad traffic in the
New England region. With dogged persistence and meticulous analysis
of information gained from the I.C.C and the Massachusetts Railroad
Commission, Brandeis eventually pieced together evidence strongly
suggesting flagrant corporate mismanagement. Despite its reputation
as a well-managed and financially sound company, the New Haven
actually juggled statistics to conceal hugh financial debits and looked to
acquire assets like the Boston & Maine to cover its own losses. Brandeis's
legal and investigative efforts triggered I.C.C. investigations of the New
Haven Railroad in 1912 and again in 1913. The final negative report
of the commission, issued on July 9, 1913, caused New Haven stock to
plummet and forced the resignation of company president Charles S.
Mellon.

On February 6, 1914, Senator George W. Norris of Nebraska, evidently at the urging of Brandeis, introduced a resolution requesting

5. *Congressional Record,* 62d Cong., 2d sess., 10177; 63d Cong., 1st sess., 195,
239, 370, 1985; *New York Times,* December 7, 1913; "A Proposed Easier Method of
Amending the Federal Constitution"; "Amending the National Constitution"; "Other
Gateway Proposals." A list of officers in the National Popular Government League can
be found in David Yancey Thomas Papers, Special Collections Division, University of
Arkansas Library, Fayetteville.

the I.C.C. to reopen its investigation of the New York, New Haven & Hartford Railroad. Norris contended that past investigations had not gone far enough to ascertain what had happened to funds expended by the New Haven or if any corporate officials found guilty of mismanagement should be prosecuted. Norris believed that if public opinion could be aroused by a full disclosure of the facts, then laws remedying such conditions might be enacted by Congress. Norris doubted the Wilson administration's resolve to move forward with antitrust enforcement, as the appointment of McReynolds had seemed to indicate, and hoped to use his resolution to force the administration to commit itself to a stronger policy. The Senate approved Norris's resolution in March, just as Folk assumed his new duties as chief legal counsel.[6]

Public hearings in the third I.C.C. investigation of the New Haven Railroad finally got under way on April 9, 1914, and the task before Folk must have seemed overwhelming. As chief examiner he had to digest the innumerable details and untangle the complex web of financial transactions connected to a case that had nearly a ten-year legal history. Despite the realization that he had to exercise caution in taking testimony of witnesses where immunity from future criminal prosecution might result, Folk made it known that he intended to hear testimony from Charles Mellon and other high-ranking officials of the beleaguered railroad whenever he deemed it necessary to get at the truth. He insisted, as he had during the St. Louis boodle investigations, that more good would be done by public exposure of wrongdoing and an awakened public conscience than by pressing for a few jail sentences and/or fines without the full story being told. The hearings, which lasted until June 7, generated over twelve hundred pages of sworn testimony and nearly as much appended material. And like Herbert Hadley's earlier investigation of the Standard Oil Corporation, Folk's glimpse into the inner workings of the New Haven provided yet another sensational example of corporate malfeasance. The final report of the I.C.C., issued on July 14, 1914, denounced the management of the New Haven Railroad in unqualified terms and labeled the operation of the company as "one of the most

6. Melvin I. Urofsky, *Louis D. Brandeis and the Progressive Tradition*, 40–46; Geiger, *Joseph W. Folk*, 156–57; Richard Lowitt, *George W. Norris: The Persistence of a Progressive, 1913–1933*, 16–17; Coletta, *Bryan*, 2:111.

glaring instances of maladministration revealed in all the history of American railroading." The report charged the directors with "reckless and profligate financiering" and criminal negligence, and recommended vigorous prosecution of a number of corporate officials.[7]

One week after the Folk report, President Wilson ordered Attorney General McReynolds to begin a civil suit seeking the dissolution of the New Haven's "unlawful monopoly of transportation facilities in New England," and to present the criminal aspects of the case before a grand jury. As Norris suspected, the administration never really intended to press a contest that might actually bankrupt the New Haven if they could achieve their objectives (break the monopoly, save the company, and maintain competition) in a peaceful settlement of the suit. As a result, both parties entered into negotiations that led McReynolds to withdraw the dissolution suit and accept a consent decree on October 17, 1914. The Justice Department proceeded with its plans to prosecute eleven of the directors of the New Haven for criminal violations under the Sherman Act, but the three-month trial yielded no convictions.[8]

Folk appeared to find his work at the I.C.C., where he remained as chief counsel for nearly four years, to be both demanding and rewarding. In addition to the New Haven investigation, which thrust him again, albeit briefly, into the public spotlight, Folk also conducted detailed inquiries into the financial relations, rates, and practices of the Chicago, Rock Island & Pacific Railroad (1914–1915), the Louisville & Nashville Railroad (1916), the Marquette Railroad (1917), and the Cincinnati, Hamilton & Dayton Railroad (1917). The historian Louis Geiger credits Folk's investigations with assisting in the inclusion of provisions

7. U.S. Interstate Commerce Commission, *Decisions of the Interstate Commerce Commission, June 1914 to October 1914,* No. 6569: "In Re: Financial Transactions of the New York, New Haven & Hartford Railroad Company," 31:32–70; Entry from the Diary of Colonel House dated May 11, 1914, (see fn. 4) in Wilson Papers; Melvin I. Urofsky and David W. Levy, eds., *Letters of Louis D. Brandeis,* 3:284 fn. 1; Geiger, *Joseph W. Folk,* 157–61. For mention of Folk's participation in the New Haven investigation, see *New York Times,* April 11, 16–18, May 1–3, 7–9, 12–18, 20–29, June 4, 6–7, 9, 1914. There is a cartoon in the *Times* on May 24, 1914, that shows Folk playing the fiddle and Charles S. Mellon dancing to his tune.

8. Link, *Wilson,* 422–23; Geiger, *Joseph W. Folk,* 160. For a readable account of the Brandeis–New Haven merger fight, see Henry Lee Staples and Alpheus Thomas Mason, *The Fall of a Railroad Empire.*

in the Esch-Cummings Transportation Act of 1920 that broadened federal regulation of common carriers. The act specifically granted the I.C.C. the authority to regulate the issuance of railroad securities and the power to prohibit interlocking railroad directorates, recommendations Folk had made years before.[9]

The Folks seemed to enjoy official life in Washington. Time spent and personal associations made at the State Department and the I.C.C., along with his continued demand as a public speaker and his prominent presence at events like the Common Counsel Club luncheon and the traditional Jefferson Day banquet, demonstrate that Folk had assumed an active role near the center of Democratic politics. Along with close friends that included Federal Trade Commissioner Joseph Davies, the journalist Mark Sullivan, President Wilson's private secretary Joseph Tumulty, and a few others, Folk enjoyed "membership" in a small group that often lunched together at what they called "The Cockroach Table" and, presumably, talked politics. In a rare interview, Gertrude Folk admitted to having succumbed to the lure of Washington. From their home in Le Roy Place, one of the exclusive residential streets in Washington Heights, she told of driving her husband to work every morning—enjoying a spin around the Washington Monument or over the Potomac River before dropping him off at his office on F Street. The Folks also dined out regularly, usually with friends, and began to enjoy regular attendance at the theater. Life seemed good.[10]

In January 1918 Folk abruptly resigned his position at the I.C.C. to accept a three-year appointment as general counsel for the St. Louis Chamber of Commerce at a salary of $12,000 a year. On the surface it seemed surprising that Folk would be willing to exchange his current employment, with its accompanying social and political attachments, for the slightly better paying position as attorney for an organization

9. Geiger, *Joseph W. Folk,* 160–61.

10. Ibid., 155, 161; letter from L. L. Leonard to David R. Francis dated January 23, 1918, in David R. Francis Papers, Missouri Historical Society, St. Louis; "Wife of Former Governor of Missouri Homesick for Friends in St. Louis," article dated October 24, 1915, in Mrs. Joseph W. Folk vertical file; "Address in part of Joseph W. Folk, Jefferson Day Banquet, Washington, D.C.," dated April 13, 1914, in Folk Papers.

that had never shown him solid political support. But as pleasant as Washington appeared to be, it had not satisfied his political yearnings. In Washington, he was connected to the world of politics but not directly involved in it as a politician. It was time to scratch that political itch.

Folk had actually been struggling with this dilemma for quite some time before deciding to make a move (he had confided to associates that he did not intend to stay long at the I.C.C.). And it was apparent that the desire to seek elective office again was never far from his mind. In the spring and summer of 1915 newspapers reported rumors of a possible Folk boom for governor of Missouri in 1916. That fall, at the urging of Ewing Y. Mitchell, a Springfield, Missouri, attorney active in the state Democratic party and a member of Folk's 1912 presidential campaign team, Folk allowed Mitchell to contact prominent Missouri Democrats for their views regarding his possible candidacy. Folk apparently supplied Mitchell with a list of names and requested him to: "Give them your views and if they are agreeable the movement may begin."[11]

Before deciding to run, however, Folk sought the advice of the administration. He apparently told Colonel Edward M. House, President Wilson's closest adviser, he wanted to run for governor but would be willing to shift his sights to the senatorship if the administration thought that would be better. Folk thought he could win the governorship if Senator William J. Stone did not intervene, or that he could defeat Senator James A. Reed if Wilson would come out strongly for him. House conveyed Folk's thoughts to Wilson and added: "He [Folk] believes he could serve the party better by running for Governor because it will probably bring about party harmony. If he runs for Senator [in 1916] he fears it will cause a bitter factional fight that might lose Missouri." In response, Wilson confessed that he was "at a loss just what to advise." House, apparently on his own, finally advised Folk not to challenge Reed as the resulting political fight would be disruptive in a presidential election year. While the administration considered, Folk conferred with former Governor David R. Francis, who offered more discouraging advice. Francis rejected Folk's contention that he would be

11. Letter from Joseph W. Folk to Ewing Y. Mitchell dated October 20, 1915, in Ewing Young Mitchell Papers, Western Historical Manuscript Collection, Columbia, Mo.

the strongest gubernatorial nominee that Missouri's Democrats could select and persuaded him not to run. In the end, with both political avenues closed, Folk had decided to remain at the I.C.C. and look ahead to 1920.[12]

By January 1918 both timing and circumstance dictated that if Folk intended to make another run for elective office, the time had come. Helping Folk make his decision was Jackson Johnson, a long-time acquaintance and one of the Washington Avenue businessmen who had supported Folk for governor in 1904. Johnson, chairman of the International Shoe Company, had recently been elected president of the St. Louis Chamber of Commerce. At a dinner honoring his election on January 9, Johnson pledged that he would make a determined and concentrated effort to have the so-called arbitrary on freight (primarily coal) entering St. Louis from the east abolished. Levied by the Terminal Railroad Association, the arbitrary was the rate (twenty cents a ton on coal) added to regular transportation charges on all shipments traveling over the bridges connecting St. Louis with East St. Louis. Businessmen like Johnson regarded the cost differential on coal as a significant factor in discouraging manufacturing enterprises from locating in St. Louis. To facilitate his plan, Johnson convinced the Chamber of Commerce's bipartisan board of directors to retain Folk as general counsel to lead the fight against the bridge arbitrary. The resulting agreement accommo-dated the self-interest of each party. The Chamber of Commerce could take advantage of Folk's newly acquired expertise on transportation questions and any possible political connections he may have gained while at the I.C.C. In turn, Folk could use his new position to reestablish his political contacts in Missouri with an eye on the next senatorial election in 1920. One final factor in convincing Folk to accept the St. Louis offer was President Wilson's recommendation to Congress in early January that the federal government be allowed to assume

12. Letters from Edward M. House to Woodrow Wilson dated November 8, 11, 1915, and from Woodrow Wilson to Edward M. House dated November 10, 12, 1915, in Wilson Papers; entry from the Diary of Colonel House dated November 5, 1915, in Wilson Papers; *St. Louis Post-Dispatch,* January 29, 1918; letter from David R. Francis to William J. Stone dated April 12, 1916, in Francis Papers; news clippings dated March 31, August 5, 1915, and letter from Joseph W. Folk to Ewing Y. Mitchell dated February 12, 1916, in Mitchell Papers.

operation of the railroads for the duration of the war. Wilson's action had, in effect, rendered Folk's position at the I.C.C. without purpose.[13]

Folk arrived in St. Louis to assume his new duties on February 11, confident that he could get a previous I.C.C. ruling (1915) that did not find existing arbitrary charges "unreasonable" overturned. In a speech before the St. Louis Chamber of Commerce two days later, Folk argued that recent I.C.C. rulings and changes in transportation conditions in St. Louis since 1915 had made a reversal possible. After a month spent in preparation, Folk filed a formal petition to end the arbitrary with the I.C.C. on March 19. His petition reviewed the history of the terminal situation in St. Louis, assessed the damage done to the business of the city by the arbitrary, and contended that St. Louis and East St. Louis formed a single industrial-manufacturing district and should be subject to the same rates. He argued that the Terminal Railroad Association was merely the agent of the railroads owning it and had no right to demand a special charge for service separate from the rate-hauling charge levied by the railroad.[14]

Attorneys for the Terminal Railroad Association filed their answer to Folk's petition with the I.C.C. on April 12. Their response denied Folk's charge that because the association was owned by the various railroads it was merely an extension of the rails of those lines. Instead, they argued that the Terminal Railroad Association was specifically formed to furnish necessary terminal facilities to distinct commercial districts naturally separated by the Mississippi River. As such, it was entitled to a rate differential for all terminal services—receiving freight from a connecting carrier on the east side of the river, handling it over the lines and through the yards on the east side, conveying it over the bridges across the river, and then handling it over the lines to the yards on the west side. With the complaint and answer to the complaint filed, all that remained was for a date to be set for the hearing of testimony and the introduction of evidence, and, eventually, the final presentation of briefs and arguments before the I.C.C. in Washington. But news of the sudden death of Senator William J. Stone on April 14 forced Folk to

13. *St. Louis Post-Dispatch,* January 4, 9, 29, February 13, June 27, 1918; letter from L. L. Leonard to David R. Francis dated January 23, 1918, in Francis Papers.
14. *St. Louis Post-Dispatch,* February 11, 13, March 11, 19, 1918.

consider terminating his arrangement with the Chamber of Commerce for another chance at electoral politics.[15]

Senator Stone's death triggered a lively discussion in the press as to who might succeed him. The decision was Democratic Governor Frederick D. Gardner's to make. And although the governor was only authorized to appoint a replacement until a regular election could be held in November, it was understood that the appointee would be a candidate in the formal election to complete the unexpired term of Senator Stone. After offering the office first to David R. Francis, who turned it down to remain as Ambassador to Russia, then to Congressman Champ Clark, who chose not to step down as the Speaker of the House of Representatives, and then to Judge Waller W. Graves, who decided to stay as chief justice of the Missouri Supreme Court, Gardner offered the seat to Xenophon P. Wilfley, one of his closest political advisers and friends. A native of Missouri, Wilfley had attended Central College, the Southern Methodist institution in Fayette, Missouri, earned his law degree from Washington University in St. Louis, and eventually established a successful law practice there. His only political office was that of chairman of the St. Louis Board of Election Commissioners, to which he had been appointed by Governor Gardner early in 1917. In announcing Wilfley's appointment on April 29, the governor noted that he had selected a "100 percent American" who would "whole-heartedly uphold the [Wilson] administration in the prosecution of the war."[16]

Left off Governor Gardner's short list of possible replacements for Senator Stone, Folk waited a month and then announced that he was resigning his position as general counsel for the Chamber of Commerce and that he would be a candidate for the Democratic nomination for U.S. Senator to be decided in the party primary on August 6. Although Gardner did not state his reasons for overlooking Folk, the *St. Louis Post-Dispatch* found the same old political forces at work: "The 'old guard' Democrats do not like Folk any better now than they did 10 years ago. . . ."[17]

15. Ibid., March 19, April 12, 15, October 25, 1918.

16. Ibid., April 15, 23, 25–27, 29–30, 1918; Shoemaker, ed., *Missouri and Missourians,* 294.

17. *St. Louis Post-Dispatch,* April 30, 1918.

In tossing his hat into the ring, Folk declared that his platform would be that of supporting the Wilson administration in winning the war and working toward a solution of transportation problems. As in his support of Wilson's domestic policies, Folk unhesitatingly backed the president in his conduct of foreign policy. Several of Folk's speeches during 1916 and 1917 exhibit a strong commitment to Wilsonianism—a belief in American exceptionalism, in its mission to uplift mankind, and in its duty to set the world right—and a passionate commitment to internationalism. They also offer numerous suggestions to that end (an international police force, an international parliament, an international court of arbitration, and world disarmament). When Wilson spoke, as he often did, about democracy, self-determination, and "a universal dominion of right," he aroused Folk's sensibilities by speaking in terms that suggested the ultimate triumph of righteousness. In elaborating on the value of his recent experience with transportation questions, Folk specifically called attention to railroad rate adjustments and improved waterways as items of special interest to both the city of St. Louis and the state of Missouri. He also added that having had the unusual opportunity to study transportation problems while chief counsel for the Interstate Commerce Commission, he could render particular service in the Senate in that area. Folk announced that he would continue as "special counsel" in the bridge arbitrary fight, and pledged to do no campaigning until after the hearings before an examiner from the I.C.C. had been completed in mid-June. Pleased at both Folk's announced candidacy and his proposed platform, William Marion Reedy, for one, editorially touted Folk's qualifications for the office and described him as "a Democrat of the Bryan school, graduated into the Wilsonian college."[18]

18. Ibid., May 20, 24, 1918; William Marion Reedy, "Our Senatorial Field." For samples of Folk's speeches during this period, see: "Address in Part of Former Governor Joseph W. Folk," University Club Banquet, Washington, D.C., February 14, 1916; "Mission of America," Cleveland Chamber of Commerce, January 30, 1917; "Address in Part of Former Governor Joseph W. Folk," at Boston, Massachusetts, February 10, 1917; "Address of Joseph W. Folk before the Cotton States Merchants Association Convention," Memphis, Tennessee, August 21, 1917, in Folk Papers. Folk filed his brief and argument in the bridge arbitrary case with the I.C.C. on October 25, 1918. The I.C.C. did not hand down its final decision, which went in favor of the Terminal Railroad Association, until May 1919. *St. Louis Post-Dispatch*, October 25, 1918; Geiger, *Joseph W. Folk*, 165.

Despite platform promises and patriotic pledges, the 1918 primary campaign, like each of Folk's previous intraparty contests, quickly degenerated into a contest where spurious allegations and bitter personal attacks threatened to tear the party apart. As in the past, nearly all the professional politicians—the county officers, rural courthouse rings, and everyday political workers—were against Folk. So, too, were the liquor dealers, who had never forgiven Folk for imposing the 'lid' as governor. This animosity became evident even before the campaign officially got under way when Ignatius J. Bauer, secretary of the Association of Retail Liquor Dealers of Missouri, wrote a letter to R. Perry Spencer, a close personal friend and supporter of Wilfley, pledging his association's opposition to Folk's candidacy. In the letter Bauer stated that the four thousand members of the Liquor Dealers Association would work "undercover" to defeat Folk. The letter fell into the hands of Folk's supporters who quickly gave it to the press for publication. Folk and his supporters apparently assumed that voters would infer from the letter that Wilfley had the backing of the evil liquor interests.[19]

In hindsight, the Folk camp would have been better served if they had ignored the "Bauer letter." It did give Folk the opportunity to pose as a "martyr of saloon vengeance," but it also injected the liquor question into the campaign. More importantly, it once again associated Folk's name with prohibition, an issue supported in rural areas where Folk had proven strength but opposed in urban areas where Folk had demonstrated weakness. By 1917, eighty-four percent of Missouri's counties were either totally or partially dry. But all the state's major urban centers—St. Louis, Kansas City, St. Joseph, Springfield, and Joplin—remained wet. The state had already conducted two unsuccessful statewide referendums on the prohibition question, with a third scheduled for the ballot in 1918. In each case hugh majorities in St. Louis proved able to defeat the closer dry majorities in the rural districts. National prohibition was coming, but many Missourians had not yet resigned themselves to that fact.[20]

The Folk-Bauer controversy took one final turn in late June when Bauer was indicted and charged with distributing anonymous literature

19. *St. Louis Post-Dispatch,* June 5, August 4, 1918.
20. Ibid., June 6, 1918; Richard S. Kirkendall, *A History of Missouri, Volume V: 1919 to 1953,* 25.

against a candidate for office. Specifically, Bauer had printed and distributed 5,000–10,000 copies of an anti-Folk circular which he had, in violation of the law, neglected to sign. The circular, the type of public exposure Folk could have done without, asked the public five questions:

> Who enforced the antiquated blue laws and cut out entertainments, picnics and pleasures of the middle and working classes on Sundays in Missouri?
> [Answer] Joseph W. Folk

> Who stopped conventions, excursions and commercial travelers from coming to large cities on Sundays in Missouri?
> [Answer] Joseph W. Folk

> Who encouraged and aided prohibition agitation in Missouri?
> [Answer] Joseph W. Folk

> Who put Missouri on the bum?
> [Answer] Joseph W. Folk

> Who wants to vote for Folk?
> [Answer] Nobody in Missouri

Unperturbed by the reaction, Bauer openly admitted responsibility for the circulars, claimed ignorance of the law, and defiantly stated: "To hell with Folk, we don't want him. . . . We would have signed them if we had known the law required it." In the end, the Bauer letter never seemed to capture the attention of out-state Missourians that Folk's managers had hoped, while the Bauer circular probably sank Folk even lower in the esteem of many St. Louisans.[21]

Folk and Wilfley officially opened their campaigns for the Democratic nomination for United States Senator on June 15. Folk stuck with his previously announced campaign themes—vigorous support for the war effort and transportation reform. He cast his address in patriotic terms, trumpeting his loyalty to the Wilson administration and quoting freely from President Wilson's war speeches. He reminded his listeners that they were "fighting to give the people of all the world self-government"

---

21. A copy of the circular can be found in the Mitchell Papers. *St. Louis Post-Dispatch,* June 24, 27, August 4, 1918.

and "waging a war to democratize the world"; he promised that if nominated and elected his policy in the Senate would be "100 percent Americanism." He also told his St. Joseph audience that he would work for the promotion of water transportation and the readjustment of railroad rates under federal supervision and control.

Wilfley, in a speech delivered to sympathizers on the courthouse lawn in Mexico, Missouri, declared that he had only one issue and cause to champion and that was supporting President Wilson in winning the war. He dismissed Folk's attempt to make transportation reform an issue and to win votes based on his expertise in that area, labeling it a wartime distraction, and, in a burst of patriotic exuberance stated: "He who now seeks to raise up old issues or to form new issues on old subjects shows that he is not alive to this emergency. The Hun is at our gates. . . ." As their opening remarks suggested, the campaign promised to be a Germanophobic debate on patriotism.[22]

First advantage in the patriotic war of words went to the Folk camp. On June 21, the *St. Louis Republic* published the text of a formal petition (referred to in the press as the "peace telegram") that had been mailed to President Wilson on March 15, 1917. The petition, which requested Wilson to keep America out of the war, included the statement "as far as we can see, the aggression of Germany and England on the law of nations differ only in method." The petition had been signed by Wilfley and thirty others, including German-Americans Hans Haeckel, editor of the *Westliche Post,* F. P. Kenkel, editor of *Die America,* and August Hoffman, treasurer of the National German-American Alliance. The peace telegram, sent after the United States had severed diplomatic relations with Germany and only twenty-one days before the official declaration of war, quickly became a campaign document used by Folk and his tacticians to cast suspicion on Wilfley's loyalty. Forced on the defensive, Wilfley conceded that he had signed the petition without carefully examining its contents and tried to atone for his mistake by issuing a public Americanism pledge. But Folk and the press showed him no mercy. Folk publicly referred to the peace telegram as being written and paid for by "friends of the brutal Huns," while the *Republic*

22. *St. Louis Post-Dispatch,* June 16, 1918. See also Folk campaign letter (n.d.) evidently prepared for mass mailing during the 1918 primary campaign in Folk Papers.

scolded Wilfley for not measuring up to a standard of "100 percent Americanism." The peace telegram undoubtedly caused Wilfley to lose some supporters, but the use made of it by Folk (who read it to his audiences for more than a week) showed signs of creating a negative reaction. After several weeks, the Folk camp toned down their rhetoric. They stated that they had never questioned Wilfley's loyalty, and that the only question raised by the telegram was the judgment of the man who would sign it.[23]

With only a month remaining in the primary race and his campaign in trouble, Wilfley tried to turn the table on Folk. Referring to a speech Folk had made in Memphis, Tennessee, on August 21, 1917, Wilfley quoted Folk as stating: "As events followed events, and the frightfulness of the German military police became more and more evident, those of us who sympathized with the German cause were little by little alienated." Wilfley implied that the phrase "those of us" included the speaker, and he asked Folk to explain exactly when he ceased to sympathize with Germany. Folk quickly issued a formal statement accusing his opponent of having deliberately misquoted his speech by inserting the word "of" in place of the word "among" and, thereby, distorting its meaning. Folk asserted that the speech was "a denunciation of Germany and a plea for 100 percent Americanism. It was a defense of the President and of the administration for going into the war. . . ." Folk also noted that the address had been read into the *Congressional Record* and made a public document, and that thousands of copies of it had been distributed by the Committee of Public Information in Washington to win support for the war effort.[24]

As the primary campaign entered its final week, Wilfley attempted to use Folk's Memphis address to trap him a second time. This time Wilfley accused Folk of trying to lighten his publicity expenses by having copies of his Memphis speech mailed to voters in Missouri under the frank of Congressman Herbert Fisher of Tennessee, who had submitted the original motion to have Folk's speech read into the *Congressional*

23. *St. Louis Republic,* June 21, 1918; *St. Louis Post-Dispatch,* June 22, 25, July 3, 5, 9, 22, 1918.
24. *St. Louis Post-Dispatch,* July 8–9, 1918; *Congressional Record,* 65th Cong., 1st sess., 7898–7900.

Record on October 6, 1918. Wilfley hoped to show that Folk's use of the franking privileges of a congressman not from his home state was not only improper, but an act too small for a man who aspired to be a United States Senator. Ewing Mitchell, Folk's campaign manager, tried to deflect the charges by stating that the Committee on Public Information had already distributed thousands of copies of the speech and that an extra twenty thousand copies had been mailed in Missouri only to correct Wilfley's initial misrepresentation of the public record.[25]

Missouri Democrats must have been relieved when the incredibly negative primary campaign finally came to an end. The two Democratic candidates gave their final speeches during a joint appearance at the annual Old Settlers' Picnic in New Florence on August 3. Most certainly under a party mandate to subdue their angry charges and provide voters with at least the appearance of party harmony and good sportsmanship, Folk and Wilfley could not resist taking one last shot at each other. Wilfley said he would "leave the muddy path of peanut politics" to his opponent, while Folk responded that he, at least, would not have to "apologize for any foolish telegram I signed." It was a fittingly petty end to an unusually vicious campaign. When the votes were tallied, Folk won by a majority of nearly 28,000 (57 percent). Obviously elated with the result, Folk sent a victory telegram to Woodrow Wilson in which he proclaimed: "I have been nominated for Senator. . . . Permit me to assure you again that I shall stand by you and in the Senate your policies will be my policies." The editors of the *Post-Dispatch* likened Folk's pledge of support as tantamount to a surrender of individual thought. "It will," said the editors, "tend to draw party lines by emphasizing the divergence between the Folk attitude of unqualified fidelity to administration policies and the Republican attitude of constructive opposition and criticism." Willing to run that risk, Folk "hitched his candidacy to the President's chariot."[26]

A closer examination of the primary, however, might have given Folk a great deal to worry about. He had won, but he had defeated

25. *St. Louis Post-Dispatch,* July 30, August 1, 1918.
26. Ibid., August 4, 11, 1918; letter from Joseph Wingate Folk to Woodrow Wilson dated August 7, 1918, in Wilson Papers; Missouri *Official Manual, 1919–1920,* 389–90.

a virtual unknown who was forced to do most of his campaigning from Washington. He had allowed prohibition back into the campaign and for his name to be reassociated with it. He had adopted campaign tactics that cast doubts on his character, allowed himself to be compromised by charges that questioned his integrity, and revived perceptions of himself as being overly ambitious. He had collected an impressive popular majority statewide, but continued to be unpopular in the state's two largest cities. In Kansas City (Jackson County), where the Democratic Pendergast machine supported Wilfley, Folk lost by over 3,600 votes, while in St. Louis, where the local party organization also backed his opponent, Folk lost by over 4,900. He had wedded himself to the Wilson administration and assumed that President Wilson's perceived popularity and popular support for the war would carry him to victory against any Republican opponent. He had also demonstrated a genuine hardheadedness. When the Democratic State Executive Committee urged both candidates to tone down their attacks on each other out of fear that there would be such bitter feelings after the primary that the nominee could not be elected in the general election, Folk seemed unconcerned. It was a mistake. In assessing Folk's future prospects, one observer commented: "Every thing seems lovely on the surface but many [Democrats] are polishing a brick to throw at Folk." Surprisingly, Folk seemed oblivious to the problems before him.[27]

Folk's Republican opponent in the general election was Seldon P. Spencer. A graduate of Yale University and the Washington University Law School, Spencer gained admission to the Missouri Bar in 1896 and opened a law office in St. Louis. Occasionally interrupting his law practice to assume other duties, Spencer had served briefly in the thirty-eighth General Assembly as a state representative from St. Louis's 5th District during the mid-1890s, as judge in the St. Louis Circuit Court (1897–1903), as vice-chairman of the St. Louis Board of Freeholders (1914), and as chairman of the St. Louis Draft Appeals Board (1918). Spencer had easily defeated Jay Torrey, an Ozark apple grower and Spanish-American War hero, in the Republican primary, a campaign

27. For comment, see letter from Hiram Phillips to David R. Francis dated September 2, 1918, in Francis Papers; Geiger, *Joseph W. Folk*, 166; and *St. Louis Post-Dispatch*, July 12, 1918.

in which he had refused to discuss any issue other than support for the war effort.[28]

The platforms of the two parties offered an indication as to how the election would be fought, and, in both cases, "win the war" served as the dominant theme. The Republicans, in their platform convention held at the Planters Hotel in St. Louis on August 27, went on record as favoring "the immediate and vigorous prosecution of the war" and stated that "in every step of legislation pertaining to the war, the Republican party has . . . given without reservation its full cooperation." The Democrats, meeting in their platform convention at the capitol in Jefferson City on the same day, pledged "to support and sustain to the utmost the administration of Woodrow Wilson," referred to the President as "the leader of a new world democracy," and stated that winning the war "speedily and worthily" was the party's highest priority. The two parties also took very similar approaches on two other issues of national importance—women's suffrage and prohibition. Both parties supported the national amendment proposing the extension of the franchise to women, but neither party would take a firm position on the national amendment proposing prohibition other than to say they favored "prompt action" "in accordance with the wishes of their constituents." With similar positions on foreign policy, the extension of popular democracy, and social control, the 1918 campaign in Missouri promised to be one fought outside the bounds of ideology.[29]

Spencer officially opened his campaign on September 16 with an address at Sedalia. Before a surprisingly small and less than festive crowd of about four hundred people, he announced that the keynote of his campaign would be patriotism. As a result, he would ignore politics in all his speeches and would say nothing about himself or his record. What he did not tell the crowd, but reporters quickly discovered, was that he would always share the platform with someone else connected to the Republican state campaign who would talk politics, dwell on Spencer's record since the beginning of the war, and attack his opponent. At

28. Shoemaker, ed., *Missouri and Missourians*, 294–95; Barry Robert Wood, " 'Holy Joe' Folk's Last Crusade: The 1918 Election in Missouri," 291–92.

29. Missouri *Official Manual, 1919–1920*, 606–9, 630–31; *St. Louis Post-Dispatch*, August 28, 1918.

Sedalia, and at Clinton the following night before a crowd of fewer than two hundred, a second speaker extolled Spencer's war record as chairman of the draft board (suspending his lucrative law practice to do so), organizer of the Fifth Missouri Regiment and captain and adjutant of the home guards of St. Louis, leader of the Y.M.C.A., and spokesman for the Red Cross and both Liberty Bond and Thrift Stamp drives. He also praised him for having two sons fighting in the army (one son had been decorated for heroism in France). Folk's record, on the other hand, paled in comparison. Prior to announcing his candidacy for the senatorship, Folk had done nothing patriotic for the Red Cross or for the sale of Liberty Bonds or war stamps. The message was clear. As a public official, Folk had been selfishly preoccupied with "personal aggrandizement."[30]

Folk opened his campaign one week later in the open-air theater of the State Normal School at Kirksville. Before a gathering of more than one thousand people, Folk ignored Spencer and took issue instead with the Republican platform. Folk noted that the Republicans had endorsed the war but not President Wilson. He suggested there was an inconsistency in the Republican platform position and the common Republican claim that a Republican majority in Congress would help the president win the war. To Folk, this was merely partisanship in the guise of patriotism. "The Republican politicians," said Folk, "are making a trojan horse campaign in Missouri to get into power, but once in, can anyone doubt that there [sic] partisanship will come out full-armed to block and hamper the President's war aims and plans, with a view of political advantage in the coming presidential campaign?"[31]

Folk had assumed a sound tactical position, but could he sell his argument? For that matter, was anybody even paying attention? Crowds were smaller and audiences seemed lethargic and indifferent to politics. At Kirksville, the old-time rebel yell that had enlivened Democratic political gatherings for fifty years was eerily missing. The band had even failed to strike up "Dixie." For the most part, the audience remained silent, apparently preoccupied with the war. In a strange twist to the start of a political campaign, the two senatorial candidates agreed that it

30. *St. Louis Post-Dispatch,* September 16–17, 1918.
31. Ibid., September 22, 1918.

was advisable to abandon political campaigning for the duration of the Fourth Liberty Loan drive (September 28-October 19). Although both parties continued to mail campaign literature during the "holiday," the candidates refrained from stump speaking until the final three weeks of the campaign.[32]

With noncompetitive party platforms, voter apathy, public preoccupation with the war, and deferred electioneering, the 1918 campaign promised to be the most peculiar and unpredictable ever waged in Missouri. Complicating matters for the Democrats was their divisive intraparty factionalism. In an effort to smooth over hard feelings and unify the party for the election, Governor Gardner gave a harmony dinner in Folk's honor. Invited to the dinner were the Democrat-appointed heads of the various state departments, nearly all of whom had been political opponents of Folk. Many of those in attendance had gone on record saying that they would vote for Folk (and presumably all other Democrats), but would not work for his election. As reported in the press, the purpose of the dinner was to give Governor Gardner the opportunity, in Folk's presence, to order his appointees to cease their opposition to Folk, to line up and work for his election, and to make such contributions to the Democratic state campaign fund as their salaries warranted. The Democratic State Committee had previously requested that appointees contribute 3 percent of their annual salaries, but almost every department head had ignored the request. After the meeting, the general sense was that 1 percent contributions would be forthcoming. Folk, for his part, "came off his high horse" and stated that he needed and wanted the support of those present. But the mere fact that the party deemed the "harmony" dinner necessary only a month before the election indicated that Folk's candidacy was in jeopardy.[33]

Two other events worked to compromise Folk's prospects in 1918—disease and presidential interference. Just as the political campaign was about to resume following the end of the bond drive, the influenza epidemic caused state authorities to prohibit public meetings of any kind. The two senatorial candidates found themselves limited to a few

32. Ibid., September 22, November 3, 1918; Wood, "Last Crusade," 293.
33. *St. Louis Post-Dispatch*, October 2–3, 1918.

outdoor meetings and to public handshaking on the streets of the towns they visited. Then, with only two weeks left in the race, President Wilson issued a statement addressed to the American people. In his message, Wilson urged voters to reaffirm his leadership in the final victory over Germany and the postwar peace settlement by returning Democratic majorities to both houses of Congress. Folk hoped Wilson's message would unite Missouri's Democrats, but no one could say with any certainty whether they would respond to even a presidential call for party loyalty. Sensing a possible advantage, Republicans quickly accused Wilson of violating his pledge to keep politics out of the war and predicted that voters would resent his appeal for partisanship over patriotism.[34]

As the contest entered its final days, both parties campaigned more aggressively. In an attempt to influence voters in St. Louis, Folk tried to link Spencer to the Republican political machine in the city and to big business interests. In the main, however, he continued to praise Wilson and asked that Missourians view the election as a vote of confidence in his leadership. He told a reporter from the *St. Louis Republic* that because the president was "the spokesman of the Allies' cause" and "the foremost citizen in all the world," he was "entitled to the help of Missourians." For their part, the Republicans tried to belittle Folk's war record and accused him of selfishly pursuing better paying jobs and nursing his political ambitions during the wartime emergency. One effective editorial cartoon in the *St. Louis Globe-Democrat* portrayed Folk, with his phony halo, wearing a tuxedo with an empty tin can (his war record) tied to his coattails, dropping one good job to run after a better one. Spencer, in contrast, appeared dressed in the uniform of his home guard unit and busy at work at his service job as chairman of the district draft board. By election day, Spencer, his campaign managers, and a supportive Republican press had demonstrated that by skillfully creating vivid, personalized images of local patriotism they could force Folk on the defensive and effectively blunt his more abstract appeal for Wilsonianism.[35]

34. Ibid., October 25, November 3, 1918; Wood, "Last Crusade," 294.
35. *St. Louis Republic,* November 3–4, 1918; *St. Louis Globe-Democrat,* October 31, November 2, 1918.

St. Louis Globe-Democrat, Nov. 2, 1918, State Historical Society of Missouri, Columbia

The election returns in the Senate race surprised Democrats and Republicans. Spencer easily defeated Folk by a vote of 302,680 to 267,397. In urban but non-German Kansas City and Jackson County, where the two rival Democratic factions (the anti-Folk Pendergast "goats" and the pro-Folk Shannon "rabbits") lined up to support the entire Democratic ticket, Folk won by a margin of 11,952 votes. But in St. Louis and St. Louis County, where Folk failed to win the support of organization Democrats, or to erase the memory of the lid, or to win over anti-Wilson German-Americans, he lost by a whopping 41,552 votes. Spencer also proved more popular among out-state voters by a 197,755 to 192,072 margin. W. J. Fleming, secretary of the Democratic State

Committee, neatly summed up the main reasons for Folk's defeat: angry German-Americans who wanted to "rebuke" President Wilson; "vicious" saloonkeepers who wanted to strike back at "Holy Joe"; and perfidious Democrats who wanted to "knife" Folk. Folk, who wrote to Wilson that he regretted the outcome "principally because I hoped to be there to aid you in your great work," seemed to agree with Fleming's evaluation. He told a reporter from the *St. Louis Star* that "the returns show the work of a combination of Germans who hate Woodrow Wilson, saloon men who hate me, and treacherous Democrats who hate anybody they cannot dominate." Editor William Reedy did not disagree, but added the prohibition issue to the list of probable causes. And a friend of David R. Francis thought he discovered an explanation in Folk's general unpopularity and the popular desire to "check" President Wilson during the period of postwar reconstruction.[36]

Each of the above arguments offered a partial explanation for the failure of Folk's last political crusade. Missouri's German-American voters were angry at the Democrats, but more at Folk than at President Wilson. In the sixteen "German-settled" counties outside St. Louis, Democratic congressional candidates received 39 percent of the vote to 35 percent for Folk. In St. Louis, the disparity was much more pronounced. Democratic candidates for Congress in the eleven German wards received 40 percent of the vote to only 28 percent for Folk. Compounding Folk's problems in St. Louis was prohibition. While voters outside St. Louis approved the statewide prohibition amendment that appeared on the ballot in 1918, St. Louisans rejected it by a 7 to 1 margin and carried it to defeat. The message was clear. St. Louisans would not willingly accept prohibition, nor would they support a candidate like Folk whom they associated with Sunday closing and prohibition.[37]

36. Missouri *Official Manual, 1919–1920,* 411–12; *St. Louis Star,* November 6, 1918; *St. Louis Republic,* November 7, 1918; letter from Joseph W. Folk to Woodrow Wilson dated November 11, 1918, in Wilson Papers; William Marion Reedy, "An Election Post-Mortem"; letter from Hiram Phillips to David R. Francis dated November 26, 1918, in Francis Papers; Charles Powell Blackmore, "Joseph B. Shannon: Political Boss and Twentieth Century 'Jeffersonian,'" 106, 249. See also *Kansas City Post,* November 5, 1918.

37. Missouri *Official Manual, 1919–1920,* 426–27; Wood, "Last Crusade," 300, 306–7.

But the factor that probably proved most deadly to Folk was party factionalism. Missouri's Democrats were not united in 1918. The state's congressional delegation had divided early over Wilson's wartime policies. Senator William J. Stone and four Missouri representatives (Hensley, Decker, Shackleford, and Igoe) had voted against the war, while Senator James A. Reed and Speaker Champ Clark had been vocal critics of the administration. The less-than-enthusiastic response in Missouri to Wilson's pre-election plea for support indicated that the situation had not improved. And with Democrats divided in their support for Wilson, a devout Wilsonian like Folk, who had alienated countless Democrats on his own, stood to be the big loser. Voting returns show that many Democrats "scratched" Folk and either voted for his opponent or did not bother to vote at all. Folk carried only forty-nine of the sixty counties he had won in 1904 and those by generally smaller majorities. He ran 2,259 votes behind Democrat Champ Clark in Clark's district in east-central Missouri, and polled 10,401 fewer votes than the three Democrats running for Congress in St. Louis. In fact, Folk ran ahead of the Democratic candidate for Congress in only one of Missouri's congressional districts. Missouri Democrats decided to give up the Senate seat to a Republican rather than see it go to Folk. As one historian put it, and in terms only slightly overstated: "The Missouri Democracy cast party loyalty aside in 1918 and jumped at the opportunity to help consign Joseph W. Folk to his political grave." It was a sad end for a good man, but Folk's once-promising political career was over.[38]

38. Wood, "Last Crusade," 309–10, 313; Missouri *Official Manual, 1905–1906,* 442–43; Missouri *Official Manual, 1919–1920,* 411–12.

Epilogue

After his defeat in the 1918 senatorial campaign, Folk abandoned his quest for public office and turned to the law as his new career. He remained in St. Louis for a time as counsel for the Chamber of Commerce, but in the summer of 1919 transferred his residence once again to the nation's capitol. Sharing a suite of offices with Frank P. Walsh, a close friend and former political ally from Kansas City who had served as head of the War Labor Board, Folk became a private attorney. With his previous experience at the State Department and the Interstate Commerce Commission, and with his connections in the Wilson administration, Folk had no difficulty attracting clients seeking influence with regulatory branches of the government such as the I.C.C. or the Federal Trade Commission. Some of the firm's more prominent retainers included the New Mexico Central Railroad, the Hearst newspapers, and several well-known movie companies.

Folk also achieved some notoriety as an attorney handling cases brought to him by foreign claimants. One case involved representatives of the Wafd, the Egyptian nationalist party seeking independence for Egypt, who hired Folk to press their case in the United States. He presented arguments in their behalf when the Senate Foreign Relations Committee heard appeals from subject peoples who felt they had not received justice under the Versailles treaty in August 1919. Folk lobbied for Egyptian self-determination at the State Department and maintained extensive correspondence in support of Egypt's cause from July 1919 to January 1920. In 1922 Folk represented the Peruvian government in the settlement of the Tacna-Arica boundary dispute with Chile. His efforts helped convince the U.S. government to invite representatives of the two countries to Washington to settle their dispute. The invitation, which both countries accepted, and the negotiations, at which President Warren Harding acted as arbitrator, eventually resulted in a peaceful settlement of the controversy. Folk had begun to establish a reputation as an influential international lawyer.[1]

As a result of his successful and lucrative law practice, the Folks lived in affluence. In 1920 they purchased a stately twenty-room Georgian mansion in Massachusetts Heights from Mrs. Clarke Waggaman, the widow of a wealthy Washington architect, for approximately $100,000. The house, which had once been the residence of the Russian ambassador under the Kerensky regime, was a Washington showplace. With extensive grounds and a grand terrace, the home was ideal for large social gatherings. In sharp contrast to their earlier days in St. Louis and Jefferson City, the Folks entertained in grand style, occasionally giving dinner parties for forty guests. One possible explanation for the turn to a more extroverted lifestyle was that Folk was no longer a public official worrying about actions that might compromise his official position. Instead, he was an upwardly mobile attorney with connections to several important government agencies and, at least until 1920, important contacts within the Wilson administration. Circumstances dictated change. He now needed to cultivate clients and enhance those contacts and connections. And if Joseph Folk's public and private roles had changed, so too had those of Gertrude Folk. As the wife of the governor in Jefferson City, she organized the annual festival for the children of the poor. Later, as the wife of a public speaker, and with a great deal of time on her hands, she returned to her love of music and served as head of the St. Louis Choral Society. Then, as the wife of a prominent Washington lawyer, she quickly became one of Washington's most popular hostesses.[2]

As busy as Folk was with his new legal career, he never totally lost sight of politics at either the national or state level. Nor did he stop being a loyal Democrat. In a letter to Woodrow Wilson in October 1920, he congratulated the president on his recent statement in behalf of the

1. Geiger, *Joseph W. Folk*, 169–70; Geiger, "Public Career," 358; Shoemaker, ed., *Missouri and Missourians*, 231; *New York Times*, August 26, 1919, May 29, 1923, March 22, 1925; *National Cyclopedia of American Biography*, 172.

2. Geiger, *Joseph W. Folk*, 169; *St. Louis Post-Dispatch*, May 28, 1923; *St. Louis Star*, May 29, 1923; Paolo E. Coletta, *William Jennings Bryan: Political Puritan, 1915–1925*, 95; "Wife of Former Governor of Missouri Homesick for Friends in St. Louis," article dated October 24, 1915, in Mrs. Joseph W. Folk vertical file.

League of Nations. Unwavering in his support of the new international order envisioned by Wilson, he wrote the president: "History will accord you immortality for the work that you have done for humanity and for world peace." That same month the *New York Times* reported that Folk had contributed five hundred dollars to the "Match the President" fund sponsored by the Democratic National Committee to be used in a publicity campaign to win support for the League of Nations. Later, when Senate approval of the Versailles peace treaty looked doubtful, Folk favored acceptance of the treaty with the Lodge reservations and supported William Jennings Bryan's movement for a compromise.[3] Both were concessions Woodrow Wilson refused to make. Folk also contributed financially to the Democratic State Committee in Missouri. He even renewed his friendship with his old adversary Harry Hawes and contributed money to two of his congressional campaigns.[4]

In working his way to the top echelon of Washington's professional society, however, Folk literally worked himself to death. He suffered a nervous breakdown in March 1922. Then, in August, while working on the Peruvian case, he suffered a relapse. Medical examinations revealed that he had Bright's disease, the common name for a severe kidney disorder that usually resulted in death from uremic poisoning. For the next few months Folk traveled from hospital to hospital looking for a cure. But there was none. While in New York City for treatment, he died on May 28, 1923; he was fifty-three. He was taken back to Brownsville, Tennessee, and buried in the Oakwood Cemetery.[5]

Folk's death at a relatively early age ended a political career that some historians have chosen to assess in negative, almost tragic terms.

3. Defeated in his attempt to amend the treaty, Senator Henry Cabot Lodge proposed (on November 6, 1919) fourteen "reservations" that would limit U.S. obligations under the treaty. When President Wilson refused to consider Lodge's proposal, the Senate rejected the treaty on November 19, 1919. Democrats like William Jennings Bryan, who sought some sort of compromise as a way out of the impasse, were held in check by Wilson. See Clements, *Woodrow Wilson*, 218–19.

4. Letter from Joseph W. Folk to Woodrow Wilson dated October 29, 1920, in Wilson Papers; *New York Times*, October 14, 1920; *St. Louis Post-Dispatch*, May 28, 1923; letter from Harry Hawes to K. G. "Jock" Bellairs dated February 16, 1925, in Bellairs Papers.

5. Geiger, *Joseph W. Folk*, 170–71; *New York Times*, May 29, 1923; *St. Louis Post-Dispatch*, May 28, 1923.

They acknowledge his record as "an uncommonly able and public-spirited government official," and then conclude that his career was a failure because he was not a "bigger" or smarter man. They chide him for setting goals—honest government and morally responsible public officials—that were too limited. They classify his labors as laying "outside the mainstream of progressivism." "With no purpose beyond disclosure and conviction and very little organized support . . . [he] captured the headlines and then disappeared." They concede that his words and actions briefly captured the public imagination from 1902–1904, but argue that they did not have the vitality to continue to attract voters over the long haul. They charge that Folk's heightened sense of public morality prevented him from forming political alliances, building political coalitions, or making the political concessions necessary to achieve ultimate political success. With no overriding philosophy of government to guide him, so the argument goes, he allowed himself, as governor, to be led away from "real" issues of vital concern to society to "trivial" issues of race track gambling, bucketshop wagering, and saloon closings. A "fumbling leader," Folk "scattered" the reform element and "stunted his own career." Later, as a presidential aspirant, he failed to display leadership or statesmanship.[6]

These criticisms, however, are too severe. They judge Folk more by what he failed to do than by what he did and adopt a judgmental tone that suggests a criticism hardened by modern-day cynicism. As one historian has noted: "Christian [moral] progressivism makes us uncomfortable. The reformers' indignation, moralism, and righteous rhetoric offends the tastes and grates on the ears of many modern people."[7] It is easy today to dismiss moral reformers like Folk as naive, innocent, smugly self-assured, or narrowly intolerant. Christianity today has become the rallying cry of illiberalism as much as liberalism. But in dismissing the moralistic rhetoric of the progressives as unimportant and in characterizing their emphasis on improved public behavior as irrelevant to the "real" goals of progressives (usually defined as

6. This negative view can be found in Geiger, *Joseph W. Folk,* 171–72, and in Robert Wiebe, *The Search for Order, 1877–1920,* 172, 179.

7. David B. Danbom, *The World of Hope: Progressives and the Struggle for an Ethical Public Life,* 81.

modernization, order, or efficiency), critics have minimalized the moral dimension of progressivism and marginalized progressive reformers like Joe Folk.

To appreciate Folk's place in history, one needs to remember just how degenerate municipal government had become in America when Folk appeared on the scene and how little had been done about it. Everett Colby, a rising political reformer in the New Jersey General Assembly, emphasized the importance of that point during a speech before the Princeton Alumni Association of East Orange, New Jersey, on November 10, 1905. Colby, soon to be praised by Lincoln Steffens in *Upbuilders* as an individual who successfully applied the Golden Rule as a means of solving social and political problems, spoke of the fight then being waged "in so many states" against "Boss" politics. Why, he asked, had this happened so suddenly? Why had it not happened before? "Why have we allowed ourselves to be imposed upon for years, sitting quietly by while the bosses, through their alliance with the corporations, sold us out and capitalized our inertia?" The answer, he said, could be explained by the simple fact that reformers did not understand the rules of the political game. At least not until "Folk, of Missouri, cleared up the mystery. We imagined the headquarters of a 'boss' to look something like the office of the criminal Moriatti [*sic*] in 'Sherlock Holmes.' We pictured a wonderful human mechanism, the ramifying parts of which reached out into every ward and district of a great city, and were controlled and governed in some mysterious way by the giant intellect of the 'boss.'" That was, said Colby, the reformers' impression of a boss—"all powerful, invulnerable, impregnable, phantom qualities, all[,] but qualities, nevertheless, that the reformers failed to analyze and understand. Then Folk came along and pricked the bubble. . . ." He showed the boss for what he was, merely a man.[8]

Folk's discovery about the boss was a revelation. So too was his comment to journalist Lincoln Steffens that good businessmen corrupted bad politicians and that good business caused bad government. As Steffens informed the readers of *McClure's,* "Mr. Folk has shown St. Louis that its bankers, brokers, corporation officers, its business men

8. "A News Report of an Alumni Dinner in East Orange, New Jersey" dated November 10, 1905, in Wilson Papers.

are the sources of evil. . . ."9 Businessmen, in search of special privileges
and public franchises, expropriated politics for their own selfish ends.
They replaced good politicians with bad ones, and, literally, put the
city up for sale. Bribery became an essential part of business, while
bribe money came to be regarded as the assemblyman's entitlement.
In tracing bribery to its source, Folk showed that politics and business
were inseparable. Steffens wrote the story "Tweed Days in St. Louis"
that launched muckraking, but Folk discovered the essential truth that
inspired Steffens. He also demonstrated the courage to do something
about it.

Folk's St. Louis investigations and the subsequent trials sounded the
alarm. "Boodle"—the practice by which monied interests bribed public officials to gain preferment—became a term everyone understood.
When the boodle trials began in St. Louis, only thirty-four cases of
bribery had ever been recorded in the United States. Folk brought forty-
one indictments for bribery during 1902 alone. "It was," as newspaperman Kenneth Bellairs noted, "Folk and his assistants who established the
law as to bribery in Missouri, and thereby clarified it in other states." As
defined by Folk, bribery was not a "trifling offense" but a heinous crime.
It was a crime against the state ("treason"), and the givers and takers
of bribes were state criminals ("traitors"). And Folk, with the help of
muckrakers like Steffens, made people aware of the implications of what
was happening in their cities. Boodle robbed the community, threatened
free government, and jeopardized the sovereignty of the citizen. The
words of one of the defense attorneys in the boodle cases accurately
captured the importance of this. "Joseph W. Folk's real contribution to
American politics was the regeneration of municipal government."10

When Folk set his sights on corruption at the state level, he and
Steffens were able to show that municipal reform without state reform
was meaningless. Steffens used Folk's successful investigation of the
"Lobby" to argue in "Enemies of the Republic" that political corruption
was a system, a "betrayal of trust established as the form of government."
Folk, using the grand jury, and Steffens, using his pen, turned the
searchlight of exposure on that system and called attention to the

9. Wetmore and Steffens, "Tweed Days," 586.
10. White, "Folk," 120; Bellairs, "The Legal Side," 66; *St. Louis Star,* May 29, 1923.

influence of political parties as well as the actions of individuals. Good-government-minded voters everywhere learned that corruption was "the process by which representative democracy was transformed, through party evolution, into an oligarchy representative of special interests."[11]

Along the way Folk began to articulate a concept that Lincoln Steffens called the "new patriotism." Central to this idea, and to progressive ideology in general, was citizenship, which, to Folk, implied the need for a revival of civic righteousness. Citizens had a civic obligation to hold every public official strictly accountable for all public acts. Folk, by example, encouraged them to do that and warned them of the consequences that would result from passivity. If citizens neglected their civic duty, the government would become corrupt, justice would be denied, and iniquity would reign supreme. For the system to work, however, the people would also have to reclaim control of the law. Folk helped them do that, too. He championed the law as the weapon with which to check political commercialism and restrain powerful corporations. And by enforcing the law, Folk reasserted the primacy of traditional, moral values over those that bribe-givers and bribe-takers embodied. As William Allen White noted: "A great moral issue was moving among the people. That issue concerned the enforcement or the annulment of law, and Folk dramatized it."[12] Folk firmly believed that government rested upon the law, and that bribery was the most dangerous crime because it struck at the foundation of all law.

As a candidate for governor in 1904, Folk gave vitality to the ideal that public office is a public trust by popularizing the doctrine that became known as the "Missouri Idea"—the idea "that citizenship in a free country implies a civic obligation to enforce the performance of every public trust; that bribery is treason, and the givers and takers of bribes are the traitors of peace; that laws are made to be enforced, not to be ignored; that officials should no more embezzle the public power entrusted to them than public money in their custody." The editors of *The Commoner* regarded Folk's campaign as "the first of the great battles for reform before the people, and the principles he

11. Steffens, "Enemies of the Republic," 590; Filler, *Crusaders for American Liberalism*, 223.
12. White, "Folk," 126.

declared are the inspiration of the crusade for higher ideals of public life."[13]

When Folk carried his reform program to the state level, he followed the natural path of progressive reform. As governor of Missouri, Folk continued to champion the Missouri Idea, working to replace partisanship with citizenship, warring against bribery and corruption, and enforcing the law. But as he did, his political vision broadened. His interaction with other state and national reform leaders, his gauge of public opinion, and his shared sense of purpose with other reform-minded politicians led Folk to expand the Missouri Idea to encompass a broad agenda of progressive reforms. In two legislative sessions (1905 and 1907) and one special session (1907), the Folk-led General Assembly established a remarkable record of legislative accomplishment. They made great strides in opposing special interests (antibribery and antilobby laws), and in encouraging greater democratic participation in the political process (state primary, senatorial preference primary, initiative, referendum, and recall). They expanded the power and scope of government in the public interest through social legislation (compulsory school attendance, child labor, maximum hour, fellow servant, and consumer protection laws), and economic regulation (of railroads, public service corporations, and monopolies). Folk, by his leadership, added texture, impetus, and a moral tone to progressivism. He accomplished a great deal. Yet as one rural Missouri newspaper editor noted in 1918, it was "his work of revolutionizing—recreating—the political thought of this country with respect to official life and official duty that . . . will stand as his most remarkable achievement."[14]

---

13. "Political Career of Joseph W. Folk."
14. *Rolla (Mo.) Herald,* October 24, 1918.

Bibliography

Manuscript Collections

Library of Congress, Manuscript Division, Washington, D.C.
    William Jennings Bryan Papers
    Benjamin Barr Lindsey Papers
    Theodore Roosevelt Papers
    Woodrow Wilson Papers
Missouri Historical Society, St. Louis.
    Kenneth G. Bellairs Papers
    Mrs. Joseph W. Folk vertical file
    David R. Francis Papers
Western Historical Manuscript Collection, Columbia, Missouri.
    Joseph Wingate Folk Papers, 1902–1952
    Herbert Spencer Hadley Papers, 1830–1943
    Ewing Young Mitchell Papers, 1840–1949

Newspapers

Cole County (Mo.) Democrat
Farmington (Mo.) Times and Herald
Gallatin (Mo.) Democrat
Kansas City Post
Kansas City Times
Kansas City World
New York Times
Palmyra (Mo.) Spectator
Rolla (Mo.) Herald
St. Louis Censor
St. Louis Globe-Democrat
St. Louis Post-Dispatch

St. Louis Republic
St. Louis Star
Washington Post

Sources

"Amending the National Constitution." *Equity* 15 (July 1913): 163.

Ashby, LeRoy. *William Jennings Bryan: Champion of Democracy.* Boston: G. K. Hall, 1987.

"Ask the Candidate." *The Commoner* 11 (July 21, 1911): 1, 4.

Bassford, Homer. "How Folk Was Nominated For Governor." *Harper's Weekly* 48 (September 10, 1904): 1388, 1397.

Bellairs, Kenneth G. "The Legal Side of Joseph W. Folk." *The Green Bag* 18 (February 1905): 65–77. [In Kenneth G. Bellairs Papers, Missouri Historical Society, St. Louis.]

"The Biennial Message of Governor Joseph W. Folk." *Arena* 37 (March 1907): 292–97.

Blackmore, Charles Powell. "Joseph B. Shannon: Political Boss and Twentieth Century 'Jeffersonian.'" Ph.D. diss., Columbia University, 1953.

Blair, James L. "The St. Louis Disclosures." In *Proceedings of the Detroit Conference for Good City Government and the Ninth Annual Meeting of the National Municipal League in Detroit, Michigan, April 22–24, 1903,* ed. Clinton Rogers Woodruff. Philadelphia: National Municipal League, 1903, 87–108.

"'Boodle' Investigation in Missouri." *Literary Digest* 26 (April 25, 1903): 603–4.

Burckel, Nicholas Clare. "Progressive Governors in the Border States: Reform Governors of Missouri, Kentucky, West Virginia, and Maryland, 1900–1918." Ph.D. diss., University of Wisconsin, 1971.

"Circuit Attorney Folk of St. Louis." *Munsey's* 29 (August 1903): 684–87.

Clements, Kendrick A. *Woodrow Wilson: World Statesman.* Boston: G. K. Hall, 1987.

Clevenger, Homer. "Missouri Becomes a Doubtful State." *Mississippi Valley Historical Review* 29 (March 1943): 541–56.

Coletta, Paolo E. *William Jennings Bryan*. Vol. 2, *Progressive Politician and Moral Statesman, 1909–1915*. Lincoln: University of Nebraska Press, 1969.

———. *William Jennings Bryan*. Vol. 3, *Political Puritan, 1915–1925*. Lincoln: University of Nebraska Press, 1969.

Danbom, David B. *The World of Hope: Progressives and the Struggle for an Ethical Public Life*. Philadelphia: Temple University Press, 1987.

Davis, Ronald L. F., and Harry D. Holmes. "Insurgency and Municipal Reform in St. Louis, 1893–1904." *Midwest Review* 1 (Spring 1979): 1–13.

Draper, W. R. "The St. Louis Bribery Disclosures." *Independent* 54 (October 9, 1902): 2402–6.

Dreiser, Theodore. *A Book about Myself*. Greenwich, Conn.: Fawcett, 1965.

———. "Out of My Newspaper Days." *Bookman* 54 (February 1922): 542–50.

Dunne, Gerald T. *The Missouri Supreme Court: From Dred Scott to Nancy Cruzan*. Columbia: University of Missouri Press, 1993.

Filler, Louis. *Crusaders for American Liberalism: The Story of the Muckrakers*. New York: Collier, 1961.

Folk, Joseph W. "The Enforcement of Law." *Independent* 59 (July 6, 1905): 9–10.

———. "The Limitations of Reform." *Saturday Evening Post* 182 (February 12, 1910): 10–11, 46.

———. "The Religion of Democracy." *The Commoner* 11 (January 20, 1911): 1–2.

———. "Respect for Law." *Youth's Companion* 82 (February 20, 1908): 87.

———. "The Rights of the Insured." *Independent* 59 (December 7, 1905): 1318–19.

Folk, Mrs. H. B. [Cornelia]. *Heart Thoughts: Papers and Addresses*. Philadelphia: American Baptist Publication Society, 1908.

"Future of the Democratic Party." *Literary Digest* 29 (November 19, 1904): 688.

Geiger, Louis G. *Joseph W. Folk of Missouri*. University of Missouri Studies, vol. 25, no. 2. Columbia: Curators of the University of Missouri, 1953.

————. "Joseph W. Folk v. Edward Butler: St. Louis, 1902." *Journal of Southern History* 28 (November 1962): 438–49.

————. "The Public Career of Joseph W. Folk." Ph.D. diss., University of Missouri, 1948.

Giffen, Jerena East. *First Ladies of Missouri: Their Homes and Their Families.* N.p., Von Hoffmann Press, 1970.

"Governor Folk on Public Servants and the Law-Defying Criminal Rich." *Arena* 39 (June 1908): 746–48.

Grant, H. Roger. *Insurance Reform: Consumer Action in the Progressive Era.* Ames: Iowa State University Press, 1979.

"The Great American Lobby: The Typical Example of Missouri." *Frank Leslie's Popular Monthly* 56 (August 1903): 382–93.

Guitar, Sarah, and Floyd C. Shoemaker, eds. *The Messages and Proclamations of the Governors of the State of Missouri.* Vol. 9. Columbia: State Historical Society of Missouri, 1926.

Harvey, Charles M. "Reform in Missouri: What Governor Folk Has Accomplished During the First Year of His Administration." *World To-Day* 8 (June 1905): 599–600.

History of Tennessee. Nashville: Goodspeed Publishing Co., 1887.

Howe, Frederic C. *Confessions of a Reformer.* Chicago: Quadrangle, 1967.

————. "Men of Honor and Stamina Who Make the Real Successes in Life: Joseph W. Folk." *Cosmopolitan* 35 (September 1903): 554–58.

Jackson, William R. *Missouri Democracy: A History of the Party and Its Representative Members.* 2 vols. Chicago: S. J. Clarke, 1935.

Johns, Orrick. *Time of Our Lives: The Story of My Father and Myself.* New York: Farrar, Straus and Giroux, 1973.

Kirkendall, Richard S. *A History of Missouri, Volume V: 1919–1953.* Columbia: University of Missouri Press, 1986.

Kirschten, Ernest. *Catfish and Crystal.* Garden City, N.Y.: Doubleday, 1960.

Landen, Frances Patton. "The Joseph W. Folk Campaign for Governor in 1904 as Reflected in the Rural Press of Missouri." M.A. thesis, University of Missouri, 1938.

Lawson, John D., ed. *American State Trials.* Vol. 9. St. Louis: F. H. Thomas Law Book Co., 1918.

Link, Arthur S. *Wilson: The New Freedom*. Princeton: Princeton University Press, 1956.

Lowitt, Richard. *George W. Norris: The Persistence of a Progressive, 1913–1933*. Urbana: University of Illinois Press, 1971.

McAuliffe, J. J. "Fighting the Good Fight in Missouri." *Leslie's Monthly Magazine* 58 (June 1904): 202–9.

McConachie, Alexander Scott. "The 'Big Cinch': A Business Elite in the Life of a City, St. Louis, 1895–1915." Ph.D. diss., Washington University, 1976.

Meriwether, Lee. "The Reign of Boodle and the Rape of the Ballot in St. Louis." *Arena* 33 (January 1905): 43–50.

Meyer, Duane. *The Heritage of Missouri: A History*. St. Louis: State Publishing, 1965.

Missouri. *Constitution of the State of Missouri, Adopted October 30, 1875*. Jefferson City: Regan and Carter, 1877.

———. *Eighteenth Annual Report of the Bureau of Labor Statistics*. Jefferson City: Bureau of Labor Statistics, 1896.

———. *Laws of Missouri Passed at the Forty-third General Assembly*. Jefferson City: Hugh Stephens Co., 1905.

———. *Laws of Missouri Passed at the Forty-fourth General Assembly*. Jefferson City: Hugh Stephens Co., 1907.

———. Secretary of State. *Official Manual of the State of Missouri*. Jefferson City: Hugh Stephens Co., 1901–1920.

———. *Missouri Reports. Reports of Cases Determined in the Supreme Court of the State of Missouri*. Vols. 171, 175, 178, 182, 185. Columbia, Mo.: E. W. Stephens Co., 1902–1904.

"Missouri's Reform Leader." *Current Literature* 36 (April 1904): 404–5.

"More Corruption Exposed in Missouri." *Outlook* 74 (May 23, 1903): 201–2.

Mosby, Thomas Speed. "Governor Joseph W. Folk." *Arena* 36 (December 1906): 602–6.

———. "The Claims of the Candidates." *North American Review* 187 (June 1908): 821–27.

"Mr. Bryan's List." *Literary Digest* 43 (July 29, 1911): 156–58.

"Mr. Folk as an Example." *Review of Reviews* 30 (December 1904): 650–51.

"Mr. Folk for Governor." *Independent* 57 (July 28, 1904): 173–74.

"Municipal Corruption: An Interview with Joseph W. Folk." *Independent* 55 (November 26, 1903): 2804–6.

Muraskin, Jack David. "Missouri Politics during the Progressive Era, 1896–1916." Ph.D. diss., University of California-Berkeley, 1969.

———. "St. Louis Municipal Reform in the 1890s: A Study in Failure." *Bulletin of the Missouri Historical Society* 25 (October 1968): 38–49.

National Cyclopedia of American Biography. Vol. 22. New York: James T. White, 1932.

"The Nomination of Mr. Folk." *Independent* 57 (July 28, 1904): 219–20.

Nord, David Paul. *Newspapers and New Politics: Midwestern Municipal Reform, 1890–1900.* Ann Arbor: UMI Research Press, 1981.

"Other Gateway Proposals." *Equity* 16 (January 1914): 18–19.

Park, Eleanora G., and Kate S. Morrow. *Women of the Mansion: Missouri, 1821–1936.* Jefferson City: Midland Printing, 1936.

Piott, Steven L. *The Anti-Monopoly Persuasion: Popular Resistance to the Rise of Big Business in the Midwest.* Westport, Conn.: Greenwood Press, 1985.

———. "Giving Voters a Voice: The Struggle for Initiative and Referendum in Missouri." *Gateway Heritage* 14 (Spring 1994): 20–35.

———. "Joseph W. Folk and the 'Missouri Idea': The 1904 Governor's Race in Missouri." *Missouri Historical Review* 89 (July 1995): 406–26.

"The Political Career of Joseph W. Folk." *The Commoner* 11 (September 15, 1911): 6.

"Predatory Interests Are Always at Work—Let Every True Democrat Lend a Hand." *The Commoner* 11 (July 21, 1911): 1, 4.

Primm, James Neal. *Lion of the Valley: St. Louis, Missouri.* Boulder, Colo.: Pruett, 1981.

"A Proposed Easier Method of Amending the Federal Constitution." *Equity* 15 (January 1913): 4.

" 'Pure Food' Corruption in Missouri." *Outlook* 73 (April 25, 1903): 940.

Pusateri, Cosmo J. "A Businessman in Politics: David R. Francis, Missouri Democrat." Ph.D. diss., St. Louis University, 1965.

Putzel, Max. *The Man in the Mirror: William Marion Reedy and His Magazine.* Cambridge: Harvard University Press, 1963.

Reedy, William Marion. "The Burning Liquor Question." *Mirror* 17 (February 14, 1907): 7.

———. "Chances of Folk's Programme." *Mirror* 17 (January 10, 1907): 4.

———. "An Election Post-Mortem." *Mirror* 27 (November 8, 1918): 565.

———. "Exit Folk." *Mirror* 18 (January 7, 1909): 7.

———. "The Fake Cry of Home Rule." *Mirror* 14 (April 21, 1904): 1.

———. "The Finish of Pharisee Folk." *Mirror* 18 (November 12, 1908): 1.

———. "Folk Boom's Progressive Demoralization." *Mirror* 14 (February 11, 1904): 5.

———. "The Folk-Clark Row." *Mirror* 21 (January 4, 1912): 1.

———. "Folk for President." *Mirror* 14 (November 17, 1904): 1.

———. "Folk's Presidential Prospects." *Mirror* 15 (October 26, 1905): 1–2.

———. "How and Why in Missouri." *Mirror* 18 (November 12, 1908): 1.

———. "Mr. Bryan and Mr. Folk." *Mirror* 14 (October 13, 1904): 3.

———. "Mr. Folk's Apparent Cinch." *Mirror* 14 (April 7, 1904): 1–2.

———. "Not a Blue Law State." *Mirror* 14 (February 9, 1905): 2.

———. "Our Senatorial Field." *Mirror* 27 (May 31, 1918): 322.

———. "Reform Raids." *Mirror* 14 (January 26, 1905): 1–3.

———. "Roosevelt, Folk, Bryan." *Mirror* 15 (January 25, 1906): 5.

———. "The Status of Mr. Folk." *Mirror* 21 (August 24, 1911): 4.

———. "Strikeography." *Mirror* 10 (June 21, 1900): 3.

———. "Why the Governor Isn't Liked." *Mirror* 17 (February 14, 1907): 6.

———. "Why Walbridge Won't Win." *Mirror* 14 (August 11, 1904): 1–2.

Roosevelt, Theodore. *The Strenuous Life: Essays and Addresses.* New York: Century Co., 1902.

Shoemaker, Floyd C., ed. *Missouri and Missourians: Land of Contrasts and People of Achievements.* Vol. 2. Chicago: Lewis, 1943.

"Sizing Up the Democratic Candidates." *Literary Digest* 44 (January 27, 1912): 143–45.

"A Slogan for Civic Righteousness." *Valley Weekly* 3 (January 13, 1904): 8–9.

"Some Facts about Joseph W. Folk." *Valley Weekly* 3 (January 20, 1904): 1.

Sparlin, Estal E. "Bryan and the 1912 Democratic Convention." *Mississippi Valley Historical Review* 22 (March 1936): 537–46.

Staples, Henry Lee, and Alpheus Thomas Mason. *The Fall of a Railroad Empire.* Syracuse: Syracuse University Press, 1947.

Steffens, Lincoln. *The Autobiography of Lincoln Steffens.* 2 vols. New York: Harcourt, Brace and World, 1931.

———. "Enemies of the Republic." *McClure's* 22 (April 1904): 587–99.

———. "The Shamelessness of St. Louis." *McClure's* 20 (March 1903): 545–60.

———. *The Shame of the Cities.* New York: Hill and Wang, 1957.

———. *The Struggle for Self-Government.* New York: McClure, Phillips and Co., 1906.

"The Story of Joseph W. Folk." *Current Literature* 39 (December 1905): 679–82.

Sullivan, Mark. "Credentials from the People." *Collier's* 48 (January 6, 1912): 22.

Taft, William H. *Missouri Newspapers.* Columbia: University of Missouri Press, 1964.

Thelen, David. *Paths of Resistance: Tradition and Dignity in Industrializing Missouri.* New York: Oxford University Press, 1986.

Thurman, A. L., Jr. "Joseph Wingate Folk: The Politician as Speaker and Public Servant." *Missouri Historical Review* 59 (January 1965): 173–91.

Towne, Ruth Warner. *Senator William J. Stone and the Politics of Compromise.* Port Washington, N.Y.: Kennikat Press, 1979.

Tyrrell, Frank G. *Political Thuggery; or, Missouri's Battle with the Boodlers.* St. Louis: Puritan Publishing Co., 1904.

Urofsky, Melvin I. *Louis D. Brandeis and the Progressive Tradition.* Boston: Little, Brown, 1981.

Urofsky, Melvin I., and David W. Levy, eds. *Letters of Louis D. Brandeis.* Albany: State University of New York Press, 1973.

U.S. Congress. House. Patriotic Address of Hon. Joseph W. Folk Delivered before the Cotton States Merchants' Association Convention at Memphis, Tenn., August 21, 1917. 65th Cong., 1st sess. *Congressional Record* (October 6, 1917), vol. 55, pt. 8.

———. Senate. 62d Cong., 2d sess., *Congressional Record* (August 5, 1912), vol. 48, pt. 10.

———. Senate. 63d Cong., 1st sess., *Congressional Record* (April 21, 1913), vol. 50, pt. 1.

———. Senate. 63d Cong., 2d sess., *Congressional Record* (December 2, 1913), vol. 51, pt. 1.

U.S. Department of Interior. *Twelfth Census of the United States, 1900: Population.* Pt. 1. Washington, D.C.: U.S. Census Office, 1901.

U.S. Interstate Commerce Commission. *Decisions of the Interstate Commerce Commission, June 1914 to October 1914. I.C.C. Reports,* vol. 31. Washington, D.C.: GPO, 1915.

Vandiver, W. D. "What Governor Folk Has Done." *Independent* 60 (February 1, 1906): 258–61.

Wetmore, Claude. *The Battle against Bribery: Being the Only Complete Narrative of Joseph W. Folk's Warfare on Boodlers.* St. Louis: Pan-American Press, 1904.

———. "Joseph W. Folk and the Force behind His Boom for the Presidency." *Reader Magazine* 4 (July 1904): 121–29.

———. "Joseph Wingate Folk: The Man and His Methods." *Valley Magazine* 2 (August 1903): 1–4.

Wetmore, Claude, and Lincoln Steffens. "Tweed Days in St. Louis." *McClure's* 19 (October 1902): 577–86.

"Where Former Governor Joseph W. Folk Stands." *The Commoner* 11 (August 4, 1911): 1.

White, William Allen. "Folk: The Story of a Little Leaven in a Great Commonwealth." *McClure's* 26 (December 1905): 115–32.

"Whom Will the Democrats Next Nominate for President?" *North American Review* 182 (April 1906): 481–91.

Wiebe, Robert. *The Search for Order, 1877–1920.* New York: Hill and Wang, 1967.

Williams, Walter, and Floyd C. Shoemaker. *Missouri: Mother of the West.* Vol. 2. Chicago: American Historical Society, 1930.

Winter, Ella, and Granville Hicks, eds. *The Letters of Lincoln Steffens.* Vol. 1: 1889–1919. New York: Harcourt, Brace, 1938.

Wood, Barry Robert. " 'Holy Joe' Folk's Last Crusade: The 1918 Election in Missouri." *Missouri Historical Review* 71 (April 1977): 284–314.

Worner, Lloyd Edson. "The Public Career of Herbert Spencer Hadley." Ph.D. diss., University of Missouri, 1946.

Yancey, Thomas Ralph. "The Election of 1912 in Missouri." M.A. thesis, University of Missouri, 1937.

Young, Dina M. "The St. Louis Streetcar Strike of 1900: Pivotal Politics at the Century's Dawn." *Gateway Heritage* 12 (Summer 1991): 4–17.

Zink, Harold. *City Bosses in the United States.* Durham: Duke University Press, 1930.

Index

Adams, Elmer B.: issues injunction in St. Louis streetcar strike, 21

Alum scandal: origins of, 62–65; investigation of, 65–67; political importance of, 68–69

Bauer, Ignatius J.: opposes Folk's senatorial bid in 1918, 171; distributes anti-Folk circular, 171–72

Bellairs, Kenneth G.: comments on Folk's abilities as a trial lawyer, 42; credits Folk for Missouri's bribery law, 189

Big Cinch: defined, 15; method of operation, 15; influence on nomination of Rolla Wells as mayor of St. Louis, 23

Boodle: defined, 51, 189

Boyd, Willard W.: supports utility regulation, 16; mediates St. Louis streetcar strike, 22, 24–25; supports bribery investigation, 36

Brandeis, Louis D.: initiates legal action against New York, New Haven & Hartford Railroad, 162

Brownsville: early development of, 2–3; religious influence in, 3–4

Bryan, William Jennings: speaks at Folk's inaugural, 91; tours with Folk, 115; confers with Folk, 135–36; role in Folk's presidential campaign, 153–57; attempts to mediate Folk-Clark rift, 157–58; advocates federal appointment for Folk, 159–60; mentioned, 18, 87, 111, 146, 147, 148, 186

Butler, Edward: background, 13–14; heads political machine, 14–15, 16, 18, 23; acquiesces in Folk's nomination for circuit attorney, 26–27; seeks patronage considerations, 29; role in Suburban scandal, 32; involvement in St. Louis Board of Health scandal, 38–39; implicated in street lighting scandal, 39; charged with bribery, 40; trial of, 46–48; acquitted in Board of Health scandal, 55; acquitted in street lighting scandal, 56; mentioned, 30, 31, 45

Campbell, James: organizes business support for nomination of Rolla Wells as mayor of St. Louis, 23; implicated in street lighting scandal, 39; mentioned, 17

Carleton, Murray: spearheads Folk-for-Governor campaign, 71

Central Traction Company: accused of corruption by *Post-Dispatch,* 17; granted municipal streetcar franchise, 17–18; bribery scandal, 37–38

Chapman, Henry: role in St. Louis Board of Health scandal, 38; testifies at Butler trial, 46

Clark, Champ: acquiesces in Missouri Democratic party's endorsement of Folk for president, 152; as presidential candidate, 155, 156, 157–58; turns down offer to replace Senator William J. Stone, 169; as critic of Wilson administration, 183

Cockrell, Francis M.: helps obtain revision of extradition treaty with Mexico, 43–44

Colby, Everett: assesses Folk's importance, 188

Combine: defined, 14–15; role in Suburban scandal, 31–33; role in Central Traction scandal, 37–38; role

203

150–58, endorsed as presidential candidate by Missouri Democratic party, 152; drops out of presidential race, 158; appointed Solicitor General, 160, 160*n2;* as point man for Wilson administration, 161–62; as Chief Counsel of the Interstate Commerce Commission, 162–65; social life in Washington, 165; as general counsel to St. Louis Chamber of Commerce, 165, 167–69; as senatorial candidate in 1918, 169–83; returns to private law practice, 184–85; dies, 186

Francis, David R.: as force behind St. Louis World's Fair, 23; opposes Folk's anticorporate stance, 121; associated with anti-Folk wing of the Missouri Democratic party, 137; as senatorial candidate in 1910, 150; works to undermine Folk's presidential bid, 157; offers Folk political advice, 166–67; turns down offer to replace Senator William J. Stone, 169; mentioned, 151

Galvin, James M. ("Red"): writes article that triggers boodle investigations in St. Louis, 30

Gantt, James B.: criticizes Meysenburg trial, 54; criticized for partisanship, 58; candidate for governor in 1904, 76–77, 78, 79, 84

Gardner, Frederick D.: appoints Xenophon P. Wilfley to replace Senator William J. Stone, 169; gives harmony dinner for Folk, 179

Graves, Waller W.: turns down offer to replace Senator William J. Stone, 169

Hadley, Herbert S.: enforces antitrust law, 118–20; comments of Folk's defeat in senatorial primary in 1908, 145; elected governor on Folk platform, 146–47; comments on Missouri Democratic party's endorsement of Folk for president, 153

Harrison, Edwin: as St. Louis mayoral candidate in 1897, 16–17

Hawes, Harry: as St. Louis power broker, 19, 23, 61; role in St. Louis streetcar strike, 20, 21; role in Folk's nomination for circuit attorney, 25; recounts Folk's nomination for circuit attorney, 26, 27; as candidate for governor in 1904, 77–84; comments on apparent decline in Folk's popularity, 111; associated with anti-Folk wing of the Missouri Democratic party, 137; mentioned, 56

Hay, John: facilitates extradition treaty with Mexico, 43–44, 59

Haywood County: early development of, 2, 3; religious influence in, 3–4

Hill, William Preston: advocates direct legislation, 122, 124

House, Edward M.: offers Folk political advice, 166

Howe, Frederic C.: recounts Folk's nomination as circuit attorney, 26; comments on graft prosecutions, 36

Initiative and referendum: campaign in Missouri, 122–24; measure approved by the Missouri legislature, 130; adopted as constitutional amendment in 1908, 146

Jefferson Club: as St. Louis Democratic political organization, 18–19; factionalism within, 25

Jerome, William T.: comments on ineffectiveness of Sunday closing laws, 99

Johns, George: helps procure return of fugitive John Murrell, 44; opposes Breeders' Law, 96

Johns, Orrick: describes St. Louis, 12; criticizes Folk, 52–53; criticizes Missouri Supreme Court, 58

Johnson, Jackson: convinces St. Louis Chamber of Commerce to retain Folk as legal counsel, 167

Johnson, Tom: confers with Folk, 103; mentioned, 26